Éamon de Valera: A Will to Power

by the same author

FATAL PATH: BRITISH GOVERNMENT AND IRISH REVOLUTION
1910–1922

Éamon de Valera

A WILL TO POWER

Ronan Fanning

FABER & FABER

First published in 2015
by Faber and Faber Limited
Bloomsbury House
74–77 Great Russell Street
London WC1B 3DA

Typeset by Agnesi Text
Printed in the UK by CPI Group (UK) Ltd, Croydon CR0 4YY

A CIP record for this book
is available from the British Library

ISBN 978–0–571–31205–4

FSC
www.fsc.org
MIX
Paper from
responsible sources
FSC® C101712

2 4 6 8 10 9 7 5 3 1

In memory of
Virginia
and our four decades together

Contents

List of Illustrations

Unless otherwise stated, all images are reproduced
by kind permission of UCD–OFM Partnership.

1 Éamon de Valera waving to crowds in New York, 1919–20
2 Catherine (Kate) Coll, de Valera's mother
3 Edward (Ned) Coll, de Valera's uncle
4 De Valera at school in his last year in Charleville in 1898
 and at Blackrock College in 1899
5 De Valera with the teaching staff at Rockwell College in 1903
6 De Valera with a hunting rifle at Rockwell, 1904
7 Éamon de Valera and Sinéad Flanagan on their wedding
 day, 8 January 1910
8 Commandant de Valera leading the 3rd Battalion of
 the Dublin Brigade of the Irish Volunteers under escort
 by British troops to Ballsbridge Barracks after his surrender
 on 29 April 1916
9 De Valera with cheering supporters at the East Clare
 by-election in July 1917
10 De Valera with Richard Mulcahy and Cathal Brugha
 on the morning of 6 December 1921, the day of
 de Valera's decision to oppose the Anglo-Irish Treaty
 signed in London hours earlier
11 De Valera and Arthur Griffith in Dublin, 13 August 1921
12 De Valera en route to speak at Ennis on 15 August when
 he was arrested by Irish Free State troops

Éamon de Valera's Homes in Blackrock

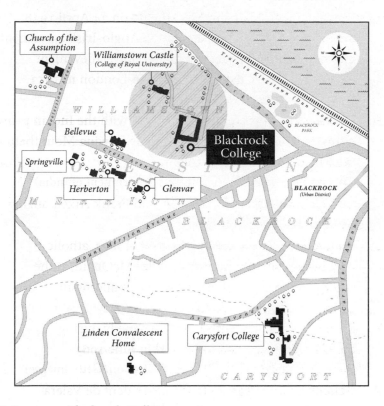

1898–1900   Blackrock College

1900–1908   Williamstown Castle

1906–12   Carysfort College, where he was Professor of Mathematics

1921   Glenvar, where he was arrested by British troops on 22 June

1930–33   Springville

1933–40   Bellevue

1940–59   Herberton

[1959–73   He lived in the President's residence in the Phoenix Park]

1973–75   Linden Convalescent Home where he and his wife died

Church of the Assumption   His parish church and a focal point
of family life

Introduction

On the eve of the centenary of the Irish revolution, the time is ripe for a biography of Éamon de Valera, incomparably the most eminent of Irish statesmen, that seeks to define the magnitude of his political achievement. From the moment of his survival as the only leader of the 1916 rebellion to escape execution until 1922 he defined and directed the course of that revolution. Even from the political wilderness (after the civil war of 1922–3 until his repudiation of anti-democratic politics in 1926) and from the opposition benches from 1927 to 1932, he continued to dictate the terms of the debate about Irish independence. Regaining power through the ballot box in 1932, he took a mere five years single-handedly to rewrite Ireland's constitutional relationship with Britain. His 1937 constitution made Ireland a sovereign, independent republic in all but name. Irish neutrality in World War II, in the face of British and American pressure to join the alliance against Hitler, was the ultimate affirmation of that independence of which he became the personification.

Éamon de Valera, teacher, revolutionary, taoiseach (prime minister), and president of Ireland, has long been acknowledged as 'the most significant figure in the political history of modern Ireland. This is a statement of incontrovertible historical fact, and it does not necessarily involve a laudatory judgment.' He bestrode Irish politics like a colossus for over fifty years, an ascendancy crowned by his election as president of Ireland from 1959 to 1973: 'We have here a span of political power and influence virtually unparalleled in contemporary Europe and in Irish history.'[1]

But Éamon de Valera also remains the most divisive figure in the history of modern Ireland because of the burden of his past:

1

the resentment and the hatred which for so many is the enduring legacy of his rejection of the Anglo-Irish Treaty of December 1921 and his consequent culpability for the Irish civil war of 1922–3. That charge is irrefutable but, if his conduct in 1921–2 cannot be excused, it can, perhaps, be explained.

By a strange coincidence my father died on the same day as Éamon de Valera, 29 August 1975, some hours before him. He was buried in Dublin's Glasnevin cemetery, again on the same day, less than a hundred yards away from where de Valera was buried an hour later in the republican plot. I was reminded on that morning that de Valera would remain as divisive a figure in death as in life. A family friend, who knew that my father was never an admirer of de Valera (despite often playing poker with Seán Lemass, his successor as taoiseach), said to me at his graveside as the under-taker was hurrying us out to make way for the state funeral, 'What's the first thing your father will say to St Peter when he sees him? "There's another Irishman, a long fellow, coming up after me and he'll cause havoc if you let him in!"'

The seed of this biography was sown at that moment. It is an attempt to reconcile the obloquy Éamon de Valera incurred for his conduct in 1921–2 that will forever scar his reputation with his right to recognition as Ireland's greatest statesman.

But this book is more than a biography. It is also a meditation on power: on de Valera's winning power in 1917, on his abuse of power in 1921, on his loss of power in 1922, and on his finding a path back to power in 1923–32. His unique understanding and mastery of state power in 1932–45 then forever identified him as the man who created a sovereign, independent Irish state.

I

From Bruree to Blackrock

Edward de Valera was born on 14 October 1882 in the Nursery and Child's Hospital, Lexington Avenue, Manhattan, New York; the only child of Juan Vivion de Valera and Catherine ('Kate') Coll, he was christened Edward (although recorded as 'George' in the baptismal register) at St Agnes Church, 141 East 43rd Street, on 3 December 1882.

Kate Coll had been born on 21 December 1856 in Bruree, County Limerick, the eldest of four children of Patrick Coll and Elizabeth Coll (née Carroll). Her father, who died when she was seventeen, was on the lowest rung of the social ladder in rural Ireland: an agricultural labourer. Kate had already worked for five years as a maid for neighbouring farmers until on 21 September 1879, aged twenty-two, she escaped through the same route as so many other women in post-famine Ireland: the emigrant ship to New York. Although she again worked as a domestic servant in Brooklyn, first with the Bennetts of Park Avenue and then with the Girauds, a French family, in Gold Street, her life was less onerous than the harsh servitude of Bruree. But she again sought a way out of domestic service and she had not been long in New York when, in 1880, she met and became friendly with Vivion de Valera, a visitor to the Girauds.

Vivion de Valera had been born in 1853 in Spain's Basque country, where his father was an army officer who later brought his family to Cuba where he worked in the sugar trade between Cuba, Spain and the United States. Edward de Valera knew little of his father. Just how little is apparent from the notes he wrote in what became his family Bible, a book he won as a school prize.

Father – born in Spain, educated abroad – knew fluently, English, German, Spanish and French. He was trained as a sculptor, but a chip injured his sight. Met mother in 1880 at Greenville – a village near New York Bay Cemetery and married mother September 1881. Died in November 1884 Denver. Was 5'7" or 5' 8" in height and could wear mother's shoes. Said he was 28 at time of marriage. Mother put things in old storage place – Reilly's (?) in Lex. Ave in October 1884.[1]

Notes so pathetically sparse that they demand decrypting. Filial pride in the father's alleged multilingual skills, information presumably gleaned from his mother, as was the bizarre nugget that his feet were so small that he could wear his wife's shoes. Vivion de Valera had suffered from bronchial illness before he was married and when it recurred in 1884 he took medical advice to go west to the drier climate in Denver, Colorado. Edward de Valera, who was not yet two years old, never saw him again. There is no documentary evidence to substantiate de Valera's account[2] that his parents' marriage took place on 19 September 1881 in Greenville, New Jersey; they then returned to New York, where they lived first in Brooklyn and then at 61 East 41st Street, Manhattan. The absence of documentary evidence of the marriage fuelled rumours of de Valera's illegitimacy that were later sporadically disseminated by his political opponents; other local rumours that he was the son of a Limerick farmer named Atkinson, for whom his mother had worked as a maid before emigrating, can be discounted on chronological grounds.

One also wonders what 'things' she put into an 'old storage place' in October 1884, given that de Valera believed that his mother did not learn of his father's death until the spring of 1885 when financial necessity dictated her return to domestic service as a nursemaid with a Dr Dawson on Fifth Avenue; as a temporary expedient she put her own child out to nurse with a Mrs Doyle, another Bruree immigrant, of Grand Street, Manhattan.

His mother's social status was a matter of sensitivity for those closest to Éamon de Valera after he had achieved fame, and the preferred narrative followed his own account that his parents first met in Greenville and not at the Girauds where his father was a family friend and his mother a maid. But whatever social aspirations Kate Coll might have entertained about her relationship with Vivion de Valera were short-lived. 'My mother had to surrender me in order to earn her living,' recalled Éamon de Valera seventy years later, and he claimed to remember a 'woman in black . . . a rather slim woman, pale face, with a handbag', visiting him.[3]

The return to Ireland on medical advice of his mother's teenage brother, Edward ('Ned') Coll (see plate 3), then working in Connecticut, offered her an opportunity to engineer a permanent separation from her son: Uncle Ned brought the infant Edward back to her family home in Knockmore, Bruree, County Limerick. De Valera, although then only two and a half, later claimed that his arrival in Ireland, at 'Cove' (then Queenstown, now Cobh) outside Cork city, on the SS *City of Chicago* on 18 April 1885 was 'the second event clearly recorded in my memory'.[4] His uncle Patrick was the head of the Coll household in Knockmore where there were two women: Edward's fifteen-year-old Aunt Hannie, of whom he became very fond, and his forty-nine-year-old grandmother, Elizabeth Coll, who became, in effect, his surrogate mother. Hers became a more enduring influence after Hannie followed her sister Kate to America in 1887. Shortly afterwards his mother briefly visited Bruree before returning to New York to marry Charles E. Wheelwright (1857–1927), a non-Catholic Englishman, who worked as a coachman for a wealthy family in Rochester, New York. They lived over the stables in the grounds of the estate and had two children, both reared as Catholics: Annie (1889–1897), and Thomas (1890–1946), who was ordained as a Redemptorist priest in June 1916. Owen Dudley Edwards's suggestion that 'two non-Irish marriages are noteworthy' and a reflection of Kate Coll's determination to escape from that Irish background[5] to which she had condemned her son is persuasive (see plate 2).

When Edward de Valera arrived in Knockmore, the Colls were moving into a new government-built, three-roomed, slate-roofed labourer's cottage with a half-acre of land; sleeping in the old pre-famine, one-room, mud-walled, and thatched family home, he recalled 'waking up in the morning and screaming . . . alone in a strange place' and being told that his uncle was in 'the new house'.[6] He also remembered saving hay, picking blackberries and mushrooms, and avoiding the police while grazing cows on the 'long acre', the grass margins by the roadside. There was very little fresh meat, only bacon; no electricity, but candles and paraffin lamps; water was usually drawn from open wells; hay and corn were cut with scythes. 'There was not an operation on the farm, with perhaps one exception, that I as a youngster had not performed,' Éamon de Valera told the Dáil at a pivotal moment during the debate on the Anglo-Irish Treaty of December 1921.

I lived in a labourer's cottage but the tenant in his way could be regarded as a small farmer. From my earliest days I participated in every operation that takes place on a farm . . . I did not learn how to plough, but until I was sixteen years of age there was no farm work from the spancelling of a goat and milking of a cow that I had not to deal with. I cleaned out the cowhouses. I followed the tumbler rake. I took my place on the cart and filled the load of hay. I took milk to the creamery. I harnessed the donkey, the jennet and the horse.[7]

The exception is revealing of the Colls' poverty: a tiny holding of half an acre required little ploughing. But the graphic catalogue of menial, back-breaking chores burned into de Valera's memory were of a life from which, like his mother and aunt, he sought only to escape. Education was his way out.

Edward de Valera's schooling began from the age of six at Bruree national school (7 May 1888–9 October 1896). 'For eight years Eddie walked the mile or so to Bruree, carrying with him a couple of quarts of milk for customers in the village.' The exoticism of the name 'de Valera' meant that from the very beginning his peers saw him as something of an outsider and some instead called him 'Eddie Coll'. His chores at Knockmore meant that his school attendance was poor and got worse; as he grew older and as his grandmother fell ill 'his home tasks grew heavier . . . he was always passed for promotion each year'. His uncle Pat was a stern taskmaster who saw no reason why de Valera should not leave school and whose ambitions for his nephew did not extend beyond wanting him to become one of the school's monitors, 'boys who had just left school and hoped to become teachers themselves later . . . but de Valera thought this a dead end unless he had enough money to pay for his teacher's training later'.[8] The death of his grandmother, who had hoped he might become a priest, in 1895 deprived de Valera of his only ally in his fight to flee from a life of manual labour by going to the Christian Brothers School at Charleville to try to win a scholarship. Although de Valera had then only just turned fourteen years old, the outcome was the first demonstration of what became his most remarkable character trait: his strength of will. He overcame his uncle's resistance by writing to his mother and insisting that 'either he was sent to Charleville or she sent him his passage money for America. Kate evidently shrank from bringing her firstborn to the USA. Charleville it was', and Frank Gallagher, a political ally in whom de Valera later confided, summed up the significance of the episode in a cryptic note in his diary: 'First Victory for E. de V.'[9]

His two years in Charleville, 1896–8, were a ferocious test of character. It was seven miles away and a bicycle was beyond his means. While a train left Bruree at 7.40 a.m., there was no return train until three hours after school ended and he had to walk home in all weathers. The scars of that ordeal never left him and he told his official biographers of how 'often on the long walk home . . . he would rest exhausted against a fence, longing to throw away the heavy pile of school books. But he persisted as so often later in life . . . At Charleville, he took Latin and Greek; arithmetic, geometry and algebra; and English and French.'[10] The Christian Brothers' unrelenting focus on ensuring that their pupils should succeed in state examinations meant that, notwithstanding the burgeoning

Gaelic cultural revolution of the time, there was no room for Irish history or the study of the Irish language; his grandmother, 'who was a native speaker . . . deliberately refrained from using Irish in his presence'.[11] Persistence paid off in 1898 when he won a scholarship known as an 'exhibition', worth £20 a year and valid for three years, in the junior-grade examination that seemed to open the door to a college education.

At first de Valera's hopes were dashed when two colleges in County Limerick, Mungret College and St Munchin's, a Jesuit college, turned him down. But a stroke of luck then changed his life for ever. The local curate, Father James Liston, had sung de Valera's praises during a chance meeting with another priest, the president of Blackrock College, Father Laurence Healy, while on holiday in Lisdoonvarna in County Clare that August. When the Jesuits rejected de Valera's application, Liston wrote to Healy. Healy's reply of 31 August 1898, which Liston later gave to uncle Pat, has survived and bears a gloss pregnant with opportunity written by the young de Valera: 'Please do not let this go astray as it may be wanting [sic] E. de V.' Healy enclosed copies of the prospectuses of both Blackrock's 'Junior Scholasticate' and of its lay college. 'If our young friend', wrote Healy, 'feels drawn to the life of sacrifice which the missions entail', he could seek a place in the Scholasticate (comprising students destined for ordination as priests). But the Scholasticate was 'very crowded' and Healy suggested that 'Master de Valera enter our College for a year, and study his vocation there'; he would accept his junior-grade exhibition in lieu of fees – a generous offer as the annual fees were £40 a year. 'The boy will come', wrote Healy in his Acceptance Book on 2 September.[12]

Admission to Blackrock College was a giant leap up the ladder of social mobility for an inhabitant of an agricultural labourer's cottage. 'I am to remain digging potatoes all my life,'[13] Eddie de Valera once said to himself at Knockmore when he heard that a schoolmate was going to a job in Limerick, the nearest city. No more was he haunted by that fear. Instead he was now in one of Dublin's leading colleges, embedded in the Catholic, bourgeois elite that would come to power in Ireland in the twentieth century. The transformation (see plates 4 and 5) was well symbolised by the presence in the same class of John D'Alton who, as cardinal and Archbishop of Armagh (the primatial see), later exercised a leadership role in the Irish Catholic Church comparable to de Valera's leadership of the independent Irish state. 'From the time I heard that I was to go to Blackrock,' de Valera recalled,

I was really walking on air. No more trudging over the interminable distance, as it seemed, from Knockmore to Charleville or from Charleville to Knockmore. No more chopping of turnips for the cows, or the drawing of water, or the attempts to do my lessons in the intervals . . . I remember well how happy I was on that night – my first night in the College. I could not understand why boys coming to such a place should be weeping. I had heard some sobbing, but for me this coming was really the entry into heaven.[14]

The passage reveals how the servitude of his years in Bruree forged de Valera's character, how it had already moulded that almost impenetrable carapace of emotional self-sufficiency that became both his greatest strength and his greatest weakness. What he 'relished from the start were the long uninterrupted hours in the study hall in the early morning before class and again throughout the evening . . . all his books there beside him in his desk with silence all round, and no other duties to disturb him'. He kept those textbooks and later presented them to the College, 'with the name Edward de Valera, French College, Blackrock, written several times even on the same page . . . staking out what were his most cherished personal possessions, and perhaps asserting a new identity'.[15]

That a teenager alone in Dublin whose father had died and whose mother had 'surrendered' him before he was three should have sought a new identity was unsurprising. De Valera's sense that Blackrock College was and would ever remain his home lay at the core of that identity. He got permission to spend his first Christmas as a boarder with the scholastics in the college, rather than returning to the domestic oppressions of Bruree, and that set the pattern for a future that included his returning to the college in later life 'to join the community for Midnight Mass at Christmas'.[16] Although he was only in the secondary school for two years (1898–1900), he also stayed in college lodgings from 1900 to 1903. He was then a student at University College, Blackrock (a college of the Royal University of Ireland), based on the school grounds in Williamstown Castle, which had been initially acquired by Blackrock in 1875 as accommodation for a civil service college. After a two-year teaching stint at Rockwell, the Holy Ghost Fathers' sister college near Cashel in County Tipperary, de Valera again returned to live in Blackrock. Not until 1908, a decade after he first entered Blackrock, did he move into lodgings in the outside world. Those lodgings, in Merrion View Avenue, were in close proximity to the college, as were most of the houses where he lived with his family – notably in Cross Avenue, Booterstown – throughout his long life. And it was to Linden Convalescent Home in Blackrock, where, as a member of the St Vincent de Paul Society, de Valera had visited the patients while a student at Blackrock, that he went to die. (See the map of Éamon de Valera's homes in Blackrock, p. xi.)

There had been few books in Knockmore, where the first novel de Valera read was Walter Scott's *Ivanhoe*. His intellectual formation at Blackrock was likewise shaped by the ethos of Victorian England: the prize books he won, apart from the Douai version of the Bible, included Scott's *The Lady of the Lake*, Pope's *Homer's Iliad and Odyssey*, Macaulay's *Essays and Lays of Ancient Rome*, Goldsmith's *The Vicar of Wakefield* and Isaac D'Israeli's *Miscellanies, or Literary Recreations*. Although his first year at Blackrock, 1898, was the centenary of the 1798 rebellion that served as a catalyst for the birth of Ireland's 'new nationalism', there is no evidence that it impinged on de Valera or that he ever challenged or was in any way uncomfortable with the Anglocentricity of the college. Unlike

Blackrock contemporaries, such as Pádraic Ó Conaire, who was among the few students 'taking Irish, or "Celtic" as it was called then, as a subject for their public examination', he did not attend Irish language classes and in later life recalled his astonishment when he saw T. F. O'Rahilly, who became a professor of Irish, reading aloud to his fellow students in the college's recreation room from the first issue of *An Claidheamh Soluis*, the newspaper of the Gaelic League.[17] De Valera himself showed no interest whatever in the League's language-revival movement or in the resurgence of Gaelic games under the aegis of the Gaelic Athletic Association (GAA). Rugby, one of the foreign games renounced by the GAA, was the dominant sport at Blackrock. De Valera was an enthusiastic, if not proficient, participant from the outset; his ignorance of the technique of tackling led to one of his ears being so mangled in his first match that he was rushed to the college doctor for stitches. Nor was he among the handful of more nationalist-minded boys who disobeyed the college president's direction to raise their caps and cheer when Queen Victoria's carriage passed the college en route from Kingstown (now Dun Laoghaire) to Dublin in April 1900.[18]

But, notwithstanding the very different path subsequently carved out by Éamon de Valera, it is scarcely surprising that Edward de Valera never sought to question the ethos of an institution where, for the first time in his life, he was happy. On the contrary, he took to the way of life in Blackrock like a duck to water. His continued standing as a scholarship boy, moreover, depended on focusing on the combination of subjects likeliest to win him more exhibitions in public examinations to pay for his further education. Careful calculation of his own best interests proved an enduring characteristic and he duly won middle-grade and senior-grade exhibitions in 1899 and 1900. He seems to have made few close friends in his first year when he had arrived late after the beginning of the autumn term. But that changed in 1899 when he got more marks than any other Blackrock student in the middle-grade examination for which he won the title 'Student of the Year', an award that led to his appointment as 'official reader of prayers in church, in the study hall, in the dormitory, etc., and . . . in the dining room during retreats . . . Until then he was something of an outsider . . . being a newcomer and otherwise undistinguished.' This was not only a valuable experience in public speaking, but marked his early emergence as the foremost among his peers, a role he clearly relished, according to the contemporary who recalled that he 'took his duties as official reader of prayers very seriously'.[19]

The seeds of the innately conservative respect for convention that always characterised de Valera were sown in his first years at Blackrock: 'He retained all his life a special liking for the prayers of that school manual, as well as for the rosary . . . These were the family prayers on which his own family were reared; and it was these prayers which were recited for him at his request up to the end of his life at Linden Convalascent Home.'[20] The deeply religious ethos of Blackrock marked the youthful Edward de Valera in other ways, most notably in creating a fertile climate for thinking he might have a vocation for the priesthood. When, in his first term, he asked if he might join the Scholasticate, the college president had demurred and counselled taking time to think it over, although he was allowed stay on with the scholastics at Christmas.[21] In 1900, after witnessing the first ordination ceremony ever conducted in Blackrock, he wrote to his ten-year-old half-brother, Thomas Wheelwright, and later to his mother, 'that he was thinking seriously of going on, this time to Clonliffe, to study for the diocesan priesthood'.[22] It came to nothing and does not seem to have surfaced again until 1904–5 at the end of his time in Rockwell College, when several of his contemporaries went to England to join a new novitiate for the Holy Ghost Fathers in Prior Park, Bath, and when de Valera was still undecided about his own future. 'At last, whether off his own bat, or the advice of someone else', he went on a weekend retreat with the Jesuit Fathers in Rathfarnham Castle.

His confessor advised that he had 'what is known as an incipient vocation'.[23] There matters rested until January 1906 when de Valera consulted the president of the seminary at Clonliffe College, where he was doing some part-time teaching, about entering the secular priesthood. Again, he was fobbed off and 'advised . . . not to come in now'.[24]

How can one explain what Tim Pat Coogan has described as the 'curious fact that, though many sources attest to his piety and deep religiosity, no director of vocations whom de Valera consulted encouraged him to become a priest'?[25] His inability to provide a copy of his mother's marriage certificate, then an essential pre-requisite under canon law for every candidate for the priesthood, offers one explanation. Kindness and sympathy of priests who admired and liked him might have prompted their sparing Edward de Valera from confronting that brutal reality. What one can say with certainty is that enduring affinity forever marked his attitude to the priests in Blackrock and elsewhere, and there is no evidence that he ever resented the discouragement of his vocational aspirations.

De Valera's involvement in the Literary and Debating Society during his time at Blackrock's University College (1903–8) is also of interest in the light of his subsequent career. He supported a motion that 'constitutional monarchy as a form of government is preferable to republicanism', on the grounds that 'constant elections disturbed the nation, and are not conducive of the prosperity of the people' and he also argued that 'there is no rule so tyrannical as that of them all'[26] – an argument foreshadowing his assertion in 1921–2, the great watershed of his political career, that the majority had no right to do wrong. But his most significant contribution to the society's proceedings was the paper of twenty foolscap pages he delivered in February 1903 on the Irish university question, then a subject of extensive political debate largely focused on the demand for a university or universities acceptable to the Catholic bishops. Two aspects of the paper merit particular attention: an originality reflecting an appetite for independent thought and an absence of any sectarian animosity towards Trinity College Dublin, long a bastion of Protestant ascendancy in Ireland.

De Valera began by insisting that he was proposing his own solution, saying that 'he was a great believer in the "man in the street solution"'; he added that his research had 'corroborated his own personal hunch' in a passage that Seán Farragher has suggested 'is the first documentary evidence we have of the process to which he was to refer later in life as "consulting his own heart" when he wanted to know what was best for the Irish people'. Citing Cicero's saying that 'to cease to think is to cease to philosophise', de Valera argued that 'the conception and expression of a single idea of one's own is of more educational value than a cartload of other people's ideas which are for the most part accepted without being boiled down, digested or assimilated'. After pointing out that Dublin University had been established in the sixteenth century with the intention that Trinity College should be but one of several colleges, he argued that no new legislation was needed for the foundation of another college of that university for Catholics with comparable funding and facilities; although the colleges would be independent in their internal organisation, they would remain integrated in a single university:

It is very prudent to have all the minds of the country shaped in one university – which does not necessarily mean shaped in one mould. If there was but one national university, it would tend to develop a strong national spirit among all students at it, whatever might be their other opinions and differences. You would have those men going out into public life with that intense common sympathy, with a common interest for which they would be ready to sacrifice their individual prejudices and inclinations. Such a spirit it is that makes patriots and constitutes the stability of a nation . . . They would have certain aims and certain affections in common, a thing which would do much to put an end to the present racial and religious strife in the country, while at the same time the religious training of all parties would not be neglected nor their consciences violated.[27]

Again, the Irish language and the 'new nationalism' are notable only by their absence and the paper reveals the independent views of a twenty-year-old on one of the rare occasions when he ventured outside the narrow realm of the four-year BA-degree syllabus on which he was by then well advanced. John D'Alton, the brightest boy in his class, recalled later that Eddie de Valera 'was a good, very serious student, good at Mathematics, but not outstanding otherwise'.[28] Hence his decision to focus on mathematical sciences for his degree and he duly continued to win the scholarships in the Royal University examinations that contributed towards his board and tuition. But he needed to supplement his income and, in 1901–2, tutored two students preparing for the Solicitors' Apprentice Examination, who showed their appreciation by presenting him with a ticket for the rugby international between Ireland and Wales at Lansdowne Road on 8 March 1902; the ticket stub, inscribed 'Given to me by my first class', became a treasured souvenir.[29] He did more part-time teaching in 1902–3 and, although he was not due to take his BA examination for another year, accepted the offer of a temporary appointment as professor of mathematics and physics for 1903–4 at the Holy Ghost Fathers' sister college at Rockwell, County Tipperary. 'So ended the five years at Blackrock which saw him develop from a raw country teenager into a sophisticated and assured undergraduate.'[30]

Why did Edward de Valera take up a full-time teaching appointment at Rockwell in September 1903 when he had yet to secure his degree in the final BA examination of the Royal University a year later? He appears to have been afflicted by a sense of insecurity about his future scarcely surprising in a newcomer to the ranks of Ireland's Catholic elite. His application in February 1903 for a job in St Wilfrid's College in England[31] is certainly suggestive of indecision about where best to pursue the teaching career on which he now seemed set. The sudden offer of a vacant post in Rockwell, a sister college of Blackrock run by the Holy Ghost Fathers, must have seemed like manna from heaven. 'Many of the staff were already known to him personally' and he would have accommodation in the college and become 'part and parcel of what was a very closed community (see plate 6), and ... accepted in a way he would not have been at Blackrock', where he had only the status of a student, albeit a university student.[32] That sense of belonging meant much to someone who, only five years before, had still been trapped in the rural isolation of Bruree, and it was to Bruree that he now returned for a summer holiday in 1903 before taking up his post with the lofty title of 'professor of mathematics and physics' in Rockwell.

Tim Pat Coogan has suggested that 'his stay in Rockwell, from 1903 to 1905, seems to have provided him with the nearest he came in life to a hedonistic interlude'[33] and de Valera himself remembered 'his period at Rockwell as the happiest time of his life; he never tired of recounting anecdotes about the conditions and people of that period ... The lay professors dined with the prefects at a raised table in the boys' refectory; they were very much part of a community with the prefects, being of the same age group and being involved in the same work for class and games. They even joined in their celebrations, authorised and unauthorised.' In 1904 he captained the Rockwell senior rugby fifteen, consisting largely of lay teachers, prefects and senior students but whose star players were two past pupils, the Ryan brothers, who had played on Ireland's triple-crown-winning team in 1899. Eddie de Valera – it was also at Rockwell that he acquired what became the lifelong nickname of 'Dev' – became personally friendly with Mick and Jack Ryan and he enjoyed the freedom of the Ryan household, participating in their other pastimes: shooting (a gun licence was issued to Edward de Valera [see plate 7], 'professor of Rockwell College' on 12 November 1904),[34] fishing, card-playing, horse racing and 'becoming an expert in the matter of punch making'. Stewart's Hotel in Cashel was a social centre for Rockwell's lay teachers where he picked up the local idiom of 'totty-twigging' for watching the girls go by and where they were entertained by the proprietor's daughters, Cissie and Mary. 'It was soon obvious to all that Mary had taken a special fancy for Dev and it was felt that there was a real romance in the making'; but it came to nothing.[35] He and some other teachers used cycle to Cashel to dances, sometimes not returning until 4 a.m. When they once found the door locked against them, it was de Valera who took the lead by climbing into the college through an open window, saying as he opened the door that 'we did not join the Rockwell staff as monks'. When they again found the door locked in the early hours, it was de Valera who once more climbed through the window; 'this time [he] removed the lock and threw it into the college lake. The door was not locked again.'[36]

But Edward de Valera seems to have paid a high price for his uncharacteristic excursion into this less than lurid self-indulgence: it allowed little time for focusing on preparing for his BA examination in the summer of 1904. Although he left Rockwell and returned to Blackrock as soon as the school year ended, only fourteen weeks remained before the examination began. It was not enough. Although de Valera's earlier university results were 'highly creditable' they were not 'particularly outstanding'. Where 10 of the 450 candidates in the first arts examination in 1902 had been awarded first-class exhibitions, he was among the 24 awarded second class; similarly in the second arts examination when 7 of 330 candidates achieved first class, de Valera was among the 11 awarded second class.[37] But neither result presaged his disastrous performance in the BA examination in 1904. 'For the first time he had to take his place with the vast majority of students and be content with a mere Pass in Mathematics. He was thoroughly disgusted and was to regret it all his life.'[38]

Edward de Valera's failure to acquire an honours degree damned his hopes of ever obtaining an academic appointment in a university. When the Irish Universities Act of 1908 dissolved the Royal University and established the National University of Ireland (NUI) in its place, de Valera's BA in Mathematical Science was automatically transmuted into a Bachelor of Science (BSc) of the NUI. But a pass degree could not be transmuted into an honours degree and, privately if not publicly, de Valera always bore the intellectual stigmata of being a mere pass graduate. Understandably, the episode was not something on which he liked to dwell or about which he subsequently encouraged discussion and his authorised biography baldly records merely that 'he was disappointed when he only obtained a pass degree'. He remained convinced, however, that teaching was his true vocation and went back to Rockwell to heal his self-esteem. But in the summer of 1905, after a second year there, 'he felt he was likely to stagnate if he remained and returned once more to Dublin to seek another post. One interview for a teaching position took him to Liverpool but after one look round he returned the very next day, determined to accept whatever post he could obtain in Ireland.'[39]

There followed a string of temporary, part-time appointments that included Belvedere College (1905–6); Dominican College, Eccles Street, Dublin (1906–8); Holy Cross College, Clonliffe, Dublin, and another sister college run by the Holy Ghost Fathers, St Mary's College, Rathmines, Dublin. Then the Blackrock connection opened yet another door for Edward de Valera. It took the form of a conversation in the unlikely setting of a cricket match – cricket was the summer sport both in Blackrock and Belvedere. Father Joseph Baldwin, the former dean of Rockwell, was well known to de Valera; he was transferred to Blackrock in 1905 where he became one of the leading players on the senior cricket eleven. He was also confessor to the Sisters of Mercy in the adjoining Carysfort Teachers' Training College. De Valera 'recalled how thrilled he was when one evening in the summer of 1906, as he came to watch the cricket', Father Baldwin advised him that the Mother Superior had just told him of a vacancy in Carysfort for a professor of mathematics. Baldwin recommended de Valera, who was duly appointed.[40]

His remarkable reluctance to sever his ties with Blackrock College was reflected in his obtaining permission to live in the

'Castle'. Its advantages have been summarised by Tim Pat Coogan: 'The Castle presented both a scholarly and sympathetic milieu for de Valera – and one, moreover, in which he was well placed to keep an eye out for employment opportunities.'[41] Another advantage was that it was only ten minutes' walk to Carysfort, where he taught from nine to eleven each morning – he later claimed to have trained over a thousand women as teachers – leaving him time to cycle around the city to his other teaching engagements but little time for postgraduate research, despite his attending courses at Trinity College and University College. But he did find time again to take part in Blackrock's Literary and Debating Society and in the rugby club where he became captain of the second fifteen in 1907–8 when their unexpected defeat in the final of the cup was attributed by his teammates to an authoritarian style of captaincy that foreshadowed his subsequent career in politics: a fixation he had about his ability to kick penalties and conversions,[42] all of which he took himself. He stopped playing rugby after another season and in 1908 finally severed the umbilical cord binding him to Blackrock when he moved into lodgings nearby.

Blackrock College served Edward de Valera well in his future quest for power. 'In its origins the Separatist movement was essentially a movement of the plain Irish people – the common man – and remained so,' the secretary to William Walsh, the Catholic Archbishop of Dublin, later wrote in his diary; 'the Intellectuals were unseen and unheard, though some toyed with it after the Rising . . . Up to May 1916, the names of Clongowes and the more "select" Catholic colleges do not appear, and only rarely and inconspicuously for years afterwards.'[43] But, as it grew in popularity, the separatist movement needed uncommon leaders, and Blackrock College proved an ideal training ground for one who came to aspire to lead Ireland's Catholic nation.

2

The Greening of Edward de Valera

The Edward de Valera who finally moved out of Blackrock College in 1908 had little in common with the Éamon de Valera who won fame as the leader of the Irish nation in 1917 when he first became the colossus of the Irish political landscape. Indeed neither the studious and religious scholarship boy in Blackrock nor the rugby-playing and totty-twigging Dev in Rockwell seems to have evinced any interest in politics. Even his address to the Blackrock debating society on the university question was reflective of his engagement in education rather than of any political aspirations.

From his teenage years de Valera had meticulously retained papers and documents of all sorts bearing on every aspect of his life; the letter from the curate in Bruree saying that he had won a place in Blackrock is a case in point. The voluminous collection of de Valera's private papers includes all kinds of papers from his early years – even such ephemera as dance cards, tickets and pro-grammes for concerts and sports days. What is remarkable about the collection in the light of his subsequent career is that it is utterly devoid of any document relating to politics in any shape or form. There is no evidence to suggest he was not part of the broadly quiescent nationalist majority that aspired to domestic self-government embodied in the home-rule programme of the Irish Parliamentary Party, led by John Redmond since 1900. But in de Valera's case it was a low-intensity aspiration and he was to remain markedly averse to any personal participation in politics until after 1916.

Nor do his papers contain any documents earlier than 1908 that indicate that he had taken the slightest interest in the Irish language. His authorised biographers refer to his having 'heard the old people, including his grandmother, converse in Irish' but there is no evidence that he was ever minded to join in their conversation. Nor is their claim remotely persuasive that 'he was inspired with an interest in the Irish language' by Father Eugene O'Growney's Irish-language lessons, published from 1896 in the weekly edition of the *Freeman's Journal*, the leading nationalist newspaper. Initially 'Pat Coll and his nephew thought they would study them week by week' but, given de Valera's remarkable capacity for self-help and for studying on his own, their contention that, because his uncle's interest collapsed after the first lesson, 'de Valera was unable to continue the studies alone'[1] is utterly implausible. Although his later expressions of regret that he had not studied Irish earlier in life were doubtless genuine, there are not even the faintest signs that he felt any such regret before 1908.

Edward de Valera's decision to leave the Castle and take lodgings in the outside world inaugurated the transformation. For a decade after his escape from Bruree, Blackrock and Rockwell Colleges had shaped his view of his place in the world. He was content, indeed understandably proud, of his achievements in state examinations, in the debating society, on the rugby field and as a budding teacher. But his career prospects were dramatically constricted on 28 October 1904 when the Royal University awarded him a mere pass degree. Although his intellectual ambitions were unimpaired, the lack of an honours degree crippled his chances of ever obtaining the university teaching appointment for which he had hoped. Nor, despite his enquiring about applying for a scholarship at Trinity College Dublin,[2] did he ever acquire a postgraduate degree in mathematics. He applied for the chair of mathematics in University College Galway in 1912, the year his appointment at Carysfort came to an end, but withdrew his application before the appointment was made, and he was also an unsuccessful applicant for the chair of mathematical physics in University College Cork in 1913. But in October 1912 he got a part-time and temporary appointment as lecturer in mathematics and mathematical physics in St Patrick's College, Maynooth, the main seminary for Catholic priests, a pontifical university since 1896 and, since 1910, a recognised college of the National University of Ireland. This Maynooth connection was 'of great value to him in subsequent years' as his colleagues on the staff included some of the brightest priests in Ireland destined for elevation to the hierarchy, notably Joseph MacRory, a future Cardinal Archbishop of Armagh.[3]

In the meantime Edward de Valera had begun plugging a gap that threatened to jeopardise his career prospects as a teacher. The first decade of the twentieth century saw two major changes in the Irish education system: the dramatic advance of Irish as a subject at all levels of education and the establishment in 1908 of the National University of Ireland (NUI). The campaign for the revival of the Irish language was a key element in the resurgence of the Irish-Ireland movement and the Education Act of 1900 (de Valera's last year at secondary school) so encouraged the study of the Irish language that by '1904 almost 30 per cent of all secondary students taking examinations took Irish . . . by 1908 this had risen to almost 50 per cent'. Controversy over the evidence presented to a royal commission on university education 'making the case for the enhanced study of Celtic/Irish . . . had given an enormous fillip to the public standing and the morale of the Gaelic League . . . That the League had the public support of leading figures in the . . . Irish Parliamentary Party, and of a broad spectrum of Catholic clergy (including bishops) was a further boost to its confidence.' The introduction of the Irish Universities Bill, which established the NUI, in March 1908 provided the backdrop for the League's insistence that 'the new university would be "an intellectual headquarters for Irish Ireland"'.[4]

'We take it for granted that from the outset Irish would be a compulsory subject at the Matriculation Examination,'[5] wrote Patrick Pearse, the editor of *An Claidheamh Soluis*, the League's newspaper, on 8 February 1908, a week after the bill's introduction.

This was but the opening salvo in a 'remarkable propaganda blitz' in the months before and after the bill's enactment on 1 August 1908. 'The decisive turn in the controversy came when a number of county councils, galvanised by the League,' resolved that the scholarships they awarded students entering the NUI be conditional on the university's insisting that Irish be a matriculation requirement; these resolutions were forwarded to the inaugural meeting of the Senate of the NUI on 17 December 1908; the Senate duly adopted a resolution to that effect by 21 votes to 12 on 23 June 1909.[6]

The national ferment about the role of Irish in education created pressure for its inclusion in the Carysfort syllabus and de Valera was also aware of the provision in the Universities Act that degrees would henceforth be awarded only to students attending the recognised colleges of the NUI (in Dublin, Cork, Galway and Maynooth) would restrict his opportunities to supplement his income by teaching elsewhere. So it was scarcely coincidental that, when he finally took the plunge of abandoning the comforts of the Castle in Blackrock in the autumn of 1908, he moved into lodgings with a native Irish-speaking landlady, Mrs Russell, in the adjacent Merrion View Avenue. But his opportunities for learning Irish there were limited since it could be spoken only when her husband, a Scot who had no Irish, was not at home. Then and only then did Edward de Valera, conscious that 'he could not afford to ignore the potential effect of the language on his future career',[7] decide to take Irish lessons in a branch of the Gaelic League in Leinster College in Dublin's Rutland (now Parnell) Square.

Falling in love with his teacher immediately intensified an interest in the Irish language, initially rooted in anxiety about his career. Jane Flanagan, an ardent language revivalist who had already gaelicised her name as Sinéad Ní Fhlannagáin, was red-haired, pretty, petite and four years older than de Valera.[8] A primary-school teacher and amateur actor, she was talented, intelligent and had been teaching Irish in her spare time for some years, winning the gold medal in the Oireachtas teaching competition in 1907. The attraction was mutual and immediate: they agreed to marry in June 1909 only months after they met, although Sinéad did not wear her engagement ring in public until just before their marriage. Having first passed the intermediate examination in Irish, de Valera spent his summer holidays that year in Tourmakeady, an Irish-speaking district in County Mayo where Sinéad was attending an Irish college. Their engagement was short – 'We hardly knew each other until we were engaged,' she later recalled – and if an impatient de Valera, who wanted to get married in August, had got his way, would have been even shorter.[9] The wedding ceremony, in St Paul's Church on Dublin's Arran Quay on 8 January 1910, was conducted in Irish by a priest who did not know the language but to whom de Valera had taught the formulaic sentences; after a short honeymoon at a hotel in Woodenbridge, County Wicklow, they began married life in Vernon Terrace, Booterstown, Blackrock, but soon moved into 33 Morehampton Terrace, Donnybrook, where they lived until 1916 (see plate 7).

Edward de Valera's foreign surname had the advantage of not requiring de-anglicisation, but by now Edward had become 'Éamonn' – 'Éamonn' became 'Éamon' in the late 1920s. He set about the construction of his new nationalist identity with the same unwavering determination as his marriage and, subconsciously at least, Tim Pat Coogan's suggestion that he 'seems to have turned to the Irish language as part of a process of creating an identity for himself to compensate for the uncertainties of his early upbringing'[10] is compelling. However opportunistic his embrace of the Irish language might have been in its origins, he brought the zeal of the convert to his involvement in the Gaelic League and became as thoroughly imbued with its ethos as he had earlier been imbued with the very different ethos of Blackrock College. Yet that Blackrock identity had the benefit of ensuring that his burgeoning nationalism was never tainted by the 'robust Anglophobia' identified by Roy Foster as an affinity uniting 'middle-class revolutionaries in Edwardian Ireland'.[11] At first Éamon de Valera was still so little known in Gaelic League circles that the reference to his wedding in its newspaper 'did not give his Christian name and gave his surname as "Devalero"'.[12] But a contemporary biographer described how the newly married de Valeras 'were to be met constantly in the places where the enthusiasts of the "Irish Ireland" movement congregated', talking Irish to each other as far as a limited vocabulary would allow, buying nothing that was not of Irish manufacture, and taking an active part in all the social and educational gatherings organised by the Gaelic League.[13]

De Valera quickly completed his Irish-language courses, winning first place for the teaching diploma in Irish while also attending lectures at the Royal University, for which he was awarded the Higher Diploma in Education of the National University of Ireland (his only postgraduate qualification) in October 1910. 'My public life might be regarded [as having started] when I joined the Gaelic League,'[14] de Valera declared in a memoir dictated half a century later and, once armed with these academic qualifications in Irish, he began to participate in the League's broader activities. He was elected to the committee of the Ard-Craobh (central committee) in 1910 and chosen as one of its delegates to the annual convention in 1911 when he was proposed for membership of the executive committee. But he was beaten by the machinations of the Irish Republican Brotherhood (IRB), the oath-bound secret society committed to winning independence by physical force. The 'first function of the IRB was . . . to get control in as many groups and organisations as possible. It was a policy of peaceful penetration in order to wield the widest possible authority in . . . trade unions . . . sports and athletic organisations and the Gaelic League.'[15] De Valera was still so ignorant of nationalist politics that 'he did not know who had defeated him. He had noticed Seán Ó Muirthile, a teller during the election "tricking with the votes", and he went home in a high state of indignation', blaming Sinn Féin because he

knew Ó Muirthile was a Sinn Féin activist. 'He thundered to
Sinéad: "If there's one organisation I will never join, it is Sinn
Féin."'[16] What he did not know was that Ó Muirthile's first loyalty
was to the IRB.

De Valera's engagement in political – as distinct from cultural –
nationalist activities was still non-existent. Patrick McCartan, a
long-time member of the IRB, wrote of how a decade later, when
they were together in the United States, de Valera recalled hearing
McCartan's speech in February 1911 at a public meeting in Dublin
protesting against a proposal that Dublin Corporation present a
Loyal Address to the visiting King George V: 'That was the first
time he heard an Irish Republic advocated and . . . he went home
thinking it was a fine ideal but one not likely to be attained.'[17]

De Valera's commitment to teaching Irish was meanwhile un-
abated and he was appointed for a three-year term as director of
the summer school in Tawin, an Irish-speaking island in Galway
Bay linked by bridge to the mainland. In 1911 he brought his wife
and Vivion, their eight-month-old son. But in August 1912, after
a second child, Máirín, had been born in April, de Valera went
alone and this first of many separations prompted a bizarre but
erotic love letter[18] mingling his feelings for his wife with, perhaps,
a subconscious longing for the mother who had abandoned him.
In the preface to his magisterial *Speeches and Statements by Éamon
de Valera*, Maurice Moynihan writes of how 'it may seem strange
that the great bulk of the material presented in this volume is in
English' and explains how English had become and remained 'the
language of politics in Ireland'.[19] For Éamon de Valera, English also
remained the language of love.

'My dear little Mummie,' his letter began,

I am very lonely without my own sweetheart and her babies . . . I am always
thinking of you darling – yet I don't wish you here for want of proper
accommodation is a desperate nuisance. There is a big big vacancy in my
heart. I feel empty, joyless without you. I do not let myself think on for I
know in a short time I'll have my own darling in my arms . . .

I love you a million, billion times more now than I did when we were in Tourmakeady. When I read in the books about love – about the Speir-Bean [term used in Irish to describe the Spirit Woman or sometimes the spirit of womanhood] and all the rest I say my mummie is a great deal nicer than all that . . .

I have felt very often whilst here that it was a great pity I was not doing some literary subjects we could talk about at home. The maths are so cold and icy . . .

The words '*beal beosac*' came into a poem a few days ago. We translated it as 'nectar lipped' – but I understand what the poet meant. Those wild kisses.

Goodbye darling,
Your husband,
and sweetheart, Dev
xxxxxxxxxxx

The census form for his family submitted by de Valera in 1911 also reflects his earlier rather than his 'new nationalist' identity, as well as a certain diffidence about his expertise in Irish. His own entry and his signature, as Head of Family, appears not as 'Éamon de Valera' but as 'Edward de Valera BA, Dip. in Educ. Math. Professor' and he entered his languages on the census form as 'English and Irish', whereas he entered Sinéad's as 'Irish and English'. The form provided that no entry should be made under Rank, Profession, or Occupation 'in the case of wives, daughters, or other female relatives solely engaged in domestic duties at home'; that Sinéad's entry under this heading was duly left blank eloquently testifies to how she had sunk into domestic anonymity within fifteen months of her marriage.

A recently discovered photograph of 164 people attending the Gaelic League's national convention in Galway in the summer of 1913, de Valera's final year as director of the summer school at Tawin, symbolises his relative anonymity in League circles. Pádraic Ó Conaire (his former classmate at Blackrock), Seán T. O'Kelly (who later served as a minister in all de Valera's governments from 1932 until 1945 when he was elected president of Ireland), and such militant IRB revolutionaries as Éamonn Ceannt and Thomas Ashe are among the thirty or so seated in the front row with the League's founding fathers, Douglas Hyde and Eoin MacNeill; de Valera stands at the back almost obscured from view.[20]

Political rather than cultural nationalism now began to command de Valera's attention as the crisis over the third Home Rule Bill, the apparent fruition of nationalist demands for domestic self-government, deepened. The bill remained the repository of the hopes of most Irish nationalists who believed it would be enacted in 1914 in the form in which it had been introduced by the Liberal government in 1912, but attention increasingly focused on unionist demands for the exclusion of Ulster from the terms of the bill. The Ulster Volunteer Force (UVF) had been established to resist Ulster's inclusion in January 1913 and in September the Ulster Unionist Council (UUC) approved plans for the seizure of power by a provisional government if the bill were enacted. Many nationalists, frustrated by the interminable postponement of home rule, admired unionist militancy. 'A wonderful thing has come to pass in Ulster', wrote Eoin MacNeill, a founder of the Gaelic League and long-time supporter of John Redmond's home-rule party, in an article entitled 'The North Began' in the League's newspaper on 1 November 1913. This was manna from heaven for the IRB and other hard-line republicans. 'I am glad the North has "begun"', wrote Patrick Pearse, who had also initially supported home rule. 'I am glad that the Orangemen have armed, for it is a goodly thing to see arms in Irish hands . . . I should like to see any and every body of Irish citizens armed. We must accustom ourselves to the thought of arms, to the sight of arms, to the use of arms.' A steering committee to set up the Irish Volunteers first met on 11 November; on 25 November Eoin MacNeill presided over the inaugural meeting of the Irish Volunteers in Dublin's Rotunda at which some 3,500 men enrolled. Among them was Éamon de Valera, who had until then also supported John Redmond's party but who identified the occasion as 'the next step in [his] public career'.[21]

De Valera was under no illusions about the gravity of the choice confronting him and later wrote of how, when 'enrolment forms were handed out after the speeches', he considered whether he should enlist.

I was married and my wife and children were dependent on me. I had no doubt that the formation of the Volunteers meant there wd. be an armed insurrection. The question was – was I justified in entering into an engagement to take part in an insurrection with its likely consequences. I decided that our manpower was such that if the movement was confined to unmarried men it would not be numerous enough to succeed. So I crossed the Rubicon and joined. From the moment I signed my name I regarded myself as a soldier with battle inevitably in the offing.[22]

His application of the logic of that decision, as with all de Valera's decisions, was remorseless: his obligations as a soldier henceforth took precedence over his obligations as a husband and father.

De Valera's commitment to any cause in which he came to believe was unswerving and, never a man to do things by halves, he immersed himself in the Volunteers as comprehensively as he had become absorbed in the life of Blackrock College in the 1890s or in the activities of the Gaelic League after 1908. Yet again his name – written as 'Emin Dilvara' on his membership card – caused initial confusion. But he was an 'enthusiastic and whole-hearted Volunteer' from the beginning. In addition to the weekly drill meetings, he also attended

the voluntary Saturday afternoon exercises . . . open to all Volunteers and . . . specially designed for picked men . . . Volunteers from all over the city gathered to do more advanced exercises in company and battalion drill . . . He paid his threepence weekly like the rest of the recruits but soon his diligence began to bring him to a more important position. He was first promoted to be a squad leader, that is something like corporal, in charge of twelve men, and then a section commander or sergeant, in charge of two such squads. Later he was elected a second lieutenant. When the Donnybrook company was formed, he was elected captain and was responsible for recruitment, collecting subscriptions and drill instruction; he also 'wrote, on request, a manual of drill suitable for the Volunteers'.[23]

Such rapid promotion was not due simply to diligence. De Valera was older, more intelligent and much better educated than most Volunteers; his experiences as a teacher, moreover, had accustomed him to exerting authority over younger men. More financially comfortable than his subordinates, he bought one of the Irish Volunteers uniforms as soon as they became available as well as his own rifle and bayonet for £2 10s, which he paid off in monthly instalments.[24] But most significant of all was that Éamon de Valera now had a growing appetite, as well as an aptitude, for leadership.

His power of initiative was evident after the gunrunning on 26 July 1914 when rifles were distributed to waiting columns of Volunteers at Howth harbour. His company was the last to receive arms and, when it seemed impossible to cross the Liffey and get back to Donnybrook after the intervention of British troops, he marched his men in a wide detour to Santry near the present Dublin Airport.

De Valera soon realised that they would never manage to circle the city by the following morning, so he changed his plan. He dismissed two-thirds of his company, making each man leave his rifle with someone in the section left behind. Then he set out to cross the city alone. When he arrived in Donnybrook he took out his motor bicycle and side-car and returned to Santry. Each one of his remaining men was now in charge of three rifles and de Valera ferried them one by one with the rifles hidden under the apron of the side-car to their homes. The operation lasted all night.[25]

The gunrunning was one of a series of episodes that led to a dramatic increase in the numbers of Volunteers: from under 2,000 at the end of 1913 to 160,000 by July 1914. This so worried John Redmond, the leader of the Irish Parliamentary Party, that he issued a statement in June demanding control of the movement.

Open dissension was at first averted when the Volunteer leadership grudgingly acquiesced but, after Britain's declaration of war on Germany, a split became inevitable. It was triggered by a speech delivered by Redmond, on 20 September, after he had inspected a Volunteer parade at Woodenbridge in a field within yards of the hotel where the de Valeras had honeymooned in 1910. He called on the Irish Volunteers 'to serve not only in Ireland but wherever the firing line extends'. His renown so soon after the enactment of the Home Rule Bill on 18 September ensured that the great majority – some 150,000 'National Volunteers' – followed him. The minority of fewer than 10,000, including de Valera, retained the title of the Irish Volunteers. On 28 September de Valera explained to the weekly drill meeting of his company why he had broken with Redmond: he believed 'the Volunteers could be more effective if not tied to a political party'.[26] As he led the small majority of those who had supported him from the hall 'he called back to the others remaining in their places. "You will want us to get that Home Rule bill yet, and when you want us we will be there."'[27] The remark shows that in the autumn of 1914 home rule remained the outer limit of Éamon de Valera's nationalist aspirations; for him, unlike the members of the IRB, the split in the Volunteers was not about the respective merits of home rule and a republic but about the best way of achieving home rule.

The numbers in his company swiftly collapsed from 130 to 7. 'Even with that small number de Valera carried on as if he had a full Company and solemnly issued orders to form fours with the seven men.' Although that reaction might seem ludicrously pedantic, it symbolised the energy and ideological commitment motivating Redmond's opponents. De Valera was also assiduous in educating his subordinate officers and Liam Tannam, who became company commander in 1915 when he was only twenty years old, recalled how 'for four weeks, twice a week' de Valera brought him to his home in Donnybrook and advised him on what to read and how to run the company.[28]

De Valera's success in rebuilding his company, which he had redesignated as a scouting corps – he attracted new recruits with the slogan 'Wanted: eyes and ears for the South City battalions'[29] – impressed his superiors. On 11 March 1915, after 'a terse interview' establishing 'de Valera's readiness to obey orders without question', Patrick Pearse confirmed his appointment as commandant of one of the four Dublin battalions – de Valera's was the 3rd battalion in the south-east of the city. Two days later Pearse called a meeting of the battalion commanders when the possibility of a rising in September was discussed. De Valera later claimed that he was the 'only one at that meeting who did not expect to survive. My age was abv [above] average of the others.'[30]

Age reinforced by education and his training as a teacher made for a 'meticulous attention to detail', which, as Charles Townshend has observed, was 'a trait that would have been immensely valuable in a staff officer – if the Volunteers had had any'.[31] Once he was told that 'his battalion would be assigned to the Westland Row–Grand Canal Street area, de Valera made a close study of the district, surveying its military possibilities. With his son Vivion, then about five years old, he walked several times from Baggot Street to Grand Canal Street along the banks of the canal.' He also travelled on the train from Kingstown, where British reinforcements might land, to Westland Row station 'checking as he did so the means of immobilising the railway'.[32] His attention to detail sometimes took bizarre forms as when, mindful, perhaps, of the symbolic association with the rebellion of the United Irishmen in 1798, he designed pike heads, which he had manufactured in Clonskeagh, although there is no evidence that they were ever distributed to his men.[33]

While Eoin MacNeill and a majority of the Irish Volunteers' executive remained resolutely opposed to armed action other than in self-defence, the IRB element in the Volunteers, personified by Pearse, was continually planning an insurrection from this point on. De Valera, whose distaste for political intrigue went back to the summer of 1911 and the defeat of his candidature for membership of the Gaelic League's executive committee, remained aloof from the IRB and he declined an invitation to join after his appointment as battalion commandant. But, as planning for a rising accelerated, he discovered that some of his subordinates knew more about those plans than he did. When he complained to the brigade commander, Thomas MacDonagh, whom he now also served as adjutant, MacDonagh explained that secret information was confined to members of the IRB and urged him to take their oath. De Valera at first resisted – saying that as a Volunteers' officer 'he could not serve two masters' – but gave way when MacDonagh argued that, because the IRB controlled the Volunteers' executive, taking the oath involved only obeying that executive. Although a reluctant de Valera then took the oath, in this case his commitment was conditional: 'he made it clear . . . that he would attend no meetings' and 'did not want to know the names of any of the members or share any of the secrets of the organisation' except those essential for his commandant's role as the plans for the rebellion of 1916 gathered momentum.[34]

3

Éamon de Valera and the 1916 Rising

Éamon de Valera, despite his rank as battalion commandant, played no part whatever in the initial preparations for the Easter Rising.

The majority of the Irish Volunteers executive was opposed to armed action except in self-defence; so were such key figures in the IRB as Bulmer Hobson. But the core militarist element in the IRB, acting on the time-honoured republican maxim that England's difficulty was Ireland's opportunity, was determined to launch a rebellion in 1916. They worked through a military committee, established in May 1915, and initially consisting of Patrick Pearse, Joseph Plunkett and Éamonn Ceannt. In September 1915 Tom Clarke (revered as the leader who had revived the IRB in Dublin in 1907) and Seán Mac Diarmada (Clarke's staunchest ally, who had just been released after a four-month jail sentence) joined the committee, which became known as the military council; in January 1916 so did James Connolly, the founder of the Irish Labour Party, who was sworn into the IRB and whose independent preparations for a rebellion with the paramilitary Irish Citizen Army were subsumed into the military council's plans; the council's composition was completed in April by the co-option of Thomas MacDonagh.[1]

These men – Clarke, Mac Diarmada, Pearse, Connolly, MacDonagh, Ceannt and Plunkett – were the seven signatories of the Proclamation of the Irish Republic that Pearse, the commander in chief of the Volunteers during the rising and the president of its Provisional Government, read from the steps of Dublin's General Post Office (GPO) on Easter Monday, 24 April 1916.

Éamon de Valera's relationship with the IRB, which he had so reluctantly joined only in 1915, was never more than tangential. He was not a signatory of the Easter proclamation and had no hand, act or part in drafting what became the foundation document of independent Ireland. There is no evidence of how he reacted to its reference to the Germans as 'gallant allies in Europe'. Nor do we know how enthusiastically he endorsed the declaration of 'its resolve to pursue the happiness and prosperity of the whole nation and of all its parts, cherishing all the children of the nation equally'. But we do know that, 'despite the proclamation's commitment to universal suffrage and equal rights'[2] and unlike other commandants in 1916, he refused to allow women into his battalion command post in Bolands mill. When asked fifty years later by John Murray, who subsequently became Chief Justice and was then a university student, about the social elements in the proclamation, de Valera was dismissive: the significance of the proclamation was the demand for self-government; a social programme would have to wait until after the achievement of independence.

De Valera's continuing aversion to any political, as opposed to military, engagement in the Volunteers was reflected in his reaction in 1915 when Thomas MacDonagh had 'pressed him strenuously to allow himself to be nominated as a member of the Volunteer executive . . . de Valera absolutely refused'. He explained why to his authorised biographers; 'He wished to concentrate on the tasks allotted to him. At this stage of his life he was above all a soldier and little concerned with politics.'[3] He then saw himself not as a leader but as a follower, as a soldier obedient to the orders of senior officers. William O'Brien, the Labour leader who was willing to join the Provisional Government envisaged in the 1916 proclamation if it became a reality, got a clear sense of this cast of mind when he met de Valera for the first time when they were prisoners together in Richmond Barracks after the rising: de Valera told him 'he was glad that he [had] had no responsibility for deciding anything and that he simply obeyed orders.'[4]

De Valera briefed his senior officers on his plan for the rising scheduled to begin on Easter Sunday, 23 April, at a meeting of his battalion council on Good Friday night. He 'went over the plan in very great detail' and 'was able to tell each Company Captain where he would enter on to his area and what he would find to his advantage or disadvantage when he got there'. The plan centred on holding the railway line from Dublin to Kingstown and the adjacent bridges at Grand Canal Street, Mount Street and Baggot Street over the Grand Canal. This was because Kingstown, some eight miles away, was the port where British reinforcements were likely to disembark, and the railway would otherwise enable them to bring fresh troops into 'the very heart of the city'. One of de Valera's company captains, Joseph O'Connor, recalled his amazement

at the amount of information our Commandant had accumulated and how thoroughly he understood about the position each Company was to occupy. He was able to discuss every detail even to the places where it would be possible to procure an alternative water supply, where we could definitely find tools for such things as loopholing walls and making communications . . . I cannot remember a query put to him that he was not able to answer immediately, and there was not a solitary suggestion to improve the dispositions made.

'A' Company, under O'Connor's command, was to occupy the railway line from Grand Canal Quay to Kingstown, including all level crossings and the railway workshops in Grand Canal Street; it was also to 'assist in dominating Beggar's Bush Barracks, front and rere [sic]'. 'B' Company was to take over Westland Row station and to send a party to Tara Street station to link up with the 2nd Battalion in Amiens Street station. 'C' Company was to occupy Bolands mill and a dispensary building at Grand Canal Street, as well as a builder's yard at the corner of the canal and Grand Canal Street where it was to barricade the canal bridge; it was also to occupy a series of buildings adjoining Mount Street bridge:

Clanwilliam House, the schools and parochial hall on Northumberland Road and No. 25 Northumberland Road commanding the junction with Haddington Road and the approach to the front of Beggar's Bush Barracks. 'D' Company was to be based in Bolands mill from where, theoretically, 'they were to hold a line from Merrion to the Liffey along the coast'. These dispositions were based on the assumption that the battalion 'would have eight to ten hundred men at [its] disposal'.

De Valera was fatalistic. 'We'll be all right, it's the women who will suffer,' he told Joseph O'Connor during a chance encounter on Easter Saturday. '"The worst they can do to us is to kill us but the women will have to remain behind to rear the children." It was one of the few times that he ever really revealed himself to me,' recalled O'Connor. But while de Valera had no illusions about the likelihood that he would not survive the rising, there is not a shred of evidence to suggest that he ever shared the enthusiasm of those few who rejoiced at the prospect of death and who revelled in the theory of blood sacrifice, as personified by Patrick Pearse.

De Valera's meticulous preparations began to go awry when Eoin MacNeill, who was still the Irish Volunteers' commander in chief, belatedly learned of the military council's intention to launch the rising, and issued a countermanding order cancelling all Volunteer movements on Easter Sunday. The confusion caused by the publication of his order in Sunday's newspapers drastically reduced the numbers mobilised when the rising began the next day. De Valera, who had planned on 'a minimum garrison of 500' to occupy his headquarters in Bolands mill on Grand Canal Street, 'found himself entirely without his battalion staff. He had no vice-commandant, no adjutant and no quartermaster; the captain of B Company had only been appointed; no captain in C Company and no captain in D Company and with scarce one hundred men . . . He had to do everything himself especially for the first few hours,' recalled Joseph O'Connor. But de Valera 'considered himself committed to carrying out whatever orders might be issued to him whether he approved or disapproved'.[5] When a surprised O'Connor responded to de Valera's telling him at ten o'clock on Easter Monday morning that they were mobilising at twelve noon by asking, 'Were they mad?', de Valera's reply was unequivocally obedient: 'I am a soldier and I know you are a soldier also'.[6]

De Valera duly led his battalion from mustering points in Great Brunswick Street (now Pearse Street) and Earlsfort Terrace to Westland Row station where he deployed an occupying detail; he then deployed other Volunteers to move along the railway line towards Bolands mill. When he reached the mill with the remainder of his force about one o'clock that afternoon, 'he met no resistance because the employees were off on holiday and he found only the horses used in pulling the delivery drays'.[7] Both Éamon and Sinéad de Valera were very fond of animals and the horses were 'one of his main concerns and he managed to have them fed and watered'. When the fodder ran out, he ordered that the horses be set free. The home for stray dogs and cats was also in his battalion area and he ordered their release when he discovered there was no one to feed them.[8]

All the Volunteer companies deployed on Easter Monday were depleted. About a third of 'the possible muster' mobilised according to one calculation – 'barely 800 Volunteers – most of them members of the IRB – and less than 200 of the Citizen Army'[9] and 'there were not more than fifty rifles' in de Valera's garrison of about 100 men in Bolands mill.[10] Isolated on the south-eastern periphery of the city and largely ignored by the British forces bent on regaining control of the city centre, they saw so little action that they suffered only eight casualties. 'There wasn't much of a fight,' Sam Irwin, one of the survivors, later observed, 'but it wasn't the fault of the men. They weren't put into the position to fight.' But Irwin tempered his criticism of de Valera's disposition of his troops with the recognition that inexperience meant that neither Volunteer 'officers [n]or men knew what they were about'.[11]

Things were very different a few hundred yards away where much the fiercest fighting of the rising took place in the battle for

Mount Street bridge. This began when four battalions of Sherwood Foresters, marching in from Kingstown on Wednesday morning, ran into a withering hail of fire from the Volunteer outposts in Northumberland Road and in Clanwilliam House. The British troops – 'merely boys . . . who had been in uniform about 6 or 8 weeks . . . many had never fired a rifle' – were sitting ducks for Lieutenant Michael Malone, 'the crack shot of the 3rd Battalion' armed with a Mauser automatic given him by de Valera and stationed in 25 Northumberland Road. 'From there, and also from Clanwilliam House, a substantial Victorian town-house block facing across the low hump of Mount Street bridge with a clear view down Northumberland Road, the soldiers appeared hope-lessly confused . . . [and] presented an almost absurdly immobile target.' Although the British had taken Baggot Street bridge, which had been undefended and was only a few hundred yards up the canal, in the early afternoon, their orders to persist in a frontal assault on Mount Street bridge led to 'potentially catastrophic' casualties. Superior manpower eventually prevailed. Malone was killed about five o'clock and Clanwilliam House burned out during the final successful assault of the British at dusk.[12] The price was high: '4 officers killed, 14 wounded, 215 other ranks killed and wounded – half the total casualties sustained by the British during Easter week'.[13]

But what Ferghal McGarry has described as 'the most significant and deadly confrontation of the week . . . did not set the pattern for the fighting that followed'. Apart from the GPO, none of the buildings occupied by the rebels 'would face a full-frontal assault; instead, they were individually isolated by military cordon', while British forces advanced on the GPO. Most of de Valera's battalion, occupying Bolands mill, 'played no part in the fighting'. British incompetence in the battle for Mount Street bridge was mirrored by de Valera's tactical ineptitude. He failed to reinforce the mere 'seventeen Volunteers in the most effective outposts, despite ample requests and opportunity to do so'.[14] Charles Townshend has argued that de Valera anticipated 'an assault on his main position, and a couple of stray encounters close to the bakery with troops trying to work their way round Beggar's Bush to outflank the Mount Street bridge positions probably convinced him that it was imminent. His misreading of the situation was not surprising, though it showed how hard it was for many inexperienced commanders to adapt their plans in face of reality.'[15]

Although other aspects of de Valera's performance in action subsequently incurred criticism, they surfaced only years after he had become a bitterly divisive figure in Irish politics. 'None of the accusations made against me by certain members of B Company', he wrote in 1964, 'were made prior to the signing of the Treaty in 1921. The members who made the accusations were those who took the Treaty side.'[16] Yet the account of his staunchest defender among the Volunteers under his command, Simon Donnelly, the officer commanding 'C' Company, 'showed that he himself had been puzzled and anxious' about some of de Valera's decisions. Donnelly 'drew a picture of de Valera as hyperactive – "a real live wire from the first moment we entered our position: he was forever on the move, ignoring dangers, and to my mind taking unnecessary risks". By Friday he was clearly worn out, but refused to rest.' Sam Irwin, one of the guards posted by Donnelly outside the office in which de Valera was finally persuaded to rest, recalled that when he awoke 'he was gesticulating and talking nonsense. I was only a boy of eighteen then, and the whole incident wasn't very reassuring.' Nor was de Valera's inexplicable decision on the Friday night temporarily to move his garrison out of Bolands mill onto the railway embankment from where they could see the city centre in flames; the experience so unnerved one officer that Donnelly had to club him unconscious when he fired at one of his comrades.[17]

But, in the aftermath of the rising, de Valera's military failings – tactical ineptitude, indecisiveness and hyperactivity – counted for nothing when set against the heroic image of the most senior officer to survive 1916; as the officer, moreover, commanding the

Volunteer company that had inflicted the heaviest losses on the British forces. What mattered, in short, in paving the way for de Valera's subsequent rise to power was not what he did in 1916 but the political purposes to which what he did could be bent.

That the garrison at Bolands mill was slow to surrender further burnished de Valera's image. After five days occupation of the GPO, which had by then been reduced to ruins, Patrick Pearse decided unconditionally to surrender. At 3.45 p.m. on Saturday afternoon, 30 April, Pearse communicated his decision in a general order to the 'Commandants of the various districts in the City and County . . . to lay down arms . . . to prevent the further slaughter of Dublin citizens, and in the hope of saving the lives of our followers now surrounded and hopelessly outnumbered.' But the messenger, Nurse Elizabeth O'Farrell, charged with delivering the order did not go to Bolands mill until Sunday morning. At first de Valera refused to accept the order for the arcane reason that his immediate superior, Thomas MacDonagh, had not signed it. But after several of his officers had confirmed O'Farrell's identity, he took the decision to surrender despite the wishes of those in his garrison who wanted to fight on. 'I obeyed the orders of my superiors in coming into this fight,' he told his men, and 'I will obey the orders of my superiors to surrender and I charge you to observe the same discipline.' More than that, he denied his men the opportunity to escape open to them because Bolands mill was not surrounded on all sides. But de Valera persuaded his garrison that, although they might all 'leave by the railway and proceed home quietly . . . this would not fulfil the terms of the surrender.'[18] Such pedantry – 'Commandant de Valera', one of his men later remembered, 'stated, as we had gone into battle on an order, the order to surrender was equally binding'[19] – was in marked contrast to the pragmatism displayed by Volunteers elsewhere, most memorably by Joe McGrath, a long-time IRB man, who responded to Con Colbert's giving carte blanche to anyone who wished to escape while announcing the surrender to the garrison of the

South Dublin Union by cheerily saying, 'Toor-a-loo, boys, I'm off', as he crossed the wall.[20]

. Yet the manner of de Valera's surrender – in particular, the photograph of his lofty figure towering over both his guards and his men as he marched behind a white flag along Northumberland Road to initial imprisonment in the showgrounds of the Royal Dublin Society in Ballsbridge (see plate 9) – ultimately added to the lustre of his image. There '117 Volunteers were herded together in horse-boxes', while de Valera 'was treated as an officer and placed under guard in the Weights and Measures office of [Balls-bridge] Town Hall'. Two days later, at midday on Tuesday, 2 May, they were marched from Ballsbridge through Dublin to Richmond Barracks in the west of the city. 'Passing through Dame Street and Thomas Street they received a hostile reception from people along the sidewalks' illustrative of the widespread popular antagonism towards the rebels in the immediate aftermath of the rising, and de Valera told his biographers of how he 'was overwhelmed with sadness that these Irish men and women should misunderstand the Volunteers' fight for Irish liberty just as he felt a pang of dis-appointment when he saw the people of Northumberland Road feeding the British soldiers'.[21]

The screening and court martial of the leaders of the rising had already begun while de Valera was apart from the main body of prisoners and isolated in Ballsbridge. On his first morning in Rich-mond Barracks many prisoners were awoken at 3.45 a.m. by the volleys signalling the earliest executions: Pearse, MacDonagh and Clarke. The shots did not waken de Valera, always a sound sleeper, but he expected to share their fate.[22] There were four more execu-tions the next day, 4 May, and another on 5 May. A weekend lull followed and de Valera's court martial did not take place until 8 May, a day that had begun with another four executions.

Between 2 and 17 May '160 prisoners were tried by Field Gen-eral Court Martial. The trials were held *in camera*. The prisoners were not represented and not permitted to give sworn evidence in their own defence . . . One prisoner [William Pearse] pleaded guilty and convictions were recorded in 149 cases . . . Ninety death sentences were passed and of these 15 were carried out.'[23] Éamon de Valera was among the 75 whose death sentences were commuted – in his case to penal servitude for life.

The record of the courts martial of all the executed prisoners are extant and have been published[24] but records of many other courts martial in 1916 have not survived. 'Repeated and thorough searches of the records held at the National Archives [of the United Kingdom] for the transcript of de Valera's court martial have revealed no indication that it has survived.'[25] The surviving transcripts show that 'most of the trials were very short – a matter of minutes'; William Cosgrave, whose trial was longer than most, - recalled that 'his entire trial lasted less than 15 minutes'.[26]

De Valera's court martial, on the afternoon of 8 May, seems to have fitted this pattern: his recollection was that it was 'short and business like'. Although 'his wife had, a few days before, approached the American Consul in Dublin to make representations that he was an American citizen and the Consul had written to the Under Secretary, Sir Matthew Nathan [the most senior official in Dublin Castle]', de Valera made no such representations on his own behalf. When questioned, he said that he had been born in New York but did not know 'whether his father was a Spanish subject or a naturalised American'. He also said that 'he always regarded himself as an Irishman and not as a British subject'.[27] Alfred Bucknill, then the deputy judge advocate general of the British forces in Ireland, later acknowledged 'the great difficulty in getting sufficient legal evidence to pin any particular offence against any particular person' because of the need to prove 'that the accused had surrendered with arms from some place which had been held by the rebels and where fighting had taken place'.[28] There was no such difficulty in the case of Éamon de Valera. A British officer, Captain Hitzen, testified that 'de Valera had surrendered to him and that the men in the Boland's Bakery area obeyed him' and further evidence was given proving that he had been 'in command in that district', evidence sufficient to ensure that de Valera was found guilty and sentenced to death. But 'the findings of the court had no validity until the process of confirmation had been completed. In the final stage of the trial process, the case papers went to General Maxwell to consider confirmation of conviction and sentence.'[29]

De Valera was transferred to Kilmainham jail – those executed had been shot by firing squad in the prison yard – to await Maxwell's verdict. He believed 'his execution was certain' and, although he did not write to his wife or his mother because his sentence had not been confirmed, he wrote other letters based on that assumption: to the nun in charge of Carysfort Teachers' Training College where he had taught mathematics; to Frank Hughes, the best man at his wedding, asking him to do what he could to help his wife and children; and to Mick Ryan, the rugby international with whom he had become so friendly at Rockwell: 'Just a line to say I played my last match last week and lost. I am to be shot, an old sport who unselfishly played the game.' It was not to be. On 10 May an officer came to his cell and read him the verdict: guilty and sentenced to death; but 'the officer then read a second document, commuting the sentence to penal servitude for life'.[30]

Robert Schmuhl has unearthed the account of how Éamon de Valera, the then eighty-year-old president of Ireland, replied when, on the last night of his visit to Ireland in 1963, President Kennedy asked him how he had escaped execution by firing squad in 1916. 'There were many times when the key in my jail cell door was turned and I thought my turn had come,' he said and 'Kennedy was "spellbound" as he listened to the ageing rebel's tale, with its emphasis on de Valera's American connection.' By 1969 the emphasis had changed. Then de Valera insisted that 'the fact that I was born in America would not have saved me'; the key factor was that the British prime minister, Herbert Asquith, 'wanted no further executions, save those of the ringleaders, which they interpreted as those who had signed the Proclamation'.[31]

It is unsurprising that the then president of Ireland, speaking privately half a century later to the president of the United States, should talk of his own American roots. Nor is it surprising that de Valera's wife and his relations in New York – notably Father Thomas Wheelwright, his half-brother, a Redemptorist priest – played the American card so assiduously in their efforts to save his life or that their campaign and the mere fact of his American birth fuelled a myth that endured.

The truth is simpler: de Valera owed his survival more to luck than to Asquith or America. He was lucky that Bolands mill was isolated on the city's south-eastern periphery. Lucky that he was first imprisoned in Ballsbridge and not with the other leaders. Lucky that he was not transferred to Richmond Barracks for forty-eight hours and that his trial was delayed until 8 May. Lucky that General Maxwell was summoned to London on 5 May by a government so alarmed at the impact on Irish public opinion that it urged him to bring the executions to an end.

Two more executions followed on 12 May, those of Seán Mac Diarmada and James Connolly – both signatories of the Proclamation. Having confirmed Connolly's fate after a discussion with William Wylie, the prosecuting officer at the trials, Maxwell asked who was next. De Valera, Wylie replied, stumbling like so many others over the strange name. 'Is he someone important?' asked Maxwell, and Wylie made what Tim Pat Coogan has described as 'the immortal reply: "No. He is a school-master who was taken at Boland's Mill,"'[32] and so de Valera escaped death. With the benefit of hindsight and in the light of all de Valera made of the life thus spared, Wylie's reply does indeed seem immortal; but in the context of the time it reveals a more mundane reality: Éamon de Valera survived in 1916 because he was unknown.

Nor was he well known outside the ranks of his own battalion when, on 10 May, he was transferred from Kilmainham to the less draconian regime of Mountjoy prison. His sojourn there, when he was visited by his wife and his two eldest children (Vivion and

Máirín), lasted only a week. On 17 May he was among a batch of prisoners sent to England under military escort. 'They had been given permission to smoke . . . and as they approached the desolate moorlands of Dartmoor and caught sight of the prison, one man jokingly resolved to give up smoking until his five years' sentence had passed, another until Ireland would be free. De Valera, taking the pipe out of his mouth, announced that he would never smoke again.'[33]

Nor did he. The episode is emblematic of the strength of will and self-sufficiency that would serve de Valera so well in prison and ever afterwards.

4

The Assumption of Power, 1916–19

De Valera was a political nobody when he crossed the threshold of Dartmoor on 17 May 1916. Thirteen months later, on 16 June 1917, he was released. A mere eleven months of liberty, until he was re-arrested in 1918, coincidentally, on 17 May, sufficed for his emergence as the unchallenged and unchallengeable leader of Ireland's revolutionary nationalists.

Why has the significance of 1917 as the pivotal year in de Valera's life been so little recognised? Largely because it is sandwiched between the bloody headlines of 1916 and the earthquake of Sinn Féin's triumph in the general election of 1918. But, although de Valera's status as the only surviving commandant of the Easter Rising provided the platform for his pretension to leadership, it was not in 1916 but in 1917 that he carved out his path to power.

In the immediate aftermath of the rising, few Irish Volunteers, outside the 3rd Battalion of the Dublin Brigade, had ever heard of de Valera. Robert Brennan, subsequently a close ally, recalled walking around the exercise yard of Mountjoy prison In May 1916 with Thomas Ashe and Harry Boland, who pointed out to him 'a morose-looking man, serious for his years, with extraordinary [sic] long legs, and a head that was small for his large frame. It was de Valera.'[1] Serious for his years: this was among the qualities that was to set de Valera apart from almost all the other prisoners.

Age was another. De Valera was then thirty-three years old when an 'overwhelming majority' of Volunteers – '82 per cent in 1917–19' – was under thirty and the median age for officers was twenty-five.[2]

Education set de Valera even further apart. A minuscule proportion of Volunteers had been educated at Blackrock or any other
fee-paying college. Fewer still had been to university, let alone
earned the title of 'professor'. An exception was Eoin MacNeill, the
Professor of Early Irish History at University College Dublin, and
it was scarcely coincidental that he was the only other prisoner
whom de Valera treated as an equal. 'The fighting men of limited
education, like myself,' observed an officer in Fianna Éireann, the
nationalist youth movement, 'devoted most of our energy to the
reorganisation of military organisations, while the men of education took over the political machinery. In other words, men of
my type were to accept the position of citizen soldiers.'[3] Robert
Holland of the 4th Battalion of the Volunteers, recollecting the
scene in Richmond Barracks after the rising when those identified
as ringleaders were separated from the rank and file, wrote
poignantly of how those left behind 'must have looked a very
squalid sight, as now our leaders and intellectuals had been taken
away from us.'[4]

'Imprisonment in England was the making of Éamon de Valera,'
David Fitzpatrick has acknowledged. 'But for his assured perform-
ance as a leader of the Irish prisoners in Dartmoor, Maidstone, and
Lewes, the tongue-tied and hesitant professor of mathematics at
Carysfort College would scarcely have seemed a credible candidate
for the republican leadership.'[5]

The arrival in Dartmoor of Eoin MacNeill after about a month
triggered de Valera's emergence as the prisoners' leader. MacNeill
had marred his reputation among revolutionary nationalists by
issuing the countermanding order on Easter Sunday in an attempt
to abort a rising he regarded as doomed to failure. 'We were all
conscious that the prisoners had mixed feelings about him, as he
had prevented the Rising from being what it might have been,'
observed Robert Brennan of what happened on the first morning
when MacNeill joined the prisoners waiting to go out to exercise.

To our amazement, de Valera stepped out from our ranks and faced us. His voice rang out: 'Irish Volunteers! Attention! Eyes left.' The command – a salute to MacNeill – was obeyed with military precision. 'Eyes front!' Again the command was obeyed and de Valera stepped back into the ranks, leaving us all a bit amazed by his amazing chivalry and courage. This was rank mutiny, one of the two offences involving corporal punishment. De Valera was marched off to the separate cells. We did not know what was going to happen to him. As it turned out, nothing did, except that he was returned to us in the afternoon.[6]

Although the episode much enhanced de Valera's stature, his attitude to MacNeill was ambivalent. He admired, even revered, him as a founder of the Gaelic League and whose pioneering scholarship on early Irish history had led to his appointment as the inaugural Professor of Early Irish History in University College Dublin, an eminence to which the would-be academic de Valera could never hope to ascend. This was bolstered by his respect for MacNeill's role as the founder of the Irish Volunteers; MacNeill had presided over their first meeting in November 1913, at which de Valera had enlisted. But admiration stopped short of deference. For de Valera resolutely refused to surrender to MacNeill that primacy of place among the prisoners to which he felt himself entitled by virtue of his status as the senior surviving commandant of the rising.

The issue came to a head when the prisoners, initially in solitary confinement, decided to elect a commandant when they were given the right to association. At first, opinion favoured reinstating MacNeill 'in his own as well as the national esteem . . . But de Valera would have none of it. He claimed that as the senior surviving Volunteer commander he was entitled to the honour of the position of the prisoners' commandant, and that, as MacNeill had . . . placed himself outside the ranks of those who had fought, he could not hold that position.' MacNeill then withdrew and supported de Valera's claim to election.[7]

Another incident in Dartmoor in October 1916, when de Valera threw a loaf of bread to another prisoner, reinforced his primacy.

When the warder reported him to the prison governor, de Valera 'pleaded that as the bread was his and he did not require it he had the right to give it to any man who required more food'. He was sentenced to three days on bread and water. 'He was the first man to get this punishment, and this, and his fight for his fellow prisoners . . . marked him out as our future leader', recorded one Volunteer.[8]

De Valera was patient with the few prisoners 'constantly urging him to take some decisive action . . . using all his powers of logic and commonsense and, invariably, he won them to his viewpoint'. But he reacted very differently to the even smaller group 'who questioned, not so much his judgement, or his decisions, but his authority'. One sympathetic observer – Robert Brennan, a fellow prisoner who became a life-long admirer – later recalled that de Valera 'resented this attitude bitterly. He held that since authority had been freely bestowed on him by his comrades, every man was bound in duty and in honour to recognise it.'[9]

Éamon de Valera 'is decidedly a "personality" and the others seem to look up to him as their "leader"', reported Dartmoor's prison governor, Major Reade. Fearing 'a sympathetic strike' if de Valera carried out his threat to go on hunger strike if again punished, Reade had him transferred to Maidstone on 21 October 1916 from where he petitioned the Home Secretary on 9 November to be put in solitary confinement 'rather than to have to associate intimately with those who ordinarily find their way to your convict prisons'. This resulted in his transfer to another prison, Lewes, where, on 13 November, the government decided that all Irish prisoners sentenced to penal servitude should be brought together and segregated from ordinary convicts under a more relaxed regime. But de Valera continued to voice the prisoners' grievances, culminating, on 28 May 1917, in his handing the principal warder a written statement demanding 'that we be made prisoners of war' and refusing to do any labour 'except those services directly necessary for ourselves'. By 4 June all the prisoners had associated themselves with de Valera's action and he and others regarded as ringleaders were sent back to Maidstone.[10] By now news of the impasse had spread to Dublin, where a big protest meeting in support of the prisoners took place on 10 June.

De Valera's first thirteen months in jail drew to a close when the British government decided to release the prisoners as a good-will gesture to mark the opening of an all-party convention ostensibly designed to solve the Irish question. On 16 June 1917, as he walked out of Pentonville, the jail where all the prisoners had been assembled in preparation for their return to Ireland, de Valera was handed a telegram that inaugurated a political career that was to extend over half a century: it informed him that he had been chosen as the Sinn Féin candidate in a by-election in East Clare. There remained a final gesture on the way home that copper-fastened the prisoners' unswerving allegiance when de Valera marched them into the first-class saloon of the ship at Holyhead and refused the captain's appeals to move to the third-class quarters for which they had been given tickets.[11]

The extraordinary scenes when the returning prisoners arrived in Dublin on 18 June 1917 cast a national spotlight on de Valera's assumption of power. 'Up to this he was not much in the limelight,' recalled one Volunteer. 'I don't remember having heard his name previously but, now that he led our prisoners home, he was hailed and accepted as our new leader.'[12] '[The] Sinn Féin prisoners arrived in Dublin about 8 a. m. They were met by thousands who had been there since 6 a. m. Many had been waiting all night. They received a tremendous ovation. It was noticed that de Valera was apparently the recognised leader,'[13] wrote Monsignor Curran, Archbishop Walsh's secretary, in what was the first of many references to de Valera in a detailed political diary. Kevin O'Shiel later wrote of their reception that he

never saw anything to equal it, save, perhaps, the reception of Fitz-maurice and the German fliers in Dublin after the [first] East–West crossing of the Atlantic . . . All Dublin went wild with delight and was left to herself to do so, the forces of 'Law and Order' being conspicuous by their absence . . . The hero of the day was undoubtedly de Valera. His exploits during Easter Week . . . that he was the last insurgent commander to surrender, and his subsequent activities in Lewes Gaol, as leader of the men's revolt against convict treatment, all united to make this hitherto unknown man the most famous and most sought-after individual in Dublin on that historic occasion, and in thus forcing him and his unquestionable qualities forward into the full public view, paved the way for his ultimate selection by the Nation as its accepted Leader.[14]

For as long as he was in jail, de Valera was preoccupied with the survival of the Volunteers, not with the electoral prospects of Sinn Féin. 'The armed force started in 1913 must not be allowed to disappear,' he wrote at Easter 1917. 'The Irish Volunteers, or whatever else you like to call them, must be kept as a permanent force at the country's back. That it seems to us is our mission as a body and we must allow nothing to make us forget it.' Hence his scepticism about fighting by-elections against the Irish Parliamentary Party – 'to provoke a contest in which *defeat* may well mean *ruin* . . . As soldiers (Irish Volunteers, etc.) we should abstain *officially* . . . and no candidate should in future be *officially* recognised as standing in our interests or as representing our ideals.'[15] When a little-known Lewes prisoner, Joseph McGuinness, was proposed as a candidate for a by-election in South Longford, it was de Valera who drafted his letter refusing the nomination. If McGuinness lost and the prisoners were identified with his candidature, he wrote, 'it would mean the ruin of the hopes – not to say the ideals – which prompted our comrades to give the word last Easter . . . His defeat would mean our defeat – the irretrievable ruin of all our comrades died for and all their death had gained.' But de Valera acknowledged that the prisoners were 'in a regular fog' and lacked the 'necessary data for the forming of a solid judgement . . . We are anxious to co-operate with you outside but we do not quite understand what you are doing.'[16] The judgement of those outside, notably

Michael Collins, prevailed. McGuinness was nominated and his victory – albeit by the slenderest of margins – in the by-election on 9 May was the backdrop for Sinn Féin's nominating de Valera to contest a by-election in East Clare two months later.

The wheel had now turned full circle. De Valera unequivocally rejected the offer of Joseph O'Connor, who had succeeded him as commandant of the 3rd Battalion of the Volunteers when it was reorganised after the rising, to resign in his favour: 'He would not accept,' recalled O'Connor, 'stating that his activity would be in the political line from henceforward.'[17] 'When this lousy war is over, no more soldiering for me': the marching refrain of British troops on the western front springs irresistibly to mind. Substitute 'splendid' or some such adjective, for 'lousy' (because de Valera never ceased to revere 1916 and those who then lost their lives) and it meets the case. In 1917 the man who in 1915 and in 1916 had turned his back on politics because he was a soldier now turned his back on soldiering because he wanted to become a politician.

Yet again de Valera was lucky. Fate in the shape of his release from jail gave him a golden opportunity to set his personal stamp on the East Clare campaign, to gain experience of all aspects of electioneering of which he had hitherto been innocent (in particular, of speaking at public meetings) and, most important of all, to win a popular mandate at the polls. He seized it with relish. His first step was to unite the Volunteers behind his campaign. He resisted the enduring antagonism towards Eoin MacNeill and agreed to go to Clare only if MacNeill accompanied him. A few objected but finally consented if MacNeill 'would declare in favour of an Irish Republic. He did so.'[18] That de Valera campaigned in his Volunteer uniform was a measure of his fidelity to the military wing of the movement and, as Michael Laffan has pointed out, 'it was during the Clare election that the Volunteers re-emerged in public as a powerful element in Irish life. They paraded through the streets, formed escorts for de Valera, acted as a private police force, and generally succeeded in making the RIC [Royal Irish Constabulary] redundant.'[19]

'First known to the people as "The Spaniard" or "The man with the strange name",[20] there was an element of the exotic about de Valera when he descended on what was to become his constituency for over forty years. One supporter, a Volunteer from Waterford, remembered meeting de Valera with his uncle 'coming along in a pony and trap' from Charleville just after his arrival: 'They went into the labourer's cottage where Dev was reared. We were asked in, but refused as we thought it better not to butt in on such an occasion.' De Valera then made his first election speech to a meeting in Bruree: 'He was a rather picturesque looking foreign type and went down well with the crowd, though his speech was halting.'[21] He told audiences that they 'must be prepared to fight against England' and that every vote was 'as good as the crack of a rifle'.[22]

But de Valera knew that he needed the support of the Catholic Church in order to broaden his electoral appeal; his most influential clerical supporter was Bishop Fogarty of Killaloe – Clare was within his diocese – and parish priests invariably presided at his election meetings. Hence his denial of allegations that he was an anarchist or an atheist, saying that 'all his life he had been associated with priests, and the priests knew him and were behind him in this election'. While he insisted that the 1916 rising 'had saved the soul of Ireland', he also declared that 'another Easter week would be a superfluity'; but 'he and his friends' 'would not altogether eliminate physical force from their programme' when that 'would mean that John Bull could kick as much as he liked'.[23] His sinuous ambivalence 'persuaded a large part of the clergy and their flock that celebration of one rising was not tantamount to preparation for another', and even parish priests who supported the Irish Parliamentary Party's candidate, Patrick Lynch, 'found their curates campaigning for de Valera'.[24] His assiduous playing of the Catholic card is neatly captured in the verses composed by the parish priest of Killaloe after a mass meeting in Ennis on 29 June; they were then set to music by the parish priest of

Clonlara and published in the *Clare Champion* three days before polling day:

> De Valera had spoken in manly appeal
> To the gallant Dalcassians, and up stood MacNeill,
> As his pleadings for Erin with eloquence fell,
> Hark, sweet came the tones of the Angelus bell.
> A reverend pause as the sound reached his ears,
> Then he called out aloud to a priest standing near,
> 'The Angelus, Father,' and bowed was each head,
> As the message of God in the old town was said.[25]

This tightrope act between the poles of clerical and revolutionary support fashioned a majority that began four decades of uninterrupted election victories in Clare and signalled de Valera's emergence as a popular hero (see plate 10). The result of the East Clare byelection, announced on 11 July 1917, sent a seismic shockwave through the Irish political landscape. Before the birth of opinion polls by-elections were the best guide to electoral attitudes and what mattered was not that de Valera won – by 5,010 votes to Patrick Lynch's 2,035 – but the magnitude of his 5–2 majority. 'The result was an amazing one, and spells the death knell of the [Irish Parliamentary] Party,' Monsignor Curran wrote in his diary the next day.

Lynch was a very strong candidate and, in addition to the support of the powerful Lynch clan in Clare, received the Unionist vote. Nobody expected anything like this result. The [Irish Parliamentary] Party was confident of winning and, until yesterday, the Sinn Féin party themselves did not expect to win by more than a small margin. The election was fought openly on the issue of an independent Irish Republic... The result gave rise to tremendous demonstrations throughout the country. The [Irish Parliamentary] Party and their journal [the *Freeman's Journal*] are frankly in a panic. A huge landslide is carrying away all their followers into the Sinn Féin camp.

The 'chief importance' of the outcome, concluded Curran, was 'the open assertion of an Irish Republic as the object of the Sinn Féin organisation'.[26]

De Valera was now the personification of Sinn Féin's success, and the way was open for his formal installation as its leader. But, first, he set about severing his ties with another organisation: the Irish Republican Brotherhood. Although de Valera 'was nominally in the IRB' he was 'never enthusiastic . . . or took an active part in it in any shape or form'; as he explained to Richard Walsh, 'he was formally introduced to and sworn into the organisation but . . . he practically had no more connection with them'.[27] His brief and reluctant membership of the IRB, in other words, was no more than a cosmetic exercise without conviction. He had joined only to consolidate his own powers of military leadership in the rising. Once the rising was over, the IRB, he argued while in Lewes jail, was redundant. Immediately after his release from Pentonville on 16 June 1917 he told Diarmuid Lynch, the Munster representative on the IRB's supreme council from 1911 to 1916, that 'he would discontinue membership, but gave no reason for his decision'.[28]

The East Clare campaign delayed the implementation of that decision but the result reaffirmed its necessity. Armed with such a stunning popular mandate, de Valera moved swiftly to sever his ties with a secret society he had always disdained and whose decisions he had little prospect of influencing and none of controlling. In August 1917

a message came to the Centres Board [of the IRB] that de Valera wished to be relieved of his oath and resign [*sic*] the organisation as he had conscientious scruples with regard to an oath and had never slept easily since he took the oath of the IRB. This was a conscientious objection provided for by the organisation that any member who had conscientious scruples with regard to the oath at any time could resign, so that de Valera did not resign as a mutineer, he resigned in the constitutional manner. Collins declared his belief that de Valera would never hurt the IRB.[29]

The procedure adopted by de Valera was characteristically pedantic but politically astute, as the reaction of Michael Collins illustrated; it also served to minimise resentment within the IRB. De Valera's relationship with the IRB, in short, was essentially opportunistic: the strength of his Catholic convictions suggests his scruples about membership of a secret society were sincere but they had not prevented his joining the IRB when he perceived an advantage in his doing so. De Valera's path to power in 1916–17, moreover, was a public path. His authority rested on the twin foundations of public acclaim as the senior surviving Volunteer of 1916, reinforced by public recognition of his role as the prisoners' leader and of his stunning electoral success in East Clare. The byzantine workings of a secret society offered no opportunity for the exercise of his new-found talent for attracting public acclamation. In this at least, Tim Pat Coogan's citing of the 'gifts with which he was increasingly finding that he could manipulate public opinion' and observation that 'what he feared was not being able to *control* the Brotherhood'[30] are convincing.

His triumph in East Clare imbued de Valera with the self-confidence to distance himself from the absolutism of the most doctrinaire republicans and he now began to elaborate what Charles Townshend has described as 'the political formula that would offer Sinn Féin a distinctive (yet also usefully ambiguous) platform for the future. "We want an Irish republic", declared de Valera, "because if Ireland had her freedom, it is, I believe the most likely form of government. But if the Irish wanted to have another form of government, so long as it was an Irish government, I would not put in a word against it."'[31]

De Valera's gaining control both of Sinn Féin and of the Volunteers was preceded by his unanimous election as 'Chief' of Fianna Éireann on the proposal of Countess Markievicz, who had founded the revolutionary nationalist youth organisation, at a convention held at 41 York Street in August 1917.[32] Although the leadership of Sinn Féin was a harder nut to crack, East Clare was the apotheosis of a phenomenon described by Michael Laffan: 'The new Sinn Féin which emerged in the opening months of that year enjoyed mass support even before it had developed an organisation.' Revolutionary nationalists were divided about whether MPs should abstain from attending the Westminster parliament, as decreed by Arthur Griffith's 'old' Sinn Féin, but Count Plunkett, father of Joseph Mary Plunkett who had been executed in 1916, had announced his intention of doing so after his own victory in the North Roscommon by-election in February. Many Volunteers, who resented Griffith's 'luke-warm attitude to the rising . . . tried to squeeze him out' and a convention, summoned by Plunkett in Dublin's Mansion House on 19 April, 'came close to splitting the separatist movement'. Plunkett's scheme to establish a Liberty League, 'a nationwide system of clubs which would duplicate and rival the existing Sinn Féin structures' under Griffith's control, fomented further dissension. But the two groups merged under the Sinn Féin umbrella in June when it was agreed that 'Griffith would remain as president until October when a convention of all the amalgamated Sinn Féin clubs would review the situation'. Although Griffith despised Plunkett, he had lavished praise on de Valera in an editorial in *Nationality* in July: 'In choosing Éamon de Valera as its representative, East Clare has not only chosen a true and gallant Irishman – it has chosen a man with the mind and capacity that Ireland will need at the Peace Conference – the mind and capacity of the Statesman.'[33]

Griffith's acquiescence in de Valera's meteoric ascent to power was decisive. The prospect of a three-way contest for the leadership between Griffith, de Valera and Count Plunkett evaporated when, a week before the convention, Griffith and de Valera met privately in the D.B.C. restaurant at the top of Dublin's Grafton Street. The discussion was 'friendly' but de Valera's appetite for power surfaced when he pressed his own claims on the grounds that 'the new Sinn Féin was largely a Volunteer movement'. Griffith not only gave way but offered to propose de Valera.[34] 'De Valera is a younger man than I am,' Griffith privately explained. 'He is a soldier and, I think, a statesman.'[35] Sorcha Nic Diarmada, a member of Cumann na mBan and the Gaelic League, recalled Griffith's using the same words in his speech proposing de Valera at the convention: 'For the first time since the time of Parnell we have a statesman and in addition a soldier.'[36]

De Valera's private interpretation as he canvassed for support at the home of Dr Kathleen Lynn, a meeting place for Sinn Féin women, reflected both his determination to secure the first place and his willingness to use IRB support to achieve his goal. He explained that he would be 'a kind of compromise' between Griffith, Plunkett and MacNeill, saying disingenuously that 'he himself was not anxious for it – he was very modest and retiring – but that that was the decision of the boys – that he would be the compromise. That was the solution.'[37] His reluctance to join 'the boys' in their secret conclaves no more inhibited him in his campaign for the presidency of Sinn Féin than it had inhibited him when he had taken the IRB oath to bolster his leadership credentials in the prelude to the Easter Rising. De Valera's distaste for the IRB was not the only example of how he tailored his leadership in line with Catholic orthodoxies. Another was the fate of the candidature of P. S. O'Hegarty for appointment as his presidential secretary. O'Hegarty was openly anti-clerical, declaring in a newspaper article in 1909, for example, that what anti-clericalism really meant was the insistence 'for the nation as a whole and for every individual in it that the Church should confine itself to such matters as come with its province and that secular matters should remain secular'.[38] So, despite Michael Collins being 'very keen' on O'Hegarty getting the post, de Valera, once 'he heard that he [O'Hegarty] had not been married in a Catholic Church, said, "No"'.[39]

When the convention, Sinn Féin's tenth *ard fheis*, attended by some 1,700 delegates, met in the Round Room of Dublin's Mansion House on 25–6 October 1917, the result was a foregone conclusion. De Valera was duly elected unopposed as president, on Griffith's nomination, on the first day. The key passage in the provisional constitution, as drafted by de Valera, sought to reconcile the views of the hard-line republicans with those of Griffith, who felt an unambiguous commitment to a republic would be a tactical error; it stated: 'Sinn Féin aims at securing the international recognition of Ireland as an independent Irish Republic. Having achieved that status the Irish people may by referendum freely choose their own form of government.'[40]

There was no such ambiguity about de Valera's acceptance speech. His election, he told the convention, endorsed Sinn Féin's aim of 'securing international recognition of Ireland as an independent Irish Republic' and 'declared to the world that the policy we put before the people of East Clare is the policy of the people of all Ireland'. He then repeated what he had said when he was elected in East Clare: that he regarded his election as a tribute to the dead of 1916.

I regard my election here as a monument to the brave dead, and I believe that this is proof that they were right, that what they fought for – the complete and absolute freedom and separation from England – was the pious wish of every Irish heart . . . the only banner under which our freedom can be won at the present time is the republican banner. It is as an Irish Republic that we have a chance of getting international recognition . . . This is not the time for discussion on the best forms of government. But we are all united on this – that we want complete and absolute independence . . . this is the time to get freedom. Then we can settle by the most democratic means what particular form of government we may have.[41]

Given de Valera's fulminations to his wife in 1911 that he would never join Sinn Féin,[42] there was a piquant irony in his sudden emergence as their leader. Indeed, when he was asked in April 1948 as a witness in the Sinn Féin funds case, which hinged on the disposal of the party's assets after the Treaty split in 1922, when he had joined 'the Sinn Féin Organisation' his answer was remarkably vague: 'It is not easy to say . . . The Organisation was reconstituted in October 1917, and at that meeting reconstituting it, I was appointed as President. After coming out of prison I was on a committee, whether it was the committee of the old Sinn Féin or not, I don't know.'[43] But what signified was that the Sinn Féin convention completed his transformation from soldier to politician. 'We should have got beyond the stage when we regard politics as roguery and a politician as a rogue,' he told his listeners, who, as David Fitzpatrick has remarked, realised that de Valera 'had become a politician and none dared call him a rogue'.[44]

On the evening of the last day of the Sinn Féin convention the Irish Volunteer convention took place in surroundings very different from the affected grandeur of the Mansion House: a building in the Gaelic Athletic Association's headquarters in Croke Park known as the Pavilion, part of which 'was filled with hay'. The delegates, numbering about 1,100, all of whom had also been delegates at the Sinn Féin convention, sat 'on portions of an open stand and around on the hay'. De Valera chaired the meeting and those 'behind him, lying on the pile of hay' included Michael Collins, Cathal Brugha, Terence MacSwiney and Ernest Blythe – 'all the prominent men in the republican physical force movement of that time were present'.[45] Although 'there was no mention of a "renewal of hostilities"',[46] de Valera's election as president of the Volunteers set the seal on his ascendancy because, in the phrase of his official biographers, 'the military and political wings of the National movement were now combined under one man'.[47] De Valera himself spelled out the magnitude of his achievement at a pivotal moment during the Dáil debates on the Treaty: 'The political leader at the time [Griffith] . . . surrendered at the Convention his Chairmanship of the Sinn Féin Organisation, surrendered it to me, and I was elected political head unanimously.' Even before that, Cathal Brugha, the Dáil's then minister of defence, 'had surrendered to me, as Senior Officer in the Army at the time, the headship of the Irish Volunteers. I combined therefore in myself for the time being, the political headship and the military headship.'[48]

The events of October 1917 marked a change not only in de Valera's accretion of political power but also in his financial circumstances. As president of Sinn Féin, he was voted an annual salary of £500 a year. All thought of a teaching career was abandoned. Politics had become what it always remained thereafter: his profession. He was well paid and, as mounting popular support in the United States as well as in Ireland swelled Sinn Féin's coffers, he could also draw on whatever expenses he deemed necessary in pursuit of his objectives as its president. His presidential salary enabled him to improve the material comfort of the family he saw so rarely between 1916 and 1925 – he and Sinéad now had five children – by renting a comfortable house in Greystones, a seaside village on the railway line fifteen miles south of Dublin. The last months of 1917 was a time of almost unparalleled domestic tranquillity – a sixth child was born in August 1918 – that came to an end only in the spring of 1918 with the eruption of the conscription crisis after the German breakthrough on the western front threatened to tilt the war in Germany's favour before America's full weight was brought to bear against it.

The crisis began on 9 April when the British prime minister, David Lloyd George, introduced a Military Service Bill that empowered his government to extend conscription to Ireland. Spontaneous outrage erupted in nationalist areas of the country. On the very next day de Valera took an independent initiative that revealed the extraordinary composure and self-confidence that was to characterise his dealings with the hierarchy of the Catholic Church throughout his political career: he went secretly to Archbishop's House in Dublin and sought a meeting with the archbishop, William Walsh. He did not see Walsh, who had been ill with a disfiguring skin disease since 1916, but he did speak at length to his secretary, Monsignor Michael Curran, of 'how deeply troubled he was by the fear that the bishops might paralyse strong action by a weak or vaguely general statement, or give the least excuse to the weak-kneed to adopt a mere passive resistance'. De Valera was especially concerned about Cardinal Logue, the Archbishop of Armagh, whose deep hostility to Sinn Féin had found expression in a pastoral in November 1917. When Curran got confirmation that 'a general meeting of the bishops' was to take place, he began planning to co-ordinate the bishops' response with 'that of the political leaders'. As de Valera's 'acute anxiety . . . coincided precisely with the archbishop's [Walsh's] anxiety over Cardinal Logue', Curran – without telling Walsh – decided to inform de Valera about the forthcoming meeting of the bishops and 'to propose to him that the political leaders should meet at once, formulate their strong policy', for which they would then seek the bishops' support. 'The bishops would thus be relieved . . . of the initiative and would find it easier to follow on in support of the laymen.' On 14 April Curran called on Dublin's Sinn Féin Lord Mayor, Larry O'Neill, and urged him to summon an immediate meeting of the Mansion House Conference established to co-ordinate resistance to conscription, saying that 'no time must be lost and that the laymen should set the headline for action'.

The Lord Mayor duly summoned a meeting of the Mansion House Conference on 18 April, the same day that the bishops were meeting in Maynooth. When O'Neill contacted Archbishop Walsh on the evening of 17 April, he affected ignorance when the archbishop told him of the bishops' meeting and it was agreed that the Lord Mayor would telephone before lunch the next day to arrange for the bishops to receive delegates from the Mansion House Conference on the grounds that 'this was vastly better than sending a statement'; but the archbishop's role in these machinations 'was to be kept secret'. De Valera sought to make assurance doubly sure by calling again at Archbishop's House at nine o'clock before the Mansion House Conference began. Although his offer to see the archbishop if he so wished was declined, de Valera again hammered home his request to Curran, who duly conveyed it to Walsh: 'that the bishops would say nothing which would hinder those who were prepared to defend themselves with arms to the last'.[49]

Nationalists of every hue duly united in opposition to conscription at the Mansion House on 18 April, the day the bill was enacted. De Valera made a striking first impression on the other nationalists who knew nothing of his secret choreography of the day's events. 'His transparent sincerity, his gentleness and equability captured the hearts of us all,' wrote the old parliamentarian William O'Brien.

His gaunt frame and sad eyes buried in their sockets had much of the Dante-esque suggestion of 'the man who had been in hell'. His was that subtle blend of virility and emotion which the Americans mean when they speak of 'a magnetic man'. Even the obstinacy (and it was sometimes trying) with which he would defend a thesis, as though it were a point in pure mathematics, with more than French bigotry for logic, became tolerable enough when, with a boyish smile, he would say: 'You will bear with me, won't you? You know I am an old schoolmaster?'[50]

De Valera steered proceedings throughout the day. He drafted the pledge unanimously agreed at the meeting in the Mansion House in the morning – 'Denying the right of the British Government to enforce compulsory service in this country, we pledge ourselves to one another to resist conscription by the most effective means at our disposal' – and a delegation then went immediately and brought the pledge to the meeting of bishops. The delegation consisted of representatives of Sinn Féin (de Valera and Griffith); the Irish Parliamentary Party (their new leader, John Dillon (John Redmond had died on 6 March), and Joe Devlin), the dissident Irish nationalist MPs of the All-for-Ireland League (William O'Brien and Tim Healy) and the Irish Labour Party (Thomas Johnson and another William O'Brien, the trade unionist and Labour leader who had been interned with de Valera in Richmond

Barracks in 1916). Some delegates were apprehensive about beard-
ing the bishops in their den and found the ecclesiastical surroundings oppressive. Not so de Valera, who felt at home in Maynooth,
where he had become temporarily head of the mathematics
department in October 1912; he was also personally acquainted
with some of the bishops.[51] 'I have lived all my life among priests,'
he reassured Tim Healy. His reception at Maynooth, likened by
one bishop to 'the descent of the Holy Ghost upon us,'[52] conferred
on Sinn Féin 'the moral sanction of a legitimate political party and
removed it from the realm of theological and moral suspicion.'[53]
His choreography included arranging the order in which the
delegates spoke. De Valera spoke first and 'made it clear that their
lordships should not say anything that could be taken as con-
demnatory of the Volunteer movement, because no matter who
decided anything the Volunteers would fight if conscription was
enforced, and they had no time for passive resistance. This last was
for Cardinal Logue's benefit.'[54]

The bishops' proclamation – that the people had the right to
resist conscription by every means consonant with God's law –
gave de Valera all he wanted. 'In no time the news of the Maynooth
visit was universally known in Dublin,' wrote Archbishop Walsh's
secretary in his diary. 'The effect was electrical. The evening papers
were grabbed by everyone and universal excitement reigned . . .
The so-called "constitutional policy" was now dead and abandoned. Newly united Ireland during those days adopted the new
policy and cut with Westminster Parliamentarianism for ever.'[55]
The episode not only set the seal on de Valera's emergence as the
leader of nationalist Ireland but also revealed the subtlety and
discrimination, as well as the remarkable assurance and sense of
authority, he brought to that role both in his negotiations with the
bishops and with older and more politically experienced nationalist leaders.

The British government, confronted with this united front
between Church and nation, shrank from the consequences of

extending conscription to Ireland and instead took refuge in a policy of coercion. On the night of 17–18 May de Valera was among 73 Sinn Féin leaders arrested on trumped-up allegations, designed to placate American opinion, of collaborating with Germany.[56] In fact de Valera had poured cold water on any such collaboration only days before in the first interview he ever gave to a foreign newspaper, the *Christian Science Monitor* of Boston. Asked if a free Ireland would 'hand over' its ports to Germany, his unequivocal reply revealed the embryo of what became his un-wavering geopolitical strategy in British–Irish relations: 'To be free means to be free, not to have a master. If England took away her troops and our independence were acknowledged, we would fight to the last man to maintain that independence.'[57]

The circumstances of de Valera's arrest in Greystones railway station are remarkable. Éamon Broy, one of Michael Collins's spies in Dublin Castle, had given clear warning not only of who was on the list of those to be arrested but of exactly when the arrests would be carried out. Indeed Broy and Patrick Tracy, the go-between who had conveyed Broy's information to Collins, were so mystified as to 'what had gone wrong' that they wondered 'if the "wanted" men wanted to be arrested'. When Broy later questioned Collins, he replied that 'a few minutes before train time de Valera looked at his watch and announced that, notwithstanding the threatened arrests, he was going home'; de Valera rejected all further attempts to dissuade him and 'left Westland Row travelling on the pre-arranged train'. Armed police duly arrested him as he stepped off the train in Greystones. When Broy pressed Collins on why he had 'allowed de Valera to do that' since he must have known from dealing with Broy over two years that his information was 'absolutely correct', Collins 'shrugged his shoulders and looked at Greg Murphy [a long-time comrade in the IRB], and Greg Murphy looked at him, and they both smiled. We did not pursue the subject further.'[58] The incident is a striking early example of the near-absolute obedience de Valera inspired both in Sinn Féin and in the

Volunteers, even in someone as powerful in his own right as Michael Collins.

Broy's account suggests that de Valera did indeed want to be arrested or, at the very least, embraced the likelihood of arrest with equanimity. 'His own arrest, if it happened, might do the cause more good than harm,' he later confided to Mary Bromage. 'What else was there for him to do by way of action till the war in Europe ended?'[59] Why else should de Valera have decided that imprisonment would not inhibit the leadership that he had wanted so badly and prized so highly? Partly, perhaps, because imprisonment in 1916–17 had been no barrier to his ambition: rather had it become the launching pad for his bid for leadership, which enabled him to seize the Irish nationalist imagination. His stature now resembled Charles Stewart Parnell's in the 1880s: the uncrowned king of Ireland and, again like Parnell in Kilmainham in 1881–2 and like Nelson Mandela in South Africa decades later, he could play the role of jailed leader as imprisoned martyr before a national and an international audience. His remarkable self-sufficiency, moreover, meant that jail held no terrors for him. But de Valera's indifference to the probability of imprisonment also illustrates the extraordinary self-confidence in which he had become cocooned within a matter of months: he clearly believed that, whether in or out of jail, his leadership was immune to challenge. That conviction sprang from the deference that had been accorded him since autumn 1917 by Volunteers and members of Sinn Féin alike, a deferance that became increasingly apparent during his imprisonment in 1918–19.

After a brief spell in Gloucester jail, de Valera was sent to Lincoln jail in early June. The terms of confinement for unconvicted internees, which included freedom of association, were lenient and he spent much of his time reading and writing in his cell; his appreciation of Machiavelli's *The Prince* dates from this time. Although he exercised regularly, his aloofness and the awe he inspired among his fellow prisoners was eloquently symbolised by his playing handball alone. Like so many successful leaders – Charles de Gaulle is a case in point – de Valera's extraordinary ascendancy was rooted in what Padraic Colum identified as 'his ability to take himself and his position seriously, even solemnly'.[60]

The arrests of May 1918 – which included Arthur Griffith, William Cosgrave and Countess Markievicz – ravaged the upper echelons of Sinn Féin's leadership. All its officers were arrested, apart from one of its vice-presidents, Father O'Flanagan, and an honorary secretary, Harry Boland, 'both of them on the radical republican wing of the party' and Michael Laffan has argued that, because 'politicians suffered more severely than the military' – Michael Collins, Cathal Brugha and Richard Mulcahy all evaded capture – the arrests 'helped shorten the "political phase" of the Irish revolution . . . and made a resumption of violence more probable'.[61]

Although revolutionary politics were relatively quiescent for much of 1918, de Valera's imprisonment meant his hand was no longer on the helm when the end of the Great War heralded a new political era. This was inaugurated by the announcement of a general election in December 1918, the first election for eight years. The prisoners' expectation that they would be released once the war was over came to nothing. De Valera was nominated to stand in four constituencies – East Clare, East Mayo, West Belfast and South Down. But he issued no election address because what he first wrote was blocked by the prison censor, instead declaring that 'silence is preferable to mutilated statements'.[62] Silence was eloquent enough to ensure his defeat of John Dillon in Mayo; his Clare seat was uncontested, but he failed to defeat Joe Devlin, the Irish Parliamentary Party's standard-bearer in West Belfast, and he had withdrawn from South Down in favour of the IPP candidate rather than split the nationalist vote.

De Valera's inability to contribute significantly to Sinn Féin's election strategy and his awareness of the momentous events that would follow in the wake of victory when Sinn Féin refused to take its seats in the Westminster parliament made the prospect of continued imprisonment intolerable. As soon as the election was called in November, he began planning to escape from Lincoln jail. But by the time his plans came to fruition, on the night of 3 February 1919, the election had come and gone, the Paris peace conference had begun, and, on 21 January 1919, an independent Irish parliament, Dáil Éireann, composed of the Sinn Féin MPs who had won a decisive majority of the Irish seats, had already met for the first time.

5

Mission to America, 1919–20

America commanded the attention of Ireland's revolutionary nationalists throughout 1918 because of President Woodrow Wilson's commitment to national self-determination as an American war aim. 'Self-determination is not a mere phrase,' he had explicitly declared in February 1918. 'It is an imperative principle of action which statesmen will henceforth ignore at their peril.' Their triumph in the 1918 election reinforced Irish-American sympathy for Sinn Féin, which had been growing since 1916, and they deluged Wilson with petitions for Irish self-determination. A series of mass meetings in the great American cities culminated in 'a gathering of many thousands' in New York's Madison Square Gardens on 10 December when 'a resolution endorsing Irish self-determination was radioed from the meeting to the President who was by then en route for Europe and the Peace Conference in the USS *George Washington*'.[1]

No one was more conscious of the predominance of the American dimension than the American-born Éamon de Valera: he had 'had his eye on America' since he drafted in April 1918 the Mansion House declaration, which denounced the threat of conscription as a 'direct violation of the rights of small nationalities to self-determination'.[2] Writing not as 'Éamon' but as 'Eddie' from Lincoln jail to his 'dearest mother' on 28 November 1918, he picked up the same theme: 'If America holds to the principles enunciated by her President during the war she will have a notable place in the history of nations – but will the President be able to get them accepted by others whose entry into the war was on motives less unselfish?'[3] From then on de Valera saw his own role as best played on the American stage.

In the meantime, a sub-committee of Sinn Féin's standing committee, steered by Seán T. O'Kelly and Harry Boland (the party's honorary secretaries), charted the way ahead. De Valera had no part in choosing Sinn Féin's election candidates, a process that Boland and Michael Collins were 'widely credited' with having manipulated 'in order to ensure the IRB's domination of the nascent republican assembly [the first Dáil]'. The same sub-committee drew up the party's election manifesto, which 'repeated the demand for an Irish republic, demanded the withdrawal of Irish representatives from Westminster, and called for the establishment of a constituent assembly. It also committed the party to using "any and every means available to render impotent the power of England to hold Ireland in subjection by military force or otherwise".'[4] This explicit threat of physical force reflected the IRB's influence, which the imprisoned de Valera was unable to counteract. Collins and Boland had insisted that 'the Republic must be made the mandate' in the election, as they told de Valera when they got him out of Lincoln jail; he responded that 'if he had been out he would have opposed this, believing that they would be beaten at the polls, but seeing that they had won the elections he was satisfied'.[5] 'You made it strong,' said de Valera to Robert Brennan, the author of the final draft of the manifesto, on the day he returned to Dublin; 'I wouldn't have gone so far.'[6] The remark implicitly acknowledged his temporary impotence and his regret at having played no part in drafting the election manifesto, just as he had played no part in drafting the 1916 proclamation.

The election manifesto was as riddled with unreality as it was strong on rhetoric. Its treatment of the central problem of British–Irish relations, the appropriate constitutional relationship between the two islands, was crude and simplistic: it denied that there could be any legitimate relationship between the two islands and so solved the problem by the expedient of denying its existence or, in the words of the manifesto, 'by denying the right and opposing the will of the British government or any foreign government to legislate for Ireland'. Cathal Brugha, in his opening speech as acting speaker (Ceann Comhairle) hammered that message home when the Dáil first assembled on 21 January: the significance of what they were doing was finally to break with Britain.

The key documents proclaimed at the inaugural meeting of Dáil Éireann on 21 January 1919 – the Declaration of Independence and the Message to the Free Nations of the World – were as 'strong' as the election manifesto and had none of the subtlety and refinement that came to characterise de Valera's pronouncements on British–Irish relations. The first, having ratified the Irish Republic proclaimed in 1916 and endorsed with a democratic mandate in the 1918 election, solemnly declared 'foreign government' an intolerable 'invasion of our national right' and demanded 'the evacuation of our country by the English garrison'. The second was even more belligerent: it spoke of 'the existing state of war between Ireland and England [that] can never be ended until Ireland is definitely evacuated by the armed forces of England'. Both documents were silent on how Ireland's independence here claimed in theory was to be achieved in fact.

The air of unreality was inevitable given that the Dáil's inaugural meeting in Dublin's Mansion House was little more than an exercise in international propaganda. The surroundings contributed to a sense of theatre, well captured in de Valera's remembrance of the backdrop for the anti-conscription conference of 1918: 'the exterior of the eighteenth-century Mansion House . . . with its gravelled approach and old-fashioned lamp-posts; the iron lace trimming over the great front windows; the glass *porte cochère* beneath which carriages used to discharge their dignitaries; the whole having the look of a birdcage'.[7] But the performance of 21 January 1919 lacked leading players. Arthur Griffith, like de Valera, was in jail and both Michael Collins and Harry Boland were also 'among those marked absent . . . though for the benefit of the press other deputies answered to their names', despite their both having left for England that morning to mastermind de Valera's escape from jail.[8]

By then de Valera's earlier indifference to his imprisonment had entirely evaporated. Now 'his great fear' was that the British 'might decide to release him before he could escape'. His anxiety was dispelled when his dramatic escape made headlines not just in Ireland but around the world; a highlight, not revealed until decades later, was Boland's giving de Valera his own fur-lined coat while he donned a raincoat and, 'arm-in-arm, like a fond couple, they ran the gauntlet – Harry, the supposed lady, adding to the pretence with an occasional "Good night, chums" to soldiers . . . bidding loving farewells to their girl friends' at the gates of a nearby military hospital.[9]

Michael Collins's plans for de Valera to go into hiding in Manchester until the hue and cry diminished went like clockwork. But Collins's report that de Valera intended to go immediately to America burst like a bombshell when the Volunteers GHQ next met. The statement, recalled Piarais Beaslaí,

was received by all of us with dismay. We felt that de Valera's departure would be a fatal mistake, that the country would misunderstand his motives and regard it as selfish, or even cowardly desertion. When this view was expressed, Collins replied, 'I told him so, but you know what it is to try to argue with Dev. He said he had thought it all out in prison and that he feels the one place where he can be useful to Ireland is in America.' The meeting took the view that the place for an Irish leader was in Ireland where the strength of the fight put up would determine the support in America, and it was decided to send Brugha to urge de Valera not to go at all or, failing that, to show himself first in Ireland so that the publicity value of his escape should not be dissipated.[10]

'He had thought it all out.' 'You know what it is to try to argue with Dev.' These two phrases well serve as epigrams for a style of leadership already set in stone. His colleagues' acceptance, however reluctant, of his decisions is of comparable significance, particularly in the case of Michael Collins, who had likewise complied with de Valera's acquiescence in his own arrest in May 1918.

Authority was the heart of the matter: what Robert Brennan had already identified as de Valera's bitter resentment of any questioning of his authority in Dartmoor, 'freely bestowed on him by his comrades [which] every man was bound in duty and in honour to recognise'.[11] By 1919 Éamon de Valera's authority had become national. Initially endorsed in the East Clare by-election, immensely reinforced by his unanimous election as president of both Sinn Féin and of the Volunteers and by Sinn Féin's triumph in the 1918 election, it would be further buttressed by his election as president of Dáil Éireann when he returned to Dublin. Small wonder, then, that de Valera and his colleagues alike were already behaving as if his pronouncements were infallible and his authority unassailable.

The task of persuading de Valera to return to Dublin fell to Cathal Brugha, who had been 'appointed President of the Ministry *pro. tem.*'[12] when the Dáil had assembled in private session on 22 January. Brugha was 'a man of very limited intelligence' but with 'unlimited physical courage, and he was very determined and obstinate in whatever line he had taken up. There was a sort of respect for him because of his heroism in Easter week, but, mixed with that, was something like contempt for the naïveté of his views'.[13] These characteristics were abundantly evident when he met de Valera, then hiding in the house of a Catholic chaplain to a Manchester workhouse, and resurrected his harebrained scheme to assassinate British cabinet ministers (first unveiled during the conscription crisis)[14] in the event of British forces moving against the Dáil. 'Theoretically, if the cabinet forced a war on the Irish people, de Valera felt any defensive action against members of that cabinet was justified'; but 'whether such an attempt would damage rather than help the Irish cause was another matter'. De Valera demurred because, as he told his authorised biographers, he 'did not feel called upon to argue the question too closely since it was not an immediate issue'. Nor was it an issue that he would have welcomed as falling within his remit as president and, although Brugha succeeded in persuading him to return to Dublin, the need for an American mission was, unsurprisingly, 'never fully out of his mind' from the moment he arrived in Dublin on 20 February. His first act was to give an interview to an American journalist highlighting the intention of putting Ireland's case to the Paris peace conference.[15] The interview consisted of points dictated by a cautious de Valera for simultaneous publication by 'some 700 newspapers served by the United Press of America . . . When eventually published on 12 March, the interview aroused controversy by explicitly condoning violence as a last resort. 'If the Paris Conference fails to take steps to extend self-determination to Ireland, violence will be the only alternative left to Irish patriots.'[16]

Seán T. O'Kelly had been ensconced in the Grand Hotel in Paris as the self-styled 'accredited envoy of the Provisional Government of the Irish Republic' since 8 February. Although his initial efforts to win admission for an Irish delegation of de Valera, Griffith and Count Plunkett were unavailing, he wrote to Brugha on 7 March urging that de Valera should come to Paris 'if at all possible in two or three weeks' time'.[17] But de Valera's obsession with going to America was undiminished; so much so that, even as Harry Boland smuggled him into the relative security of the gate lodge of Archbishop's House in Drumcondra on 24 February, de Valera commissioned him to get him a large-size fountain pen for use on board ship. As the archbishop's secretary, Father Curran, unbeknownst to the ailing Archbishop Walsh, guided him through the adjoining and deserted grounds of Clonliffe College past 'the brilliantly lit windows of the College, de Valera recalled his own personal associations with Clonliffe'. After a week spent revising the text of Ireland's statement for presentation to the Paris conference – the historical section had been drafted by Father Curran in collaboration with two Jesuits – de Valera hastened his departure from Dublin and returned to Liverpool on 3 March to await embarkation to New York.[18] He seemed indifferent to the risks of recapture and 'the hazards to which [he] exposed himself by attempting to leave for America left Collins [who masterminded such enterprises] aghast'.[19]

But the political climate changed overnight when the post-war influenza epidemic caused the death of Pierce McCann, the Sinn Féin deputy for East Tipperary, in Gloucester jail's hospital on 6 March. The British government, alarmed by Irish anger at McCann's death and by the prison doctor's apprehensions about the likelihood of further deaths, released the other 'German plot' prisoners. This effectively relieved de Valera of the risk of re-arrest. Michael Collins, acting on his own initiative and without consulting Sinn Féin's executive, put notices in the newspapers advertising a reception on 26 March on Mount Street bridge, the scene of the Volunteers' greatest battle in 1916, when the Lord Mayor, Laurence O'Neill, would welcome de Valera back to Dublin and present him with the keys of the city. The plan initially appealed to de Valera but when the British banned the meeting, he sided with Arthur Griffith, who consulted him after chairing a bitter debate at a belated meeting of Sinn Féin's executive. 'I think you will all agree with me', wrote de Valera, 'that the present occasion is scarcely one on which we would be justified in risking the lives of citizens. I am certain we would not . . . We who have waited know how to wait. Many a heavy fish is caught even with a fine line if the angler is patient.'[20] In yet another early demonstration of the unquestioning acceptance of his presidential authority, de Valera's colleagues duly acquiesced in his wishes.

The episode also reflected the very different attitudes of Collins and de Valera to the prospect of politically inspired violence. When the British proclaimed the meeting, de Valera later recalled, he 'considered that the occasion would not justify the shedding of blood'.[21] Although he accepted de Valera's decision, no such qualms troubled Michael Collins. 'We are having our "Clontarf Friday",' he raged, drawing an analogy with Daniel O'Connell's contentious cancellation of his mass meeting at Clontarf in 1843 because it had been proclaimed by the British. 'It may not be as bad but it is bad and very bad'.[22]

So de Valera returned to Dublin unobtrusively and was reunited with his wife and six children in Greystones for the first time in ten months; he had never before seen Emer, his younger daughter, who was born in August 1918. But, as always, family counted for little when set against politics. 'Give us freedom,' he declared in a written statement for a reporter awaiting him after a walk on the beach, 'freedom to enter voluntarily into whatever associations with England we may desire'[23] – a formula eschewing identification with the absolutist nomenclature of the republic.

De Valera used his brief time in Ireland to consolidate his personal authority. Cathal Brugha duly tendered his resignation as president of Dáil Éireann as well as the resignation of his ministry when the Dáil met in private session in the Oak Room of the Mansion House on 1 April. A resolution amending the Dáil's constitution and empowering the president to nominate a president-substitute 'in the event of the President becoming unable by reason of enemy action, or absence abroad, or illness or other emergency, to perform the functions of his office'[24] ensured that the chain of command would remain firmly in de Valera's hands when he was in America. A further amendment, moved by de Valera and seconded by Collins, provided that the Dáil ministry of four appointed in January could be expanded to include 'not more than nine Executive Officers . . . each of whom the President shall nominate and have the power to dismiss'.[25] The consolidation of de Valera's power was complete when the meeting concluded by his preordained and unanimous election as president.

De Valera duly nominated his new ministry when the Dáil met, again in secret session, the next day. Only Count Plunkett retained his place as secretary for foreign affairs from the first ministry and he was a mere figurehead since it was already clear that de Valera himself would play the key role in framing foreign policy. De Valera switched Michael Collins from home affairs (where he was replaced by Arthur Griffith, who had been in jail in January) to finance and Eoin MacNeill from finance to a new portfolio of industries; and he dropped Richard Mulcahy from the ministry and replaced him in defence with Cathal Brugha. He also created two other new portfolios, putting William Cosgrave into local government and Countess Markievicz into labour[26] – the first woman ever elected to the House of Commons at the 1918 election and who now became Ireland's first woman minister.

De Valera deferred his 'Ministry's Declaration of Policy' until 10 April when the Dáil met in public session for the first time since its inaugural meeting of 21 January. The achievement of international recognition that 'there is in Ireland at this moment only one lawful authority, and that authority is the elected Government of the Irish Republic' again took pride of place. Having announced that 'accredited representatives' would be sent to the Paris peace conference, de Valera concluded a brief address by reminding his audience of 'how our best energies are being absorbed by the international situation of the moment'.[27]

But de Valera made another, more heavily pregnant contribution to the proceedings on 10 April when he proposed that 'members of the police forces acting in this country as part of the forces of the British occupation and as agents of the British Government be ostracised socially by the people of Ireland'. He explained why in language much more provocative than this bland formulation. 'Spies in our midst . . . England's janissaries . . . the eyes and ears of the enemy' were but some of the phrases peppering his speech. The RIC, he declared hyperbolically, 'unlike any other police force in the world, is a military body armed with rifle and bayonet and revolver . . . The more brutal the commands given them by their superiors the more they seem to revel in carrying them out – against their own flesh and blood, be it remembered!' If Ian Macpherson, who as chief secretary was the minister responsible for the implementation of British policy, 'may incite the police', he continued, 'the Irish people, as an organised society, have a right to defend themselves'. He declared that 'the social ostracism' for which he was seeking the Dáil's sanction was but 'a first step in exercising that right'. Before formally moving his motion, he further inflamed the emotions of his listeners by asking them to stand as a mark of respect to Pierce McCann, 'the first of our body to die for Ireland'.[28] What mattered was the invocation of emotion rather than the fact that McCann had died not in Ireland as a consequence of any action of the RIC but of influenza in an English jail and de Valera's proposal, formally seconded by Eoin MacNeill, was agreed without debate.

Here, in embryo, was what became the theoretical justification for the guerrilla campaign of 1919–21: when the IRA killed policemen – whether of the RIC or the Dublin Metropolitan Police (DMP) – they claimed to be acting in defence of the Dáil and of 'the Irish people'. Although Éamon de Valera, in stark contrast with, say, Michael Collins, played no personal role in any of the carnage of 1919–20, he had, in effect, written a presidential blank cheque covering the killings that would take place while he was away in America.

On 4 May 1919 de Valera dispatched Harry Boland to New York to prepare the ground for his American mission; only the prospect of presenting Ireland's case for self-determination on the international stage in Paris delayed his own departure. The grandiosely entitled American Commission on Irish Independence, appointed by the Irish-American umbrella organisation, the Irish Race Convention, which had met in Philadelphia in February, arrived on 11 April in Paris, where they were welcomed by the Dáil's envoys, Seán T. O'Kelly and George Gavan Duffy. Their efforts to meet Lloyd George were unavailing but he authorised their being issued with diplomatic visas to visit Ireland. De Valera met them when they arrived at Kingstown on 3 May, and on 9 May the three Irish-American commissioners all addressed a special public meeting of the Dáil. Their speeches identifying the Irish and American struggles for independence and another incendiary speech by de Valera precipitated a storm of protest in the British press. 'There is no Irish Republic and there is no President de Valera', thundered the *Morning Post*, 'but there is a rebel faction in Ireland which is allowed the most extraordinary licence by the Government.'

Outrage spilled into the Westminster parliament and destroyed any prospect of getting de Valera a hearing in Paris. The commissioners, Lloyd George complained, 'so far from investigating the Irish problem in a spirit of impartiality, announced on arrival in Dublin that they had come there to forward the disruption of the United Kingdom, and the establishment of Ireland as an independent Republic'.[29]

By 24 May O'Kelly and Gavan Duffy, in conjunction with the commissioners who had returned to Paris, had 'definitely decided to recommend [to de Valera] not to come . . . there is now no chance of the Dáil delegates being allowed to appear before the Peace Conference . . . it would not be wise or proper to bring you here to have you and the Irish Republic snubbed'.[30]

De Valera left for New York within a week. His sudden departure when Michael Collins unexpectedly arrived in Greystones on the morning of 1 June to tell him that the plans were in place for his voyage, in the midst of his children's preparations to mark their mother's birthday that day, well symbolised his unwavering subordination of the domestic to the political. 'I trust you will not be lonely', he scribbled next day to Sinéad on a page torn from a notebook. 'It will be but for a short time.'[31] It was couched in terms of an instruction rather than a question. In fact, his absence lasted for eighteen months, the longest yet of their many separations.

Not even Arthur Griffith, appointed deputy-president by de Valera in a letter read to the Dáil when it next met on 17 June, was advised of his departure. Griffith looked for de Valera at 5 Fitzwilliam Square, where he had stayed during the American commission's visit, 'and was astonished not to find him. He had been to the house in Greystones to look for him before that.'[32] There were also unwonted murmurings in the docile Dáil about his disappearance. Seán MacEntee, a senior minister in de Valera's governments from 1932 to 1959, 'asked for an explanation of the absence of the President. No Member of the Dáil had been consulted. It was neither right nor fair to them that they should be unable to say whether the President had gone away and where he was.' A motion amending article 2 of the Dáil constitution and proposing that 'all Executive Power shall be vested in Committees composed of members of the Dáil', although withdrawn after brief debate, also reflected unease at the plenitude of presidential power.[33] In fact, de Valera's powers as president of Dáil Éireann remained undiminished while he was in America.

Meanwhile he had wielded arbitrary power in a minor key on the first leg of his voyage to New York. Michael Byrne, a stoker on the ship from Dublin to Liverpool, had got a bottle of whiskey before embarking and put it in his bunk, where de Valera was to hide. 'De Valera found the whiskey and, thinking it would be a danger to himself if the stoker drank it, put it out through the port-hole'; Byrne, unaware of his stowaway's identity, abused him in 'very strong language' when he looked in vain for his whiskey.[34] The transatlantic crossing on the SS *Lapland* was rough and de Valera, 'violently sick' and 'secreted away . . . could only lie on his coffin-like bunk all day', sustained by an occasional sip of brandy until the ship moored in New York on 11 June 1919. 'His first sight of New York since leaving it at the age of two and a half remained impressed upon his mind a city of "straw hats and sunshine".'[35] At ten o'clock that evening he 'just walked off the boat [dressed] as a sailor' and was handed over to Harry Boland and Joe McGarrity, an affluent and staunchly republican leader of Clan na nGael who took him to his home in Philadelphia. McGarrity, born in Carrick-more in County Tyrone, immediately became de Valera's closest ally in America, a role he held for over a decade.

At first de Valera lay low, to deny the British any clue as to how he had got to America. 'I have been trotting about,' he wrote to Michael Collins on 21 June, 'Rochester, Philadelphia, Washington, Boston, New York.' Why Rochester, in upstate New York, ahead of the great cities of the east coast? To see his mother, then in her six-ties and living there with her retired husband in 'a pretty wooden bungalow . . . in a long avenue of framehouses'.[36] 'Am anxious to travel to Rochester tonight – hope it can be arranged,' he had scribbled to Harry Boland before he had even disembarked. Boland, who now became 'de Valera's valet, shepherd, and manager instead of acting as an envoy in his own right',[37] did what he was told and went on doing what he was told for the next eighteen months. De Valera never wrote or spoke of what was said when he was reunited with his mother and their conversation might well have consisted of no more than a stilted exchange of pleasantries. But his making Rochester his first port of call in America is suggestive. His sense of personal satisfaction, of achievement and of vindication at returning to her in such circumstances can only be imagined but must have been immense. Abandoned by his mother before he was three, to the penury and uncertainties of life in an agricultural labourer's cottage in Limerick from which she herself had fled, he now returned in triumph to America as Ireland's elected leader who had already won headlines around the world. Again and again during his American mission he returned to Rochester and he spent Christmas in 1919 with his mother for the first time for thirty-five years.

'I am in America as official head of the Republic established by the will of the Irish people in accordance with the principle of Self-Determination,'[38] proclaimed the opening sentence of his press statement at his first public appearance at New York's Waldorf Astoria before excited crowds on 23 June. It was the beginning of his American cavalcade of which the next highlight, on 29 June, was a monster meeting in Boston that was so successful that it became a template for conventions of America's Democratic Party. 'The Chief addresses 70,000 at Fenway Park,' home of the Boston Red Sox, recorded Kathleen O'Connell, a thirty-year-old immigrant from Kerry whom de Valera appointed as his personal secretary to deal with his deluge of invitations, a role she played until her death in 1956.[39]

The objectives of de Valera's American mission were threefold: to seek official recognition of the Republic, to dissuade the US government from pledging to maintain Ireland as an integral part of the United Kingdom, and to spearhead the launch of an external loan. He failed in the first two but succeeded in raising nearly $6 million – more than was raised in Ireland. Criss-crossing the country, he addressed invariably large and enthusiastic audiences at public meetings as well as state legislatures: 'It was a spectacular performance . . . de Valera's travels throughout America, more than any event since the 1916 Rising, dramatised for the American people the dimensions of the Irish struggle.'[40] He also had a series of meetings with state governors and received a plethora of honorary doctorates. But the most bizarre and, from Harry Boland's perspective, most enjoyable day of the tour was a visit on 18 October to the reservation of the Chippewa Indians in Wisconsin; this had its origin, according to Liam Mellows, in the Indian veneration for 'the Chief as a person holding the same ideals regarding Ireland as they hold regarding their own rights'. De Valera is 'now a Chief of the Chippewa Nation', wrote Boland to his mother; 'his Indian name is "nay nay ong a ba" which means "the Dressing Feather".'[41]

Such was the eminence accorded de Valera by Irish-Americans that he was often incorrectly described as 'President of Ireland' or 'President of the Irish Republic' rather than as 'President of Dáil Éireann' or 'An Príomh Aire' ('First Minister'). This usage began at his very first press conference on 23 June when Joe McGarrity, mindful of the propagandist advantages, successfully persuaded de Valera to drop his objections to the more grandiose title, arguing 'that it was the same thing' as he was 'already . . . President of the Republic in the minds of the American people'.[42] There was a downside to such adulation: Patrick McCartan, a sometime travelling companion, detected 'an unconscious contempt' for the opinion of others. The 'Chief', as he was now commonly addressed, 'presides and does all the talking. Has a habit of getting on to side issues and shutting off people who want to speak and thus makes a bad impression if not sometimes enemies. Tends to force his own opinions without hearing from the other fellows and thus thinks he has co-operation when he only gets silent acquiescence.'[43] Harry Boland, 'exasperated by [de Valera's] interminable petty demands for service and attention', put it more succinctly in a diary entry after an evening in New York in December 1919: 'De V. talks all night, no one else.'[44]

This authoritarian style became a hallmark of de Valera's leadership throughout his political career; it was reinforced by his entanglement in Irish-American factional disputes when he sided with Joe McGarrity against the leaders of the Friends of Irish Freedom – John Devoy (a leading Fenian since the 1870s and the editor of the *Gaelic American*) and Judge Daniel Cohalan of the New York Supreme Court. One cause of contention was their differing attitudes to the League of Nations, which had been established by the Paris peace conference. Devoy and Cohalan were isolationists irrevocably opposed to American membership of the League, even if Ireland were admitted – now a remote prospect in the light of Article X of the League's Covenant preserving the existing boundaries of member states, which conflicted with de Valera's objective of dissuading the American government from pledging to maintain Ireland as an integral part of the United Kingdom.

These differences came to a head when the *New York Globe* of 6 February 1920 carried an abridged version of an interview de Valera had given for publication in the following day's *Westminster Gazette*. Why, he had asked, would Britain not do with Ireland as the United States had done with Cuba 'and declare a variant of the Monroe doctrine stipulating that an Irish government must never enter into a treaty with any foreign power which might pose a threat to British security'? The interview, charged the *Globe* – and the charge was reiterated in the *Westminster Gazette* – constituted a 'withdrawal by the official head of the Irish Republic of the demand that Ireland be set free'. Devoy and Cohalan followed suit and accused de Valera of reneging on Ireland's right to sovereignty.

'It will be hailed in England as an offer of surrender,' claimed Devoy's *Gaelic American*.[45]

The accusations penetrated de Valera's usually impregnable carapace of self-confidence to the point where he decided to send Patrick McCartan back to Dublin to explain the context of his feuding with the self-appointed tribal chieftains of Irish-America. He was sufficiently unnerved to write to Arthur Griffith 'presuming . . . that the moment the Cabinet or Dáil feel the slightest want of confidence in me they will let me know *immediately*'. Although he believed that 'the trouble is purely one of personalities', he took the opportunity to assert that 'no American has a right to dictate policy to the Irish people . . . Fundamentally Irish-Americans differ from us in this – they being Americans first would sacrifice Irish interests if need be to American interests – we, Irish first, would do the reverse.'[46]

As acting president, Griffith's support was crucial. Patrick Moylett, who was present at a meeting with Griffith and Collins when the Cuban statement was discussed, recalled that Collins was initially 'critical of de Valera's action. Griffith disagreed with him. "We know the President better than we know the men who are opposed to him in America. It is our business to be perfectly loyal to him."'[47] Although Patrick McCartan's 'personal view of the Cuban interview was that it was "clearly an intimation that the President of the Republic of Ireland was prepared to accept much less than complete sovereignty for Ireland"', he 'did not say a word about [its] merits or demerits' when he briefed the cabinet in Dublin. Despite some 'marked hostility' voiced by Cathal Brugha, Countess Markievicz and Count Plunkett, Collins and Griffith 'shut down the discussion and led in the acceptance of de Valera's explanation' because they 'took the view that they had sent their elected leader to the USA and now had no option but to stand behind him'.[48] Their response can only have reassured de Valera that, even when he made the analogy with US–Cuban relations of which his cabinet colleagues had been uninformed, he could nevertheless rely on their unswerving loyalty and support.

Stung by the persistent criticisms led by Cohalan and Devoy, de Valera said no more about Cuba. This, perhaps, explains why his biographers have failed to recognise the enduring significance of his interview with the *Westminster Gazette*. Although his commitment to the *theory* of sovereignty was absolute, de Valera's Cuban analogy demonstrates that as early as 1920 he understood and accepted that small states within the spheres of influence of great powers must accept the constraints on their liberty of action in the conduct of foreign policy. Not for nothing did de Valera commend Machiavelli's *The Prince* to his colleagues. No one realised earlier than he that realpolitik dictated that Ireland could never enter into an alliance against Britain if it were to achieve in practice the independence to which it laid claim in theory.

Indeed the key passages in his interview provide the blueprint for de Valera's foreign policy after 1932 and, in particular, during World War II:

With a free Ireland, *the preservation of its independence* would be as strong a moving force as *the recovery of its independence* has been a moving force in every generation since the coming of the Normans.

An independent Ireland would see everything to lose in losing its independence – in passing under the yoke of any foreign power whatsoever. An independent Ireland would see its own independence in jeopardy the moment it saw the independence of Britain seriously threatened. Mutual self-interest would make the people of these two islands, *if both [were] independent*, the closest possible allies in a moment of real danger to either.

If they are not so today, it is because Britain, in her selfishness, has robbed Ireland of every natural motive for such an alliance. The fish in the maw of one shark does not trouble about the possible advent of another shark. The mouse quivering in the jaws of the cat does not fear the approach of the terrier but, if anything, welcomes it.

And so Ireland, deprived of its freedom by Britain – in dependence, and persecuted because it is not satisfied to remain in dependence – is impelled by every natural instinct and force to see hope in the down-fall of Britain and hope, not fear, in every attack upon Britain. *Whereas, in an independent Ireland, the tendency would be all the other way.*[49] [Author's italics.]

Although he shrank from repeating the Cuban analogy, de Valera hammered home the essence of its message in an open letter to President Woodrow Wilson on 27 October 1920 that accompanied his abortive formal petition seeking Ireland's recognition as a sovereign, independent state: 'Ireland is quite ready *by treaty* to ensure England's safety and legitimate security against the danger of foreign powers seeking to use Ireland as a basis of attack against her.'[50] (Author's italics.)

By now de Valera was preparing to return to Ireland. He had been 'very surprised and perturbed' on 18 August when Sinéad had arrived in New York out of the blue on a visit organised by Harry Boland (who had gone back to Dublin in May) and Michael Collins (who had got her a false passport). She got short shrift from her husband because, as de Valera explained to his official biographers, 'he was so taken up with the serious strife with Devoy and Cohalan during his wife's visit and was so busy with meetings and work on the Irish cause that they had little time together',[51] although he did make time to bring her to meet his mother in Rochester.[52] Sinéad went home in October regretting that she had ever come: 'It was such a big mistake to go for such a long journey for such a short stay', she wrote to Kathleen O'Connell in November.[53] By then de Valera saw no reason why he should remain in America. The bond drive for the external loan had been set on a firm footing – 'five times the amount initially contemplated by the Irish Cabinet had been collected' – and he had just established the American Association for the Recognition of the Irish Republic under his control, in opposition to the fractious and divided Friends of Irish Freedom. He had also fulfilled the cabinet's wish that he postpone his return until after the formal presentation of the demand for the recognition of the Republic of Ireland had been met, although he ignored the addendum in its decision of 9 October that 'this should not be done before the new Congress and President come into office'.[54] Whether de Valera interpreted this caveat as indicating that his colleagues were less persuaded than he was that his immediate return was imperative is a moot point. But what is beyond doubt is that the key factors determining its timing were the 'rumours reaching America . . . that peace moves were being made in Dublin' and de Valera's conviction that 'he would be urgently needed in any negotiations impending'.[55]

Patrick Moylett, acting secretly on Griffith's behalf, had begun talking to Lloyd George's intermediaries in October 1920, and on 21 November, the day after Bloody Sunday (when the IRA had shot dead fourteen suspected British secret service agents in their Dublin homes), had met the British prime minister, again in secret, in 10 Downing Street. Lloyd George had then, to Moylett's surprise, urged him to 'ask Griffith to keep his head and not to break off the slender link that had been established'.[56] On 4 December the Dáil cabinet decided that, 'if the English Govt calls off its present aggressive campaign, we can respond by urging the cessation of the present Acts of Self-Defence [sic!]. All pursuit of members of the Dáil & others must cease, and the entire Dáil freely meet to arrange the terms of truce'.[57] Bloody Sunday and the Kilmichael ambush a week later (when the IRA killed every one of an eighteen-strong patrol of auxiliary police) made nonsense of British army intelligence claims that they were on the verge of a military victory. These events, together with the imminent enactment of the Government of Ireland Bill partitioning Ireland and satisfying the demands of the Ulster unionists and their allies in the Conservative Party, on whom Lloyd George was dependent for his parliamentary majority, gave him more freedom of manoeuvre to explore talking to Sinn Féin. Griffith's arrest, moreover, as a result of Bloody Sunday, created a vacancy in the presidency of Dáil Éireann that de Valera now moved to fill.

6

1921: War and Peace

Éamon de Valera returned to Dublin on 23 December 1920, the same day that the Government of Ireland Act, partitioning Ireland by providing Ulster's unionists with their own parliament and government in six counties of Northern Ireland, became law. The Act also provided for the establishment of a second parliament in Dublin for the other twenty-six counties – in effect, home rule – which Sinn Féin had rejected out of hand just as the British government had anticipated.

Ireland had been utterly transformed in the eighteen months of de Valera's absence in ways over which he had had no control. He could not have directed the course of the republican revolution at long distance if he had so wished and he never tried to do so; all his time and energy had focused instead on the struggle for power in the parallel universe of Irish-America. He had played no part in directing the affairs of Sinn Féin, of the Irish Volunteers (now known as the Irish Republican Army) or of Dáil Éireann (the three entities of which he had remained nominally president). In particular, he had no role in the direction of an increasingly violent guerrilla war. The Dáil had not met in public session since his departure and its last private session had taken place on 19 September 1920. British proclamations suppressing Sinn Féin and the Irish Volunteers had been followed in September 1919 by a declaration that Dáil Éireann was illegal. Meanwhile de Valera's blank cheque urging hostility towards the police was again and again cashed in blood as his policy of ostracism became a campaign of killing. The comparison with Parnell, who had correctly predicted when jailed in Kilmainham in 1881–2 that Captain

89

Moonlight would take his place, is again apposite. Not even the viceroy was immune, although the IRA's attempted assassination of Lord French in December 1919 had failed. The guerrilla war intensified throughout 1920: the enrolment of thousands of British recruits to serve in the RIC, who became notorious as the 'Black and Tans', began in January; between March and May the British drastically restructured their machinery of Irish government – key appointments included General Nevil Macready as general officer commanding (GOC), Hamar Greenwood as chief secretary and John Anderson as effective civil service head of Dublin Castle; the recruitment of an Auxiliary Division of the RIC from British officers who had served in the Great War began in July; then came the spectacular violence of Bloody Sunday on 21 November and the Kilmichael ambush a week later. After his return from America de Valera had singled out Bloody Sunday, 'represented in the American papers as brutal murders of British officers in their beds', as a 'deplorable' example of poor communications: 'He had had no knowledge of the facts and was compelled, willy nilly, to let the reports go uncontradicted until it was too late.'[1] While he did not explicitly disown the killings, de Valera's remarks suggest that he would not have authorised them if he had been told of them in advance. On 10 December the British proclaimed martial law in Cork and three adjoining counties and on the night of 11 December Auxiliaries and Black and Tans sacked Cork city.

This, then, was the Ireland in which de Valera now reassumed his presidential role. The contrast between the circumstances of his time in America and his circumstances in Dublin at Christmas 1920 was so stark that it must have been disorienting, notwithstanding his remarkable composure and self-discipline. In America, using New York's Waldorf Astoria Hotel as his headquarters, he had enjoyed open adulation and had travelled from coast to coast and from north to south appearing before state legislatures amid fanfares of publicity, receiving honorary degrees from eminent universities, giving press conferences and addressing mass meetings whenever he was so minded. In Dublin he was a 'president in hiding' in the phrase of his official biographers: on the run from the British, unaware that the order that he should be arrested on sight had been secretly rescinded because Lloyd George knew he would eventually have to negotiate with 'the one man who could deliver the goods'.[2] 'Speculation has been rife as to the whereabouts of de Valera,' recorded a British intelligence report for the week ending 4 January 1921. 'Several of our raiding operations have been viewed by the public as searches for him, whereas the policy is to leave him alone.'[3]

When de Valera's ship docked at Dublin's Custom House Quay, de Valera went first to the home in Merrion Square of Dr Robert Farnan, an eminent gynaecologist whose patients included the wives of British army officers and who became and remained one of de Valera's most intimate friends until his death in 1962; Sinéad visited him there next day. He asked Michael Collins to find him a secluded safe house where he could work and on New Year's Day 1921 he moved into Loughnavale, a detached house by the sea on Strand Road, Merrion, equidistant between Blackrock and Dublin city centre, where the other members of his household were a housekeeper, Maeve McGarry, the daughter of the house's owner, and his private secretary, Kathleen O'Connell, who had also returned from America.[4]

De Valera's ignorance of the state of affairs on the ground became painfully apparent when he spelled out his distaste for guerrilla warfare to the IRA's bemused chief of staff, Richard Mulcahy, on Christmas Eve. 'You are going too fast. This odd shooting of a policeman here and there is having a very bad effect, from the propaganda point of view, on us in America. What we want is one good battle about once a month with about 500 men on each side.'[5] The identification with Irish-America implicit in that 'us in America' says volumes about how out of tune with the temper of the times de Valera had become. His attitude – fed by ignorance, by his innate conservatism, reinforced by his fear of episcopal criticism and, perhaps, by a lingering nostalgia for the set-piece modalities of 1916 – might have been naive but it was rooted in his determination immediately to reaffirm his presidential authority and to establish political control over the gunmen. The Dáil, he complained to Robert Brennan at their first meeting in Loughnavale, had never taken responsibility for the IRA. He was going to get them to do this and to take the first available opportunity 'to make it clear to all and sundry that the Dáil took full responsibility for the operations of the Army'. In effect, de Valera explained to Brennan, this meant getting 'the Cabinet to stand over the actions of the IRA, which they had never done before'. He also said that 'it should not be impossible to get a [peace] formula which we could accept and which the British could accept'.[6]

The quest for peace was a matter of urgency, de Valera told the Dáil cabinet: 'We would get the best settlement from the Coalition Government then in power in Great Britain and ... must endeavour to negotiate and agree with them before they went out of office.'[7] For that was what would happen whenever the Conservative and Unionist Party decided to use its majority in the House of Commons to oust the Liberal prime minister, David Lloyd George, from 10 Downing Street, a fate he contrived to evade until October 1922. But Lloyd George had first to secure his unionist flank by establishing Northern Ireland as a separate political entity before he could risk opening formal negotiations with Sinn Féin.

In the meantime de Valera set about re-establishing his personal power base. This meant curbing the power of Michael Collins, whose reputation as the effective leader of the Irish revolution had blossomed throughout 1920. As minister of finance, Collins was the key figure in the Dáil cabinet and, as director of military intelligence, the key figure in prosecuting the war; as president of the supreme council of the IRB, moreover, he also commanded the unquestioning allegiance of a cadre of the most effective political and military activists. His appointment as acting president of Dáil Éireann, after Arthur Griffith's arrest in the aftermath of Bloody

Sunday, then crowned Collins's power. This happened by accident rather than design when Cathal Brugha (who never relinquished his job as a travelling salesman and director of a Dublin candle-making firm and who refused his ministerial salary, which he remitted to Richard Mulcahy) declined the appointment; the Dáil never met under Collins's presidency, moreover, which immediately reverted to de Valera.

Michael Collins had been unswervingly supportive of de Valera as president throughout his time in America and never then or after his return challenged his decisions. Although he could be contemptuous of de Valera's questions about military matters,[8] he always deferred to him when they were face to face or at meetings with colleagues. But Tom Garvin's contention that 'de Valera simply could not cope with Collins's decisiveness, realism and ability to learn quickly'[9] is suggestive. De Valera also realised that, even if only inadvertently, Collins had filled a power vacuum in his absence and, in effect, had emerged as an alternative source of authority for the first time since his own elevation as president of Sinn Féin and of the Irish Volunteers in 1917. So it was unsurprising that he 'effectively demoted Collins by appointing Austin Stack as Acting President should anything happen to himself'.[10] He also tacitly backed Cathal Brugha, nominally Collins's superior as minister of defence, in their running and rancorous disputes about the direction of military policy.

'In military matters Collins should have acted as Brugha's subordinate,' de Valera later observed, 'but as Cabinet Minister he was Brugha's equal. It is difficult to be an equal and a subordinate at the same time and it rarely works well.' Brugha resented what he saw as the usurpation of the Dáil's nominal control of the army because 'many of the leading GHQ officers were members of the IRB and recognised prior allegiance to that body in which Collins was dominant'.[11] His 'antagonism to Collins . . . was very widely known in Sinn Féin and IRA circles . . . "Cathal Brugha hated Collins like poison," wrote one witness. "It was pathological . . .

Brugha was Minister for Defence but never did anything. He was not able, but he was never on the run . . . Collins was so energetic that he had usurped many of Brugha's functions.'"[12]

On 9 January 1921 the Dáil cabinet met for the first time since de Valera's return. The minutes reveal a marked change in the way business was conducted. What had previously been a terse but full record of decisions now became a staccato litany of agenda items marked 'not reached' or 'wait'. The most significant minute, again unusually, is recorded under 'Other Business'. 'Once a month the President may summon some members for consult[atio]n. as required.'[13] The new presidential style of leadership – in particular, de Valera's interviewing 'his cabinet and [IRA] headquarters, man by man' and inquiring 'minutely into the military position' – increasingly disillusioned Collins who 'made no real attempt to impress de Valera' and who attended the meeting in 'a queer humour – almost melancholy'. He was particularly irritated by what he saw as de Valera's habit of wasting time by repeatedly regaling his colleagues with accounts of his American experiences. 'Oh, I have it off by heart,'[14] he growled after yet another of the president's interminable American narratives.

Collins and those closest to him in the IRA were not alone in their disillusionment. Patrick Moylett was incensed when Erskine Childers, appointed by de Valera as director of publicity after Desmond FitzGerald's arrest, repeatedly denied him an appointment with the president, to whom he wanted to explain his role as Griffith's secret messenger to Lloyd George. There was a new 'inner cabinet or advisory board to de Valera', observed Moylett, of the 'peculiar position' after his return; it also included John Chartres, a retired British civil servant and 'a new star . . . over the republican horizon'. Collins was 'somewhat demoted' . . . Collins 'up to this time . . . the highlight in the country . . . was officially dimmed'; de Valera disingenuously explained that 'these men were to be trusted and that they were always available, whereas Michael Collins and others were not always available'.[15]

In fact, de Valera tried to make Collins permanently unavailable when on 18 January, less than a month after his own return, he proposed sending him on a mission to America. De Valera's rationale, as recounted by his official biographers, was threefold: to obtain 'money and munitions', to organise 'a boycott of British goods' and to 'help to restore unity in Irish-American forces'.[16] Collins was having none of it: 'the Long Whoor [whore] won't get rid of me as easily as that', he exploded; he was 'convinced that it had originated with Brugha and Stack, and with no other idea than to get rid of him'. Confronted by 'consternation' among IRA officers who talked of resigning,[17] de Valera dropped the proposal. But that he should have ever proposed it clearly signalled his lack of confidence in Collins and his determination to suppress any perceived threat to his own authority.

Reluctant to share collegial authority within the cabinet, de Valera sought instead to use Dáil Éireann as an instrument for reaffirming his leadership. He made a false start when, acting on the advice of Cathal Brugha who warned against the danger of his being re-arrested, he irritated deputies by failing to turn up for a meeting arranged for 21 January 1921 to mark the second anniversary of the Dáil's inauguration. But he did attend the meeting rescheduled for 25 January when his 'President's Statement' addressed 'the question of the general policy to be pursued throughout the country'. He argued that

the policy demanded now was a delaying policy. Time was on their side and they ought to make up their minds to hold out. They should not seek a decision. A strong aggressive policy to bring a decision would be right if they were strong enough, but seeing they were not strong enough, the delaying policy was the right one. Their policy should be to stick on, to show no change on the outside as far as possible, and at the same time to make the burden on the people as light as they could. This policy might necessitate a lightening off of their attacks on the enemy. The change was so slight it could best be initiated by the machinery of administration rather than by public proclamation or acts.

Although this attitude smacked of defeatism to some deputies – Piarais Beaslaí saying 'if easing off was to be interpreted as a cessation . . . it would be disastrous'; Joe McDonagh said that 'the proper policy was to be as aggressive as possible', and Liam Mellows that 'they could not afford to slacken off'[18] – de Valera escaped direct criticism.

His presidential statement at the next session, on 11 March 1921, decreed that 'the Dáil should let the world know that they took full responsibility for all the operations of their Army', although 'that would practically mean a public acceptance of a State of War'. He met with no opposition and, after a brief debate, the Dáil gave him carte blanche by unanimously adopting a motion approving 'the President's being empowered to draw up a statement on the lines indicated verbally by him . . . at whatever time was considered most opportune'.[19]

De Valera's preference for the set-piece military tactics of 1916 was unwavering despite the scepticism of Collins and Mulcahy; he argued that 'the time had come to deliver a smashing blow to England, some bigger military operation than anything yet attempted', suggesting either the occupation of the British barracks at Beggar's Bush, the headquarters of the Auxiliaries, or the destruction of the Custom House, a focal point of British administration in Ireland. A hundred and twenty would be assigned to the operation and he argued, in language redolent of the Easter Rising, 'that if these 120 men were lost and the job accomplished, the *surrender* [author's italics] would be well justified'.[20] The attack on the Custom House on 23 May 1921, the only armed action discussed and approved by the Dáil cabinet in the war of 1919–21, was a military disaster, resulting in the capture of some hundred members of the IRA's Dublin Brigade and the deaths of several others.

But the prospect of peace, by then looming large, mitigated its worst effects. Although a meeting between de Valera and Lord Derby, an intermediary from Lloyd George, in Dublin on 21 April came to nothing, Derby then wrote to de Valera asking if Lloyd

George might tell the House of Commons that 'those controlling the Irish movement will not consent to meet him . . . unless the principle of complete independence is first conceded'. De Valera responded with his own question on 26 April: would Lloyd George 'not consent to meet me or any Representative of the Government of Ireland unless the principle of consent be first surrendered by us'? Lloyd George's reply took the form of a message for de Valera from a *New York Herald* reporter who had interviewed him on 11 May: 'I will meet Mr de Valera . . . without conditions on my part or without exacting promises from them. It is the only way a conclusion can be reached . . . we may find common ground upon which we can refer to our respective people for a settlement'. De Valera responded by saying that, if Lloyd George said as much 'in public', he undertook to give him 'a public reply'.[21]

In the meantime Alfred Cope, Lloyd George's go-between in Dublin Castle, had set up another clandestine meeting on 5 May between de Valera and James Craig, the Ulster unionist leader and by then Northern Ireland's prime minister in waiting, who was in Dublin visiting the viceroy. That also came to nothing, unsurprisingly given that Cope had given each man to understand that the meeting had been requested by the other. Although de Valera was dismissive of both meetings in his report to the final session of the first Dáil on 10 May – Derby, he said, was 'a mere political scout, and he spoke to him as he would to a Press man' and the Craig 'interview was of no significance'[22] – they had planted seeds of progress.

By May 1921 de Valera had already devised a formula that, in his earlier words to Robert Brennan, 'we could accept and which the British could accept'. He explained 'the scheme which became known as Document No. 2 or External Association' to Brennan and to Erskine Childers as they watched him use a compass to 'finish a very neat drawing he had already begun. There were five separate and independent circles, all contained within a very large circle. Dev completed the design by drawing another circle outside the large circle but contacting it. "There you have it," said Dev; "the large circle is the British Commonwealth, having within it five circles which are members of the Commonwealth. Outside the large circle, but having external contact with it is Ireland."' Despite personally disliking the scheme and getting the impression that Childers, 'though willing to accept the scheme was not enthusiastic about it', Brennan recalled that he 'could not but admire the rare political genius which had brought it into being'. While they were still talking, Michael Collins came in but, when de Valera 'explained the design to him', Collins, 'who seemed to be thinking of something else, said nothing at all'.[23] Although he did not publicly unveil his external-association formula until months later in the tempestuous cauldron of the Dáil debates on the Treaty, the episode shows that, unlike his cabinet colleagues, de Valera was already thinking about the shape of a possible settlement before negotiating the final stage of the path to peace.

The elections to the parliaments established under the Government of Ireland Act 1920 raised the curtain on that stage. Although Sinn Féin rejected the Act, they treated what the British conceived as an election to the southern parliament as an election to the second Dáil to which 124 of their candidates were elected unopposed. But it was the election to the Northern Ireland parliament, on 24 May, that was the key to removing the last obstacle on the path to peace. On 28 May the British used the American consul in Dublin as an intermediary to tell Patrick Moylett, Arthur Griffith's interlocutor with Lloyd George in 1920, that they wanted to meet de Valera. 'We are willing to acknowledge that we are defeated', Alfred Cope told Moylett in Dublin Castle on 30 May. 'There is nothing else for us to do but to draft . . . four hundred thousand men and exterminate the whole population of the country, and we are not willing to do that . . . We are willing to withdraw our whole establishment, from the lowest policeman to the highest judge.' There was only one exception to this offer of a complete British withdrawal: 'They would want the use of the ports in wartime.'[24]

A preliminary meeting on 7 June of Northern Ireland's House of Commons appointed a cabinet with James Craig as prime minister. On 22 June the speech of King George V appealing for reconciliation, when he formally opened the Northern Ireland parliament, provided the platform for peace. Coincidence decreed that de Valera was arrested on the same day when a detachment of British troops raided Glenvar, a large house in its own grounds off Merrion Avenue in Blackrock into which he had moved from Loughnavale in mid-May. His arrest was inadvertent and Alfred Cope appeared in evening dress in his cell in the Bridewell and arranged his immediate transfer to an officer's room in Portobello Barracks. 'Released,' he wrote in his diary next day. 'Did not know what to make of it.'[25] His immediate release so disconcerted de Valera that it initially shattered his self-esteem. 'We could not make head or tail of it,' remembered his housekeeper of the moment when she saw him walking back up the drive to Glenvar, 'a lone figure with his raincoat thrown over his shoulder'. 'I have been thrown out,' he said when he entered the house. That evening, 'making no effort to disguise himself', he went by train to Greystones to see his family for the first time since June 1920 when he had left for America. 'There is nothing for me to do now except to go out with the boys on the hills,' he told her as she walked with him to Blackrock station.[26] The observation, fifty years afterwards, of his official biographers reflects their subject's enduring paranoia about the episode. 'The most obvious reason for his release seemed to be a desire to undermine his authority, to make little of him, and even to make him suspect among his own followers . . . His political usefulness seemed over. All he could give now were his services as a soldier.'[27] Such extravagant despair shows the importance of the cocoon of self-belief to de Valera. But it soon dissipated. When he returned to Glenvar next day, 'as he was walking across the lawn, he took a letter out of his pocket and waved it . . . It was the first letter from Lloyd George asking for an interview.'[28]

No longer needing to hide, de Valera moved into an office in the Mansion House. He jibbed at Lloyd George's invitation, to 'the chosen leader of the great majority in Southern Ireland', because it was coupled with an invitation to James Craig, as 'Premier of Northern Ireland' and denied 'Ireland's essential unity' – an early airing of a mythical concept to which Irish nationalists remained wedded despite the de facto partition of Ireland in June 1921. So, before sending a comprehensive reply to Lloyd George, de Valera invited Craig and Lord Midleton (as the leader of the southern unionists) to a conference in the Mansion House. Midleton accepted but Craig, inevitably, refused.

On 5 July General Smuts, the South African premier, who was in London for a meeting of the Imperial Conference, came to Dublin as an 'unofficial' intermediary. Smuts did not take issue with de Valera's demand for a truce as a precondition to a conference but he warned him that, 'in replying to Lloyd George and proposing a conference of two instead of three . . . [to] avoid any form of language which will reflect on or belittle the position of Ulster. I see no objection to your stating that the dispute is now between the Irish Majority and the British Government, and the conference for a settlement should be between the two.' De Valera was impressed by Smuts and took his advice: he sent an anodyne telegram to Lloyd George on 8 July simply saying that he was ready to meet him to discuss 'on what basis such a conference as that proposed can reasonably hope to achieve the object desired'.[29]

The terms of the truce were duly settled on 9 July at a meeting with Cope and General Macready and it came into effect at noon on 11 July 1921. Three members of his cabinet accompanied de Valera to London: Arthur Griffith, Austin Stack and Robert Barton. Michael Collins raged in vain at his omission, which he not unreasonably interpreted as yet another slight, as he and de Valera walked up and down the garden in Glenvar. As usual, de Valera – who claimed that the reason for his exclusion was to reduce the opportunities for photographing Collins in case the talks broke down and the war resumed – got his way. In fact, the composition of the Irish delegation on this occasion mattered little since de Valera and Lloyd George met alone.

Their first meeting took place at 4.30 p.m. on 14 July in the cabinet room in 10 Downing Street. But de Valera had first to make his way through an emotional crowd singing and saying the rosary. Not even David Lloyd George, a veteran of innumerable international conferences, was immune. Frances Stevenson, his secretary and mistress, had never seen him

so excited as he was before de Valera arrived . . . He kept walking in and out of my room & I could see he was working out the best way of dealing with Dev . . . He had a big map of the British Empire hung up on the wall in the Cabinet room, with its great blotches of red all over it . . . to impress upon Dev the greatness of the B[ritish] E[mpire] & the King . . . D[avid] said he was very difficult to keep to the point – he kept on going off at a tangent, & talking in formulas and refusing to face facts.[30]

A year later de Valera painted a strikingly similar

word-picture of his session with Lloyd George – how he was received, offered spirits to drink and cigars to smoke, refusing both, how the discussion developed and how, as things got hot, Lloyd George walked across the Cabinet Room, and drawing de Valera's attention to all the red markings on the map, put the end of his fountain pen on the spot representing Ireland, which was completely covered by the pen, saying: "This is Ireland, Mr de Valera", before proceeding to talk of how Britain had mobilised 10 million men during the Great War.[31]

De Valera said little but one British official was 'surprised at the way in which [his] staff treated him as royalty and walked out backwards from his presence'.[32]

'The position is simply this', de Valera wrote to Collins next day: Lloyd George 'is developing a proposal which he wishes me to bring in my pocket as a proposal to the Irish Nation for its consideration . . . I am not dissatisfied with the general situation. The proposal will be theirs – we will be free to consider it without prejudice.'[33] After two more abortive meetings on 15 and 18 July, Lloyd George's formal proposal was hand-delivered to de Valera late on the evening of 20 July. 'Briefly it is "Dominion status" with all sorts of important powers,' explained Tom Jones, Lloyd George's foremost official on Irish policy; 'but no Navy, no hostile tariffs, and no coercion of Ulster.'[34]

De Valera 'always maintained that Dominion status for Ireland would never be real. Ireland's proximity to Britain would not allow it to develop as dominions thousands of miles away could'[35] and he rejected the proposal out of hand at what Lloyd George described as a 'pretty hopeless' final meeting on 21 July when he

demanded that Ireland should have Dominion status *sans phrase*, any condition such as that regarding the Royal Navy, which we consider vital to the safety of these islands to be left for arrangement at a subsequent date between the British and Irish Governments. He also demanded that Ulster should become a part of the Irish Dominion. Failing this, he demanded, as his only alternative, complete independence for Southern Ireland.[36]

Lloyd George replied that if that was de Valera's last word there was nothing left to discuss except when the truce should end, but, after he had accepted that the truce should continue, de Valera agreed to send a considered reply after he returned to Dublin.

De Valera unveiled his concept of Ireland's external association with the British Commonwealth to the cabinet on 27 July when 'the general line on which the letter should be sent' was agreed. Although the detail and timing were, as usual, left to the president's discretion, it was minuted that 'the basis of reply was "external association"'.[37] De Valera was in no hurry to reply. Better, if negotiations were to collapse, that they 'should be prolonged into the late autumn if possible so that, if hostilities did recommence, the advantage of the long winter evenings would favour . . . guerrilla tactics.'[38] He also decided that the document he had brought to the

Dáil cabinet on external association 'would be too revealing if sent to Lloyd George in that form'.[39] The key to his thinking was that, while he envisaged external association as a compromise he might ultimately be persuaded to accept, he was not prepared to *offer* a compromise that fell so far short of the republic pure and simple. A 'revised draft reply containing a less definite offer of association' was accordingly approved at another meeting of the Dáil cabinet on 6 August.[40]

De Valera later claimed that his reply, dispatched on 10 August, 'was designed to initiate a long correspondence'.[41] It certainly had that effect when, in the prime minister's absence in Paris, Tory ministers interpreted it as 'practically refusing' their terms. But Lloyd George had returned when his cabinet discussed whether de Valera's answer was an outright rejection of dominion status or a 'clumsy attempt' to keep negotiations going; a telegram from Alfred Cope in Dublin Castle favouring the open-door interpretation proved decisive. There followed a seemingly interminable exchange of letters between de Valera and Lloyd George, then accompanied by both his wife and mistress on a strange holiday in the rain-swept Scottish highlands. The impasse was broken after the British cabinet, at an unprecedented meeting in the bizarre surroundings of Inverness Town Hall, havered between inviting de Valera to an 'unconditional' conference or 'to a conditional conference on the basis of no separation, no republic'. The British response, which went through nine drafts, sought a 'definite reply' as to whether de Valera was 'prepared to enter a Conference to ascertain how the association of Ireland with the community of nations known as the British Empire can best be reconciled with Irish national aspirations'.[42]

On 22 August a meeting of Dáil Éireann, in private session, was notable for de Valera's blunt response when he was also asked to define his Ulster policy. 'They had not the power and some of them had not the inclination to use force with Ulster. He did not think that policy would be successful. They would be making the same mistake . . . as England had made with Ireland. He would not be responsible for such a policy.' His frankness provoked some dissent but the focus quickly returned to the reason why the Dáil had assembled: the ratification of de Valera's reply to Lloyd George's proposal. Here he met with no dissent and he wrote again to Lloyd George saying that the Dáil had unanimously endorsed his 'anticipatory judgement'.[43]

When the Dáil cabinet met on 9 September, it agreed on a reply that simply reiterated Lloyd George's formula for negotiations: 'to enter a Conference to ascertain how the association of Ireland with the community of nations known as the British Empire can best be reconciled with Irish national aspirations'. The meeting then decided on the composition of the Irish delegation, having first taken the fateful decision 'that the President would not take part in the Conference as a representative'.[44] Arthur Griffith was appointed as chairman of the delegation whose other most eminent member was Michael Collins; the other three delegates were less well known: Robert Barton, minister of economic affairs; Éamonn Duggan, a lawyer and the chief liaison officer for implementing the truce; and George Gavan Duffy, another lawyer and the Dáil's envoy in Rome. De Valera later dismissed his appointment of Duggan and Gavan Duffy as mere 'legal padding' but hoped that Barton 'would be strong and stubborn enough as a retarding force to any precipitate giving-away by the delegation'. He also hoped that Erskine Childers, 'an intellectual republican', whom he appointed as secretary to the delegation, 'would give Barton, his relative and close friend, added strength'.[45]

Éamon de Valera's refusal to lead the delegation that signed the treaty of 6 December 1921 establishing the Irish Free State as a self-governing dominion within the British Empire was the most controversial decision of his political career. It drew criticism from the start. For once, Dáil Éireann, meeting in private session in the Oak Room in the Mansion House on 14 September to ratify the appointment of the delegates as plenipotentiaries, departed from its usual practice of rubber-stamping presidential decisions without debate. The first critic was William T. Cosgrave, the minister for local government, who immediately spoke against the proposal for ratification, citing de Valera's 'extraordinary experience in negotiations' and the 'advantage' of his having already been 'in touch' with Lloyd George, who, he surmised, would lead the British delegation. An attempt to rule Cosgrave out of order on the grounds that this was a cabinet motion collapsed when de Valera explained that, because 'it was his own vote put him off' the delegation at the cabinet meeting on 9 September, 'he gave permission the matter could be raised' when the Dáil met. Arguing that while 'they recognised themselves' as a republic,

no one else did. He really believed it was vital at this stage that the symbol of the Republic should be left untouched and that it should not be compromised in any sense by any arrangements which it might be necessary for our plenipotentiaries to make . . . It was not a shirking of duty, but he realised the position and how necessary it was to keep the Head of State and the symbol untouched and that was why he asked to be left out.

Cosgrave stood his ground and, after pointing out 'that this was a team they were sending over and they were leaving their ablest player in reserve . . . formally moved that the President be chairman of the delegation'. George Gavan Duffy, one of the proposed delegates, seconded Cosgrave's amendment and also criticised describing the delegates as plenipotentiaries, saying they were not so described in Lloyd George's last letter and 'if they sent him plenipotentiaries they would be making him a present of plenipotentiaries with full powers'.[46] The British duly fastened onto the opening identified by Gavan Duffy before the conference had even begun. 'Remember they are plenipotentiaries', Lord Fitzalan reminded Lloyd George, 'and must not take advantage of de Valera's absence to delay and refer back to him.'[47] But, again, de Valera proved obdurate, telling the Dáil that 'he understood plenipotentiaries were people who had power to deal with a question subject to ratification. They would go first with a Cabinet policy and on the understanding that any big question should be referred home before being decided by them.' This was the fatal flaw in the delegation's terms of reference: they were plenipotentiaries who should not take decisions on 'any big question'. But most Dáil deputies were so deferential to de Valera that there were only four other speakers on Cosgrave's amendment and they all supported the president; after the amendment had been put and lost, de Valera's original motion was carried unanimously.

Expressions of unease at the composition of the delegation did not end there. The delegates were proposed one by one for ratification and when Michael Collins was nominated, he intervened saying that he, too, 'believed that the President should have been part of the delegation. He did not wish to go himself and he would very much prefer not to be chosen.' De Valera repeated that 'if he were not the symbol he would go', adding that Collins 'was a man for that team. He was absolutely vital for the delegation.'[48] De Valera also argued that, because Collins was 'looked upon by the British as the leader of the fighting men, no delegation of which he was not a member would get the highest British offer, that if he were absent the British would feel they had still to deal with him, and still to conciliate him, and that they would hold back something from the other plenipotentiaries'.[49] Collins yet again gave way before presidential insistence and the Dáil approved his nomination.

Although Arthur Griffith, like Cosgrave and Collins, had urged de Valera to lead the delegation in the cabinet discussion on 9 September, he kept silent during the Dáil debate on its composition. This might have been because his admiration for de Valera was then unstinting. 'He seems to know by instinct what it has taken me years of thought and political experience to discover,' he had confided to friends during a Dáil meeting in August.[50] Nor, unlike Collins, did he demur and it seems likely that he was pleased, if not flattered, by his appointment as the chairman of the delegation.

Indeed his most authoritative and not unsympathetic biographer has concluded that 'there is no evidence whatsoever of Griffith displaying any reluctance to go to London'.[51]

The criticisms voiced in the Dáil on 14 September are suggestive in the light of what happened later, but the immediate significance of the debate is that, yet again, de Valera got what he wanted: the unanimous approval of his plan. Although he himself beat no retreat from republican absolutism, he made it clear that entering into negotiations meant admitting the necessity of compromise. This, he reminded the Dáil, was the significance of the bland and neutral formula, making no mention of a republic or of a sovereign, independent Irish state that had paved the way for the conference. Only on that basis, he said, could they negotiate: 'If they had asked Lloyd George to recognise the Republic he [the president] would say it would be an unreasonable request.' He also reminded them, in a manner reminiscent of a schoolmaster talking to a class of dim pupils, that 'the fight was not finished'. If the British had 'recognised the Republic the fight would be over and there would be no question of negotiations. Negotiations were necessary because they held one view and the British another.' The ultimate question was 'whether any form of association with Britain is one which the Irish people can stand for . . . He felt it was', and that they had a duty to try to reconcile the differences between the Irish and British positions by negotiation. Yet he offered no compromise proposal but said only that, although he 'would have a definite policy to put before the Dáil when the time came', that time was not yet. 'It would be harmful to take it up now.'[52]

De Valera, in short, had signalled that he was prepared to compromise but only on his own terms and in his own time and that was how matters rested when the delegation set off for the opening session of the conference on 11 October.

7

Catastrophe

Mr de Valera may gradually come to personify not a cause but a
catastrophe. It is difficult for us over here to measure truly, but it is
obvious that in the long run Government, however patient, must assert
itself or perish and be replaced by some other form of control.

Winston Churchill to Michael Collins, 12 April 1922[1]

Éamon de Valera issued the plenipotentiaries with their final written instructions under five headings on 7 October 1921, the day
before they departed for London.

The first affirmed that they had 'full powers as defined in their
credentials', which made no mention of a republic.*

The second stipulated 'before decisions are finally reached on
the main questions that a despatch notifying the intention of making those decisions will be sent to the Members of the Cabinet in
Dublin, and that a reply will be awaited by the plenipotentiaries
before that final decision is made'.

The third specified that 'the complete text of the draft treaty
about to be signed will be similarly submitted to Dublin and reply
awaited'. The fourth that, if the negotiations broke down, the text
of the final Irish proposals 'will be similarly submitted'. And the
fifth that the cabinet in Dublin 'will be kept regularly informed of
the progress of the negotiations'.[2]

* The plenipotentiaries were vested with such powers from Dáil Éireann
'to negotiate and conclude on behalf of Ireland with the representatives
of His Britannic Majesty, George V, a Treaty or Treaties of settlement,
association and accommodation between Ireland and the community of
nations known as the British Commonwealth' (NAI DE/2/304/1).

The instructions were designed to ensure that de Valera's presidential authority was not diluted by his refusal to go to London. The second and third instructions, in particular, guaranteed that the plenipotentiaries could make no major decisions without the prior approval of the president and their other cabinet colleagues in Dublin – Cathal Brugha, Austin Stack and William Cosgrave, the first two of whom were most unlikely to oppose de Valera in the event of any difference of opinion. Despite the unease that had surfaced at the meeting on 14 September, there was no provision for a draft treaty to be referred to Dáil Éireann which did not meet again for three months, on 14 December, over a week after the treaty had been signed.

The plenipotentiaries were also each given a copy of draft treaty proposals marked 'Combined alternative drafts for work on by Delegation. Passed by President.' Again, the drafts made no mention of a republic. Both drafts instead provided that 'the British Commonwealth recognises Ireland as a sovereign and independent state' and embodied de Valera's concept of external association;[3] but his thinking as to how and when that concept might be introduced was so tortuous and opaque that the drafts were useless as instruments that the plenipotentiaries could use in negotiation. De Valera had, however, explained his strategy – in so far as it can be described as a strategy – to Patrick McCartan just before the negotiations began:

In plain English he virtually said that if we talked too much republic we might not get dominion status accepted. He was in a sort of confidential mood and said that the voting would be rather interesting as the real men would be for peace and those of the Dáil who did nothing would be immutable. He believed association with the British Empire would be best for Ireland.[4]

What passed for the Irish treaty proposals that the plenipotentiaries brought to London were fragmentary and slight; they made no mention of Ulster, for example, and, all told, ran only to six articles. Draft Treaty A was a memorandum de Valera 'had drawn up for Lloyd George on his return from the July talks, but had decided not to send. Treaty B . . . was intended for use as propaganda should the talks break down. Nowhere was there written down a clear, rounded statement of what the delegation was actually supposed to work towards and settle for.'[5] The conclusion that de Valera refused to be identified with any such statement is inescapable and the delegates were consequently unable to submit any written proposals at the opening plenary session of the conference on 11 October.

The British were better prepared and circulated copies of their own document: the very same document that Lloyd George had given to de Valera on 20 July. 'However much amended, the basic paper at any conference', as Nicholas Mansergh has pointed out, 'is apt to determine the parameters of subsequent discussion. This was to prove no exception.'[6] The British document duly dictated the terms of engagement in the opening sessions of the conference, which focused on redrafting the five restrictive reservations in the proposals of 20 July: naval access to Irish ports, air facilities, the constitutional position of dominions in relation to war and defence, and a free-trade area between Britain and Ireland.

'Dear Dev . . . I never felt so relieved at the end of any day', scribbled Michael Collins on 12 October. 'I need hardly say I am not looking forward to [sic] any pleasure to resumptions – such a crowd I never met . . . This place [the] bloody limit. I wish to God I were back home.' Arthur Griffith's postscript in a letter to de Valera next day suggests that, at least at this early stage, he was more relaxed: 'Ll G is a humorous rascal. He talked today of the vast amount of produce England bought from us. I said, "You don't buy it for love of our beautiful eyes." Whereupon, with a smile he yielded, saying, "No, on account of your beautiful butter."'[7]

There was no discussion of the two issues likeliest to cause the talks to collapse – Ulster, and Ireland's relationship with the crown – until the fourth plenary session, on 14 October, when Lloyd

George asked Griffith for his views on Ulster. Again, the Irish delegation was lamentably unprepared because de Valera was still tinkering with the so-called 'Ulster clause' in Dublin. But the discussion ran into the sands when Griffith's classic nationalist critique of 'the unnaturalness of partition' was countered by Lloyd George's impassioned exposition of the rationale underlying the British government's refusal to coerce Ulster's unionists. Nor did de Valera's draft of the 'Ulster clause', which was to hand on 17 October, help matters. Its provisions were so tortuous and con-voluted[8] that, rather than tabling the draft, Griffith returned to his theme of 14 October, urging that 'those in the Six Counties should be allowed to choose freely whether they would be in North or South'.[9] Again, the discussion went nowhere. Thereafter what de Valera offered from Dublin was little more than an eloquent silence. This aloofness, as Tim Pat Coogan has noted, was 'totally uncharacteristic . . . and completely at variance with the inter-ventionist role he played, or attempted to play, in every other political activity . . . during his career'.[10]

Only once in the early phases of the conference did de Valera's behaviour in Dublin impinge on the proceedings: when he published a telegram he sent to Pope Benedict XV on 20 October complaining about the reply of King George V to a papal message hoping for the success of the conference. He protested that the king's language might 'mislead . . . the uninformed into believing that the troubles are "in" Ireland, or that the people of Ireland owe allegiance to the British King . . . The trouble is between Ireland and Britain, and its source that the rulers of Britain have sought to impose their will upon Ireland'.[11] Lloyd George reacted as soon as the conference met in plenary session the next day. De Valera's telegram, he protested, 'deals with the very issues in controversy. It is challenging, defiant and, if I may say so, ill-conditioned; it will make our task almost impossible . . . We must know whether allegiance to the King is to be finally repudiated by you, whether the connecting link of the Crown is to be snapped,' he told the

Irish delegates and he demanded an answer within three days. Arthur Griffith, forced into the invidious position of justifying a telegram to the pope that 'he himself thought a grave mistake', realised that the conference's 'atmosphere of benevolent inquiry and mutual instruction' had collapsed and 'one of blunt ultimatum substituted'.[12] But he loyally defended de Valera's ham-fisted intrusion, even though it had gifted Lloyd George 'the opportunity to make the Crown the central concern of the negotiations, something which the prearranged Irish strategy had sought hard to avoid'.[13] De Valera was unrepentant. 'I am sure this was somewhat disconcerting,' he wrote loftily to Griffith the next day, 'but it could not be helped.' The exchange of messages between the British and the Vatican was, he claimed, the kind of 'propaganda stunt' that 'will not be allowed to pass unchallenged'.[14]

The crisis prompted Collins to go back to Dublin that weekend (22–3 October) to tell de Valera that the delegates wanted him to join them in London. But the president was obdurate and wrote dismissively to Griffith of 'the considerations of tactical advantage which determined me in holding the view that I should remain here'.[15] His obduracy was rooted in a style of leadership that paid little heed to the opinion of others, even to the views of such senior and critically important colleagues as Collins and Griffith. Leadership had been a solitary exercise for de Valera ever since he had first acquired political power in English prisons in 1916–17. President of Sinn Féin and of the Irish Volunteers since October 1917, of Dáil Éireann since April 1921, and happy to be hailed as 'President of the Republic' throughout his time in America, it was unsurprising that his method of leadership was overwhelmingly presidential. He even compared himself with the American president and 'used a large number of arguments based on [Woodrow] Wilson's alleged mistakes in heading [the] US delegation in Paris' as reasons for resisting Michael Collins's pressure that he should go to London.[16] Camaraderie, a key component of Collins's style of leadership, meant nothing to de Valera. Nor could any kind of consensual leadership evolve when he saw so little of Griffith or of Collins in 1920–21. The twin impact of adulation and isolation in America – 'a good man whom America spoiled' was Arthur Griffith's judgement[17] – was compounded after his return by the constraints inhibiting easy intercourse between revolutionaries on the run; Griffith, moreover, was in prison when de Valera returned and was not released until after the truce.

De Valera's retrospective explanations for his refusal to go to London have been well summarised by Patrick Murray: they included 'that he remained at home to avoid compromising the Republic, as a reserve against the tricks of Lloyd George, to be in a better position to rally a united nation, and to influence extreme Republicans to consent to External Association if the British accepted it'. By staying in Dublin he believed he had not only obliged 'the delegates to refer home before taking decisions' but that he had also 'created, through himself, a final court of appeal to avert whatever Britain might attempt to put over, and if anything went wrong, he would be on hand to rally the people and prepare them for resistance'.[18]

De Valera knew from his own talks with Lloyd George in July, moreover, of the extreme difficulty of the negotiations that lay ahead. He knew, too, that any Irish negotiating team would be callow and inexperienced compared with their British counterparts who would also enjoy the advantage of playing at home. In theory, his strategy of denying finality to what might happen in Downing Street by insisting that the final decision be taken in Dublin seemed shrewd. In practice, it was naive because of the inherent contradiction between the plenipotentiary status of the delegates and their agreement to sign nothing in London that had not first been endorsed by the Dáil cabinet in Dublin. Firstly, because de Valera failed adequately to explain his reasoning to the plenipotentiaries before the talks began; the corollary was that it had never occurred to him that the ultimate decision about an agreement might be made in London and not in Dublin. He was so certain on this score that he gave Seán T. O'Kelly, the Dáil's envoy in Paris and one of his own staunchest supporters, short shrift when he returned to Dublin in early November to voice his concerns about how Collins and Griffith were conducting the negotiations. 'De Valera took him coolly, almost coldly, and told him everything was safe inasmuch as the delegates could not sign anything without first submitting it to the cabinet and getting their approval'; he also rebuked O'Kelly, saying 'he should not have left Paris without permission and . . . to return there at once'.[19] Secondly, because the bonding that took place between the plenipotentiaries on their wearying journeys by sea and rail and during their long days and nights in London silently corroded de Valera's authority with consequences that proved catastrophic.

The atmosphere of crisis again pervaded the seventh and final plenary session of the conference, on Monday, 24 October, when the Irish delegates finally tabled their proposal of external association. Lloyd George was suspicious but not utterly dismissive and discussion was adjourned but continued by mutual agreement at a sub-conference. This was the format throughout the final phase of the negotiations. Twenty-four sub-conferences took place between 24 October and 6 December, of which Griffith attended twenty-two and Collins nineteen; the minor Irish delegates were largely excluded: Barton attended three and Gavan Duffy and Duggan two each.[20]

The first sub-conference, on the evening of 24 October, was attended by Griffith, Collins, Lloyd George and Austen Chamberlain (as leader of the Conservative Party). Lloyd George and Chamberlain talked 'freely – Chamberlain frankly', Griffith wrote that night to de Valera; they stressed that 'on the Crown they must fight. It was the only link of Empire they possessed.' But, when they pressed Griffith to 'accept the Crown', he replied that he 'had no authority' but that, if they reached 'agreement on all other points', he would 'recommend some form of association with the Crown'. He also 'told them the only possibility of Ireland considering association of any kind with [the] Crown was in exchange for essential unity – a concession to Ulster.' Griffith's letter prompted another intervention from de Valera:

We are all here at one that there can be no question of our asking the Irish people to enter an arrangement which would make them subject to the Crown, or demand from them allegiance to the British King. If war is the alternative, we can only face it, and I think that the sooner the other side is made to realise that the better.[21]

The plenipotentiaries bitterly resented de Valera's intervention and Collins, in particular, flew into a towering rage. They saw it as 'tying their hands in discussion and as inconsistent with the powers given them on their appointment'. The next day, 26 October, they all signed Griffith's reply, threatening to withdraw from the conference and return immediately to Dublin: 'The responsibility, if this interference breaks the very slight possibility there is of settlement, will not and must not rest with the plenipotentiaries.'[22] For once de Valera backed down, pleading that it was 'obviously a misunderstanding. There can be no question of tying the hands of the Plenipotentiaries beyond the extent to which they are tied by their original instructions.' His memoranda, he wrote to Griffith next day, were 'nothing more than an attempt to keep you in touch with the views of members of the Cabinet here on the various points as they arise'. But the episode was the first portent that there were outer limits to Arthur Griffith's hitherto unfailing deference to de Valera.

Indeed de Valera hereafter communicated with Griffith less frequently and less assertively. Whereas he had previously responded to each of Griffith's letters by return of post, six such letters between 27 October and 8 November elicited only a brief, blanket reply on 9 November; this merely endorsed the delegates' view without commenting on Griffith's reaffirmation in writing (in a letter requested by Lloyd George) of his preparedness 'to recommend a free partnership of Ireland with the other States associated within the British Commonwealth, the formula defining the partnership to be arrived at in later discussion ... [and] to recommend that Ireland should consent to a recognition of the Crown as head of the proposed association of free States'.[23] De Valera's only caveat was mildly expressed: 'I think, as far as the "Crown and Empire connection" is concerned, we should not budge a single inch from the point where the negotiations have now led us.'[24] He was also conciliatory at a meeting of the cabinet in Dublin, which Collins, Barton and Duggan attended, saying that while 'the utmost co-operation should exist between Dublin and London the plenipotentiaries should have a perfectly free hand but should follow original instructions re important decisions'. After a long discussion of the state of the negotiations, de Valera suggested that 'it would be advisable to come to concrete proposals as soon as possible and that if a break is inevitable Ulster would be the best question on which to break'.[25]

The negotiations now ground to a temporary halt because the British government was preoccupied with surviving tests of strength on their Irish policy in the House of Commons and at the Conservative Party conference in Liverpool. But, once he had secured his parliamentary majority against the danger of a revolt of the Tory diehards, Lloyd George set in train the preparation of a draft British treaty. On 16 November Tom Jones presented what Griffith described to de Valera as 'not the draft of a treaty but tentative suggestions' to which the Irish were asked to reply 'with a similar document'. But, again, it was the British draft that determined the course of the continuing negotiation. It was yet another reiteration of the reservations in their proposals of 20 July, coupled with a formulation of what Lloyd George had agreed with Griffith about Ulster: that the Northern Ireland parliament be allowed to opt in or out of a treaty settlement and, if it opted out, that a boundary commission would determine the border of Northern Ireland.[26]

The Irish response, delivered on 22 November, reduced Lloyd George to despair. 'They are back on their independent state again', and there was nothing 'about Ulster's right to contract out of an All-Ireland Parliament'. The conference teetered on the brink of collapse when Lloyd George instructed Tom Jones to tell the Irish delegates that 'unless they withdrew their document he would have to break off the negotiations'. Tom Jones prevented a breakdown by soft-pedalling his instructions when he met Griffith and Collins that afternoon. He 'did not tell them they could "pack up and go home" but made . . . them understand that, unless the letter was withdrawn or explained away, the PM . . . would have no option but to send them a letter that day breaking off negotiations'.[27] Although Lloyd George remained pessimistic, he avoided further confrontation at a sub-conference the next day with Griffith, Collins and Barton and instead awaited the outcome of their deliberations in Dublin where they returned on the night of the 24 November.

On 25 November the Dáil cabinet unanimously approved the formula 'that Ireland shall recognise the British Crown for the purposes of the Association as symbol and accepted head of the combination of Associated States' – transmuted to 'Ireland will agree to be associated with the British Commonwealth for all purposes of common concern, including defence, peace and war, and political treaties, and to recognise the British Crown as Head of the Association'[28] in the Irish reply brought by Tom Jones to Chequers on Monday, 28 November. 'This means war,' said Lloyd George, but when Birkenhead and Robert Horne arrived at Chequers they were more sanguine. 'They did not think this was the Irishmen's last word', and Lloyd George was also more hopeful after talking for over an hour to Griffith and Éamonn Duggan, who came to Chequers at ten o'clock that night.[29]

Lloyd George quickened the pace the next afternoon at a series of three meetings in Downing Street that pushed the conference into its final phase. A meeting of the British delegates on the oath of allegiance at three o'clock was followed at four by another meeting of Lloyd George, Chamberlain and Birkenhead with Griffith,

Collins and Duggan when the British 'specifically offered to put a phrase in the Treaty ensuring that the Crown should have no more authority in Ireland than in Canada'.[30] The British triumvirate then hammered out their final offer with their parliamentary draftsmen and constitutional lawyers when Lloyd George came up with the wording that Ireland 'have the same national status as the Dominion of Canada and be known as the Irish Free State'.[31]

The draft treaty was delivered to Arthur Griffith on the evening of 30 November. The draft oath to be taken by members of the Irish Free State's parliament swore 'to bear true faith and allegiance to the Constitution of the Irish Free State; to the community of nations known as the British Empire; and to the King as the Head of the State and of the Empire'.[32]

Griffith left for Dublin on the morning of Friday, 2 December, in order to give de Valera the draft treaty without delay and they met privately at eleven o'clock that evening in 53 Kenilworth Square, where de Valera was staying. 'I told him definitely that I would never consent to or sign any such agreement,' wrote de Valera three weeks later. 'He said he would not break on the Crown. We parted at that.'[33] A collision between the mail-boat and a schooner delayed the return of the other plenipotentiaries that evening. They were exhausted when they arrived at Dublin's Mansion House for a meeting the next morning between the cabinet and the delegation when Cathal Brugha poisoned an already tense atmosphere by charging that the British had 'selected its men' in respect of Griffith and Collins having done most of the negotiating in the sub-conferences. The cabinet was split, as were the plenipotentiaries. Griffith was 'in favour of the Treaty' and refused to break on the Crown, thereby handing 'Ulster the position from which she had been driven'. Duggan agreed with Griffith and believed the 'Treaty to be England's last word'. Collins was 'in substantial agreement' with Griffith and Duggan; 'the non-acceptance of a treaty would be a gamble as England could arrange war in Ireland in a week'. Barton and Gavan Duffy opposed acceptance.

Barton thought 'England's last word had not been reached and that she could not declare war on question of allegiance'. Gavan Duffy wanted the Treaty to be rejected by the Dáil and 'sent back amended'.

The president then entered the fray, saying that the Treaty

could not be accepted in its then form. He personally could not subscribe to the Oath of Allegiance nor could he sign any document which would give N. E. Ulster power to vote itself out of the Irish Free State. With modifications, however, it might be accepted honourably, and he would like to see the plenipotentiaries go back and secure peace if possible. He believed the Delegates had done their utmost and it now remained to them to show that they were prepared to face the consequences – war or no war. He would deal with the present document exactly as with that of 20th July – say it cannot be accepted and put up counter-proposals.[34]

This time it was Robert Barton who pressed de Valera to return with the delegation, saying that it would be impossible 'to get the maximum terms without his being present'. Yet again he refused and insisted on staying at home as 'the last defence', arguing that, if negotiations broke down when he was in London, 'that would be the end, but, if they broke down without him, there was always a last recourse to him'.[35] De Valera's lordly and inflexible conclusion can only have infuriated those bearing the burden of negotiation he refused to share. The message was unmistakable: I will not go to London but do as I now say and do as I did in July. His performance at that fateful cabinet meeting on 3 December indicates that, 'from de Valera's point of view, the negotiations were only the overture to the main performance he would deliver'.[36]

De Valera's suggested amendment to the oath – 'I _____ do solemnly swear true faith and allegiance to the constitution of the Irish Free State, to the Treaty of Association and to recognise the King of Great Britain as Head of the Associated States' – was duly incorporated in the Irish delegation's amended Articles of Agreement. It was a measure of the sense of make or break in both delegations that the next meeting took place on a Sunday, when Griffith, Barton and Gavan Duffy met Lloyd George, Chamberlain, Birkenhead and Horne in Downing Street at five o'clock on 4 December. Michael Collins was so '"fed up" with the muddle' that he stayed away.[37] After Griffith had read out de Valera's 'counter proposals', the British retired for a ten-minute private conclave. When they returned, Lloyd George declared that, 'although they might have considered some change in the form of the oath, this was a refusal . . . to enter the Empire and accept the common bond of the Crown'. The discussion broke down with an agreement that the Irish delegation would formally submit its proposals the following day and that the British would respond with 'a formal rejection'; they would also inform Craig that 'the negotiations were broken down'.[38]

The high drama of what happened in London the next day has been told and retold. For a biographer of de Valera, the unrelenting focus must be on why the plenipotentiaries flouted their instructions and signed the Treaty in the early hours of Tuesday, 6 December, without first referring it back to Dublin.[39]

A tête-à-tête between Arthur Griffith and Tom Jones at midnight on the Sunday led to another tête-à-tête, this time between Lloyd George and Michael Collins, on the Monday morning. Lloyd George then postponed telling his cabinet, which was meeting at noon, that that the negotiations had broken down 'on the question of "within or without" the Empire'. He was encouraged to keep talking because, although Collins queried the wording of the articles relating to the oath, he never referred either to the nomenclature or to the constitutional status of the Irish Free State; nor did he offer any objection to dominion status or make any mention of external association. This enabled Lloyd George to act on the assumption that Collins, like Griffith, would not break on the issue of Empire. There remained the issue of Ulster, in regard to which Lloyd George hoped that Collins would interpret the establishment of a boundary commission as providing for the essential unity of Ireland.

These were the considerations that shaped Lloyd George's strategy when, accompanied by Chamberlain, Birkenhead and Churchill, he met Griffith, Collins and Barton at three o'clock that afternoon. Lloyd George immediately confronted Griffith, saying that he had already agreed to the Ulster clauses. There followed the dramatic scene, recorded by Robert Barton,[40] when Lloyd George 'shook his papers in the air, declared that we were trying deliberately to bring about a break on Ulster because our people in Ireland had refused to come within the Empire and that Arthur Griffith was letting him down where he had promised not to do so'. A disconcerted Griffith, stung by his honour being impugned, was trapped into a fatal mistake. He agreed that he personally would sign the Treaty regardless of whether his fellow plenipotentiaries did so.

For the head of a delegation in a bilateral negotiation suddenly to announce while the conference is in session without prior consultation with his own negotiation team that he intends to sign the document under discussion was vain, naive and tactically inexcusable. Griffith not only utterly transformed the chemistry around the cabinet table in 10 Downing Street; he also tore apart what ties remained between the plenipotentiaries and their colleagues in Dublin. In so doing Arthur Griffith did something he had never done since surrendering the leadership of Sinn Féin in 1917: he set himself up as an alternative source of authority to Éamon de Valera. Despite his insistence 'that his colleagues were in a different position from himself in that they were not party to the promise [on Ulster] not to let Lloyd George down' and despite his 'repeated efforts to avoid the question being put' to Collins and Barton, Griffith's personal pledge to sign the Treaty meant that he was effectively siding with Lloyd George and forcing his colleagues to choose between breaking with him or flouting their instructions not to sign the Treaty without referring it back to Dublin.

Lloyd George seized the opening, saying that 'he had always taken it that Arthur Griffith spoke for the Delegation'; that they 'were all plenipotentiaries and that it was now a matter of peace or war'. Every delegate must 'sign the document and recommend it, or there was no agreement'. He then spoke melodramatically of how 'a special train and destroyer' was waiting to convey word of acceptance or rejection to James Craig in Belfast and he demanded an answer that evening. Griffith, Collins and Barton then went back to their colleagues at 22 Hans Place. Collins's attitude was decisive: the boil of resentment, his sense that he had been cast as a scapegoat to do the dirty work de Valera had shirked, now burst, and he followed Griffith's lead. The Irish delegation returned to 10 Downing Street and signed the Treaty at ten minutes past two on the morning of 6 December.

Lloyd George's theatrical behaviour – his apparent rage, his brandishing of papers in the air, his threats of war, his talk of Belfast deadlines and of trains and destroyers – has led to interminable but ultimately irrelevant debate about whether ot not he was bluffing. If bluff it was it worked, for what mattered to Éamon de Valera was that, for whatever reason, the Treaty had been signed. His strategy was based on two false premises. The first and, in his eyes, overwhelmingly the most important premise was that the Irish delegates would sign nothing without his prior approval. His second premise, unlike the first, was not so much a confident expectation as a hope: that the British would be unable to prevent the negotiations collapsing on the issue of Ulster.

De Valera had presided over a review of Irish Volunteer brigades in Ennis on 5 December and spent that night in Limerick after receiving the freedom of the city. He and his entourage – minister for defence, Cathal Brugha; chief of staff, Richard Mulcahy; and Mulcahy's aide-de-camp, Michael Rynne (see plate 11) – were still sitting at the fireside when Mulcahy received a phone call from the IRA's adjutant-general, Gearóid O'Sullivan, in Dublin informing him that a treaty had been signed. De Valera received the dramatic news 'quite unmoved . . . even quite unsurprised' and simply said 'no' when invited to speak to O'Sullivan himself.[41] It was the first act in a pattern of behaviour over the next forty-eight hours so bizarre that it makes sense only in terms of presidential outrage at the fact that a treaty – *any* treaty – had been signed without his prior approval.

Mulcahy's recollection, moreover, makes nonsense of de Valera's retrospective and self-justificatory account to his official biographers:

His immediate reaction was one of joy and surprise. He had assumed all along that the delegates would carry out their instructions and sign no agreement that had not been submitted to Dublin in its final form. Still, he could imagine circumstances in which the delegates might have risked a formal rebuke for the sake of some dazzling bargain to be clinched immediately if at all. Under some lucky combination of circumstances the British must have collapsed. 'I did not think they would give in so easily,' he said.[42]

No joy was evident – 'there was no uplift in the air', in Mulcahy's phrase – on the journey back to Dublin. Indeed de Valera, on hearing that Mrs Tom Clarke was on the train, went to sit with her and summoned Cathal Brugha to join them, leaving Mulcahy and his aide-de-camp to sit by themselves. His behaviour on arriving in Dublin was even stranger: he made no effort whatever to find out the truth about the Treaty but instead went to Greystones where he spent the afternoon with his family. He returned to Dublin that night to chair a symposium at 7.30 p.m. in the Mansion House commemorating the sixth centenary of Dante's death. But he could no longer evade the truth when he was met by Cathal Brugha and Austin Stack. 'Showed me a copy of the *Evening Mail* – incredible,' he wrote in his diary. Just then, begowned as chancellor of the National University of Ireland and about to lead the way into the Round Room for the symposium, he was approached by Éamonn Duggan, hotfoot from London, who gave him a copy of the Treaty and asked him to read it. 'What should I read it for?' answered de Valera, only to be told it would be simultaneously published in

Dublin and London within the hour. '"What," said the President,' recorded Austin Stack, '"to be published whether I have seen it or not – whether I approve it or not."'[43]

Piarais Beaslaí, a speaker who sat near de Valera during the symposium, was 'astonished at [his] state of suppressed emotion' when he had not even read, let alone 'taken the trouble to study' the Treaty. 'That a Treaty had been signed, without first being referred to him, was the source of his agitation.'[44] Writing to Joe McGarrity three weeks later, emotion still reigned: the plenipotentiaries having signed without first consulting him was, de Valera claimed, 'an act of disloyalty to their President and to their colleagues in the Cabinet such as is probably without parallel in history. They not merely signed the document but in order to make the *fait accompli* doubly secure, they published it hours before the President or their colleagues saw it.'[45]

Rage and emotion likewise fuelled de Valera's conduct on 7 December when he summoned a meeting of the cabinet ministers who were in Dublin – Brugha, Stack, Cosgrave and Kevin O'Higgins (Cosgrave's assistant minister for local government). 'P[resident] in an awful state,' wrote Kathleen O'Connell, his devoted personal secretary, in her diary. 'What a fiasco.' And so it was. De Valera immediately announced his intention of demanding the resignation of the three plenipotentiaries who were in the cabinet – Griffith, Collins and Barton – and was dissuaded only by Cosgrave's arguing that they should be given a chance to explain their action. Until that moment de Valera probably 'still viewed Cosgrave as an ally and . . . he agreed to postpone the decision for one day in order to keep him on side'.[46] 'Instead of taking drastic action,'[47] he told his official biographers, he decided to issue a press statement for immediate publication:

In view of the nature of the proposed Treaty with Great Britain President de Valera has sent an urgent summons to the Members of the Cabinet in London to report at once so that a full Cabinet decision may be taken.

The hour of the meeting is fixed for 12 noon tomorrow Thursday. A meeting of the Dáil will be summoned later.[48]

De Valera might have been dissuaded from sacking the pleni-potentiary ministers in their absence. But he had thrown down the gauntlet as the self-appointed champion of resistance to the Treaty without even discussing its terms with its signatories. So much was immediately apparent to Desmond FitzGerald, Sinn Féin's director of publicity. 'This might be altered, Mr President,' he said to de Valera. 'It reads as if you were opposed to the settlement.' De Valera was unyielding: 'And that's the way I intend it to read. Publish it as it is.'[49]

At that moment the factions for and against the Treaty were formed, leading, within months, to civil war.

De Valera's strategy in the treaty negotiations failed because it was based on an exaggerated perception of his own authority. As his leadership was challenged for the first time since the autumn of 1917, his authority disintegrated and his power ebbed away. This happened in three stages. The first stage was the plenipotentiaries' rejection of his presidential veto by signing the Treaty without his prior approval. The transition to the second stage, when he was denied a majority in the Dáil cabinet, was immediate. His loss of a majority in Dáil Éireann, the third and more protracted stage, was played out in the debates that began on 14 December 1921 and culminated in the approval of the Treaty on 7 January 1922.

The meeting of the cabinet and the plenipotentiaries on 8 December had confirmed the impossibility of compromise. Griffith, Collins, Barton and Cosgrave declared that they would recommend approval of the Treaty to the Dáil: Griffith 'on basis of its merits', the others on the basis of its having been signed. De Valera, Brugha and Stack refused so to recommend it. But, after a bitter and protracted meeting that lasted from 12 noon until 9.30 p.m., de Valera succeeded in preventing the cabinet's majority verdict being recorded as a decision. Instead of an announcement that the cabinet had accepted the Treaty, the waning, residual legacy of deference to de Valera led to an extraordinary announcement that the president would issue a press statement 'defining' the position of the minority. The only other announcement was that the Dáil would meet in public session on 14 December.[50] After the meeting ended, de Valera told Erskine Childers that 'he intended to rely on "extremist support" to carry his opposition to the Treaty'.[51]

'A quarter of an hour before midnight the Pressmen were called in and Mr De Valera's address "to the Irish people" was handed to them. The importance of the situation that had arisen was immediately realised,' recorded next day's *Irish Times*. So was the split: it also reported that the two ministers who had supported de Valera, Brugha and Stack, 'remained with him during the preparation of the address'.[52] What his official biographers describe as de Valera's 'proclamation', a flagrant attempt to evoke echoes of the minority decision that launched the 1916 rising, alleged that the treaty was 'in violent conflict with the wishes of the majority of this nation, as expressed freely in successive elections during the past three years'.[53] But the substance of the proclamation mattered less than the fact that it bore the public, presidential imprimatur. In effect, de Valera thereby asserted his right to refuse to accept the majority verdict of his cabinet and began campaigning against the terms of the settlement before the Dáil had even assembled. Indeed, de Valera dismissed as irrelevant what he described as 'an accidental division of opinion of the Cabinet' in his opening remarks to the Dáil on 14 December.[54]

He was more honest as the Dáil went into private session that afternoon: 'I have only one thing to say, one thing I feel hurt about, with respect to the delegation and that is that when a Treaty was signed in London, and when I heard of it first the signatures were appended to it.'[55] The admission goes to the heart of the fatal flaw in de Valera's position, a flaw already apparent to the members of the cabinet and that now became apparent to the members of the Dáil: he opposed the Treaty not because it was a compromise, but because it was not *his* compromise – not, that is, a compromise that he had authorised in advance of its conclusion. He introduced his own compromise of external association in the document christened as 'Document No. 2' by Michael Collins on the second day of the private session. John Regan has argued persuasively that, 'tactically, its introduction so early in the debate was a gross miscalculation . . . Neither the doctrinaire republicans, pro-Treaty deputies, nor those occupying the no-man's-land of the undecided were prepared to attempt to find any common ground within its provisions and Document No. 2 was ignominiously withdrawn by its author.'[56]

Swaddled in the comfort blanket of four years of deference and obedience, de Valera tried to chart a course too subtle to be understood by those less intellectually astute than he was. He then compounded his error by trying to prevent his own compromise becoming known to the wider public, protesting immediately when Kevin O'Higgins mentioned 'the external association idea' in the Dáil in public session on 19 December. 'Cabinet matters are matters for Private Sessions,' claimed de Valera. 'I do not care what the Irish people are at liberty to get of communications and documents; but as responsible head of the Government, I protest against Cabinet matters being made public.' Griffith's reply was crushing and prevailed: 'This is a document submitted by the President' as the alternative to the Treaty 'and the Irish people ought to see it.'[57]

Again and again de Valera's procedural interventions, citing his presidential authority, sought to alter the terms of the debate to his own advantage. But he suffered another setback on 22 December when an amendment to Michael Collins's motion (designed to give all deputies who wanted to speak the opportunity of doing so), adjourning the debate until 3 January, was lost by 77 votes to 44.

De Valera plumbed the depths of the anti-democratic contempt for majority rule in seeking to maximise his support among the extremists in his notorious speech on 6 January:

I have been brought up amongst the Irish people. I was reared in a labourer's cottage here in Ireland [applause]. I have not lived solely amongst the intellectuals . . . whenever I wanted to know what the Irish people wanted I had only to examine my own heart and it told me straight off what the Irish people wanted. I, therefore, am holding to this policy, first of all, because if I was the only man in Ireland left of those of 1916 – as I was Senior Officer left – I will go down in that creed to my grave. I am not a member of the Irish Republican Brotherhood, but I hope when I die I will get a Fenian grave.

He concluded by offering the Dáil his 'personal resignation' as president.[58] His ploy of personifying the split, through postponing a vote on the Treaty by first forcing a vote reaffirming his status as president, failed and at eight o'clock on the evening of Saturday, 7 January 1922, Dáil Éireann approved the Treaty by 64 votes to 57.

But de Valera still tried to cling to power even after he had resigned as president when the Dáil reassembled on 9 January. Seizing on Collins's proposal for the establishment of a committee of public safety comprised both of supporters and of opponents of the Treaty, he interpreted it as meaning that 'the majority party' would not oppose his re-election as president; then he 'would carry on as before and forget that this Treaty has come'. It was Cosgrave who exposed the extraordinary effrontery of his proposal:

The minority of this House takes over the government of the country . . . The President dictates to the House what the policy is regardless of the decision of this House. The minority is to regulate whether a decision of this House is to be put into operation or not . . . The advisers of the President seek to take advantage of his personal popularity and the respect in which the people of this Assembly hold him – that they desire to establish here an autocracy.

De Valera persisted, challenging Griffith to say that if he were elected president he would 'act and function as the [Chief] Executive of the Republic'. But his last throw of the dice was in vain. Realising Griffith's election was inevitable, he led the deputies who had opposed the Treaty out of the Dáil 'as a protest against the election as President of the Irish Republic of the Chairman of the Delegation, who is bound by the Treaty conditions to set up a State which is to subvert the Republic'.[59] The deputies who remained then unanimously elected Griffith as president of Dáil Éireann.

8

A Glass Wall

'Of all human troubles the most hateful is to feel that you have the capacity of power yet you have no field to exercise it.' Thus did a British prime minister, Herbert Henry Asquith, quote Herodotus to explain how he felt in the political wilderness. Much the same feeling assailed Éamon de Valera in January 1922. What made it worse was that in his case, unlike Asquith's, he knew his fate was of his own making. His colleagues had not sought to depose him but had pleaded with him to remain. But by rejecting Collins's proposal that he participate in a committee of public safety comprised of supporters and opponents of the Treaty and by abandoning the Dáil, he rejected the opportunity to retain a residue of his power by vainly insisting that he hold power only on his own terms. By February 1923 he was already fretting at his impotence: 'I have been condemned to view the tragedy here for the last year as through a wall of glass, powerless to intervene effectively. I have, however, still the hope that an opportunity may come my way.'[1]

De Valera's life over the next decade is best understood in terms of his carving out a path back to power.

Once the Dáil had approved the Treaty, power shifted to the Provisional Government. This was the body established under the terms of the Treaty at a special meeting of Irish elected representatives summoned by Arthur Griffith on 14 January and boycotted by de Valera and his supporters. The Provisional Government took over all the powers and apparatus of government that the British surrendered before 6 December 1922 when the Irish Free State was formally established. Theoretically, the Dáil system of government, to which de Valera and his supporters continued to give the allegiance they denied to the Provisional Government, continued to exist. In practice, such allegiance became increasingly meaningless. The new locus of power was well symbolised in the British handover of Dublin Castle on 16 January not to Arthur Griffith, the new president of Dáil Éireann, but to Michael Collins, the chairman of the Provisional Government.

De Valera was meanwhile reduced to attending the portentously entitled World Congress of the Irish Race in Paris on 21–8 January. This was a meeting of 'representatives of Irish organisations throughout the world', to which he travelled on the passport of a priest with whom he had been friendly in Rockwell. Playing the priest was an eloquent metaphor for his loss of power. Although the meeting duly elected him president, it disintegrated in dissension over the Treaty and 'behind a confessional in Notre Dame Cathedral de Valera put on once more the Roman collar' to travel home.[2]

He then tried to come to terms with the collapse of his authority in Sinn Féin. Although 'the Sinn Féin party never voted formally on the Treaty', voting for the election of a new standing committee on 12 January 1922 was on pro- and anti-Treaty lines. 'The result of the election was a triumph for the moderates, who won eleven posts as opposed to a mere three gained by the republicans . . . All opponents of the Treaty were soon labelled "republicans", even though some of them (most notably de Valera) had neither hoped nor attempted to achieve a republic during the negotiations with Britain.' Although de Valera then argued that the two sides 'should cleanly and definitely divide', it was agreed to postpone a decision until a special *ard fheis*. 'Dev looked dreadfully badly, fanatical almost,' an onlooker at a big anti-Treaty party demonstration in O'Connell Street wrote in her diary. But there was a republican majority when 3,000 delegates assembled in the Mansion House on 21 February and 'de Valera was not deposed as president of the party in the same way as he had already been replaced as president of the Dáil and of the Irish republic. He remained leader of the

Sinn Féin party (or rather, of *a* Sinn Féin party) for the next four years.' The meeting was characterised by a desire for unity, however tenuous. After prolonged private negotiations between de Valera and Collins, it agreed to adjourn for three months in order to avoid a party split and an immediate election. 'De Valera was particularly anxious that a new Dáil should not be chosen for at least three months, and not until the Free State constitution had been published [because] . . . he wanted the electorate to be confronted with questions other than the Treaty.'[3] This enabled him 'to preserve an institution – the Officer Board – within which he had position and influence while postponing imminent electoral defeat. It also afforded him time to regroup and campaign.'[4] On 15 March he formally established Cumann na Poblachta (the Republican Party) under his presidency, with its headquarters in 23 Suffolk Street, the same building that housed senior officers of the IRA antagonistic to the Treaty.

But de Valera's lingering influence in Sinn Féin did not extend to the anti-Treaty IRA. 'Anti-Treaty sentiment in the IRA began to crystallise rapidly once de Valera condemned the agreement', and the likelihood of violent resistance was apparent weeks before the crucial vote in the Dáil. The senior officers of the 1st Southern Division, commanded by Liam Lynch, unanimously passed a resolution urging the Dáil to reject it on 10 December (before it had even assembled) and 'divisional headquarters informed Dáil deputies from Cork that failure to vote against the settlement would be considered treason to the Republic'. In February 1922 'the IRA translated vocal opposition into action . . . and carried out a series of arms raids.'[5]

The speed of withdrawal of British troops posed the problem of whether their evacuated barracks would be occupied by local IRA units regardless of their attitude to the Treaty. 'Large areas were dominated by anti-Treaty units', which meant that before the Provisional Government 'could build up any reliable military force a large proportion of the country was potentially outside their control. To contest the taking over of posts was to risk civil war.'[6] This came to a head when the evacuation of Limerick, scheduled for 23 February, provoked a confrontation between pro- and anti-Treaty forces. On 6 March de Valera wrote to Richard Mulcahy, the minister for defence, asking him to mediate and warning that 'the crisis may well be the beginning of a civil war and a general break-up of the army and the defensive forces of the nation'. Mulcahy, who had only begun trying to recruit a national army, played for time. His negotiated compromise enabled the peaceful evacuation of Limerick to be completed by 11 March but it was opposed by Griffith for whom 'civil war was preferable to abdicating the authority of the Provisional Government and repudiating the Treaty'. The Limerick episode pointed to the shape of things to come and was interpreted by some anti-Treaty forces not as a compromise but as a victory.[7]

This was the inflammable atmosphere in which de Valera now delivered a series of incendiary speeches during a speaking tour of Munster. The Treaty, he warned at Dungarvan on 16 March, 'barred the way to independence'. On St Patrick's Day in Carrick-on-Suir he told a large audience, which included 700 young members of the IRA, that 'if the Treaty was accepted the fight for freedom would still go on; and the Irish people, instead of fighting British soldiers, would have to fight the Irish soldiers of an Irish Government'. He then moved on to Thurles where he made his most notorious speech to a crowd that included 200 Volunteers carrying rifles. 'If they accepted the Treaty . . . they would have to wade through Irish blood, through the blood of the soldiers of the Irish government, and through, perhaps, the blood of some of the members of the government in order to get Irish freedom.'

He returned to the same sanguinary theme in Killarney, 'again in the presence of armed men', on 19 March:

In order to achieve freedom, if our Volunteers continue and I hope they will continue until the goal is reached – if we continue on that movement which was begun when the Volunteers were started and we suppose this Treaty is ratified by your votes, then these men, in order to achieve freedom will have, [as] I said yesterday, will have to march over the dead bodies of their own brothers. They will have to wade through Irish blood.

And it was also on this occasion that Éamon de Valera made his infamous declaration reeking of contempt for democracy: 'The people had never a right to do wrong.'[8]

This gory litany, recited before armed audiences, was ever afterwards defended by de Valera and his followers as being intended not as incitement but as prophecy.[9] But such speeches, which attracted nationwide publicity in the *Irish Independent*, were, at the very least, insensitive, provocative and grotesquely irresponsible. Joseph Curran's conclusion is indisputable: 'For a leader of his stature to utter prophecies of bloody domestic conflict only increased its likelihood.'[10]

Such prophecy, moreover, offered rhetorical comfort and encouragement to the anti-Treaty elements in the IRA at the very moment when they were on the point of rejecting all authority but their own. On 22 March they held a press conference in the offices of de Valera's Cumann na Poblachta party when Rory O'Connor boasted of not even having read the Treaty and 'made it clear that radical republicans in the IRA did not recognise any Irish government and that they had no interest in democratic politics'. When asked if they intended to establish a military dictatorship, he replied, 'You can take it that way if you like.'[11] De Valera's official biographers claim that he 'heartily disagreed with O'Connor's action and outlook' but also acknowledge that he believed that if the IRA 'could save the nation from the calamities which he considered to flow from [the Treaty], he would consider it justifiable for it to use its strength to do so'.[12] So he uttered no criticism of the army convention on 26 March, held in defiance of the Dáil cabinet's prohibition, that reaffirmed the IRA's allegiance to a notional republic and appointed an army executive independent of the Dáil. Indeed on 6 April de Valera 'followed O'Connor's lead and publicly repudiated the Dáil' and on 11 April he told the *Manchester Guardian* 'that the political aims of the anti-Treaty forces were identical with his own'.[13]

De Valera, in short, did nothing to arrest the descent into militarism, despite privately maintaining that O'Connor's 'action and outlook' were 'a painful embarrassment' with which 'he heartily disagreed'.[14] This ambivalence guaranteed that his power base among rank-and-file republicans remained intact. Yet, as Michael Laffan has observed, 'because he kept his distance from the republican IRA during the early months of 1922 and because he made no effort to assume its leadership, the extremists were able to push him aside and ignore him'.[15]

The resort to arms became inevitable on 13 April, Holy Thursday, when in imitation of Easter week 1916, O'Connor's executive occupied a number of buildings in central Dublin, most notably the Four Courts, the focal point of the Irish legal system. This became the military headquarters of what, in effect, was the embryo of an alternative, republican government that insisted that no election could be held on the Treaty under the duress of a British threat of war. O'Connor had 'decided to act independently of political leaders henceforward'. Despite his proclaimed 'respect and trust' for de Valera, he neither consulted nor informed him.[16] Confronted with this fait accompli, de Valera was again reduced to applauding from the sidelines: he issued his own Easter proclamation to the youth of Ireland 'declaring that the goal was at last in sight and exhorting them "Ireland is yours for the taking. Take it." . . . His intransigence was for public consumption, while his moderation and his efforts to avoid civil war were concealed from view.'[17]

But on 20 May those efforts came into the open with the publication of a pact secretly negotiated between de Valera and Collins. The pact covered the impending general election to the provisional parliament (or Third Dáil): supporters and opponents of the Treaty would not run against each other but would stand jointly, all as Sinn Féin candidates, on a national coalition ticket in numbers proportionate to their existing strength in the Second Dáil; de Valera and his followers would get four of the nine seats on the executive to be appointed after the election. The anti-democratic character of the pact disturbed the British who correctly interpreted it as an attempt to evade the terms of the Treaty. It also upset some of Collins's ministerial colleagues, particularly Arthur Griffith, who gave way only when Collins made it an issue of confidence.

Collins was unrepentant; he defended the pact as a last attempt 'to avoid strife, to prevent the use of force by Irishmen against Irishmen'[18] and to safeguard against the prospect that the IRA would otherwise disrupt the electoral process. De Valera, on the other hand, signed the pact in order 'to re-establish the position of Sinn Féin, and his own leadership position within the nationalist movement'. But, as Michael Hopkinson has observed, Sinn Féin 'had already disintegrated'.[19] His hope that the pact would postpone an electoral decision on the Treaty by freezing the balance of power was dashed because, in effect, the election, on 16 June 1922, was a decisive defeat for opponents of the Treaty. Fifty-eight pro-Treaty Sinn Féin candidates, as opposed to 36 anti-Treatyites were returned; the rest of the 128 seats were divided among Labour, the Farmers' Party and independent candidates, none of whom ran on an anti-Treaty ticket. But without the pact the anti-Treaty candidates would have done even worse; it enabled 17 of them to be elected unopposed; no anti-Treaty candidate topped the poll in any contested constituency.

De Valera was pushed even further into the sidelines when the outbreak of the civil war on 28 June heralded a shift of power among republicans into the hands of the militarists. Although he re-enlisted in his old unit (the 3rd Battalion of the IRA's Dublin Brigade) and joined the beleaguered garrison occupying the block centred on the Gresham Hotel across O'Connell Street from the GPO, that he did so as a private symbolised his powerlessness for as long as the civil war continued. But this affectation of self-effacement on the military stage went hand in hand with a re-affirmation of his political leadership in the shape of another incendiary press statement publicly acclaiming the IRA's garrisons: 'The men who are now being attacked by the forces of the Provisional Government are those who refuse to obey the order to yield – preferring to die. They are the best and bravest of our nation.' The Gresham block was the last republican redoubt to fall to the Provisional Government's troops, on 5 July. After Oscar Traynor, the officer in command, ordered the survivors to retreat or surrender, de Valera and Austin Stack were among those who escaped from the burning building – Cathal Brugha chose instead to charge the surrounding cordon with gun in hand and was fatally wounded. Privately, de Valera admitted from the outset that defeat was inevitable. 'Dev I think has collapsed,' wrote Erskine Childers to his wife on 12 July. 'Says we should surrender while we are strong.'[20]

De Valera elaborated on this theme in Clonmel, where he went with Childers and Robert Brennan on a grandiose southern tour of military operations; when he inspected a map showing that the republicans still held some territory south of a line between Waterford and Limerick, he declared that 'this was the right time to make a peace when we still held territory we could hand over without fighting'. Things were worse in Cork, recorded Brennan: 'In Fermoy, Mallow and other towns, the people looked at us sullenly as if we had belonged to a hostile invading army. Dev had seen all this . . . and that was . . . why he was so desperately trying for peace while he still had some bargaining power.' But bargaining was a delusion for, as Brennan acknowledged, the Provisional Government's forces were 'winning all along the line' and would listen to nothing short of unconditional surrender.[21]

'Meditation,' de Valera wrote in his diary on 13 August, the day after Arthur Griffith died of a stroke and nine days before Michael Collins was shot and killed in an ambush in his native west Cork. 'Any chance of winning? If there was any chance, duty to hold on to secure it. If none, duty to get the men to quit – for the present. The people must be won to the cause before any successful fighting can be done. The men dead and gloomy – just holding on. How long will it last . . . This situation has not been brought about by my will, nor could my will end it.'

But neither did de Valera have the strength of will to break ranks with the fighting men and his apparent readiness 'to call off the civil war' collapsed when Liam Lynch, the IRA's chief of staff, threatened to repudiate him if he did so; there were even rumours that Lynch wanted to replace de Valera as leader of the Republican Party with Erskine Childers. 'There seems to be no way out of it,' de Valera complained to Joe McGarrity on 10 September. 'I am almost wishing I were deposed for the present position places upon me the responsibility for carrying on a programme which was not mine.' He saw no prospect that the Irish Free State could 'secure independence' and took refuge in a crude reworking of 'the Sinn Féin idea in a new form . . . *ignoring* England . . . acting as if Document 2 were the Treaty'.[22]

'*Almost wishing*'! Perhaps, but still manoeuvring at self-aggrandisement in a secret tête-à-tête with Richard Mulcahy on 5 September for which neither man had sought the prior assent of his senior colleagues. 'We met one another standing and remained standing,' recorded Mulcahy. But it quickly came to nothing when de Valera declared that '"some men are led by faith and some men are led by reason. Personally, I would prefer to be led by reason but as long as there are men of faith like Rory O'Connor taking the stand that he is taking, I am a humble soldier following after them." . . . There was no room for discussion.'[23] Just as de Valera's throwing in his lot with the occupants of the Four Courts had shaped the dimensions of the civil war, so did his refusal to seek peace in the autumn of 1922 when the republican IRA had already been effectively defeated – after 11 August it no longer controlled a single town – ensure its prolongation. What followed, moreover, was the bloodiest phase of the war as the government resorted to a draconian policy of executions without trial in response to Liam Lynch's order to shoot on sight certain supporters of the Provisional Government.

'Reason rather than faith has been my master,' de Valera despaired to Mary MacSwiney in September 1922. 'I have felt for some time that this doctrine of mine unfitted me to be leader of the Republican Party.' Although expressing his regrets for not having insisted on Cathal Brugha's 'assuming the leadership', he yet again justified his refusal to surrender primacy: 'For the sake of the cause I allowed myself to be put into a position which it is impossible for one of my outlook and personal bias . . . I must be the heir to generations of conservatism. Every instinct of mine would indicate that I was meant to be a dyed-in-the-wool tory or even a bishop, rather than the leader of a revolution.' This *cri de coeur* reflected de Valera's enduring resentment at being bound in the straitjacket of the republic and his further tortuous protestations foreshadowed his behaviour after the end of the civil war: 'I have honestly and faithfully endeavoured to discharge the duties of every position I occupied so as to realise the ideals of those who elected me to those positions. I have made myself a slave at times in order to do so. As soon as I can do it without injuring the cause, I intend to claim my own personal freedom again.'[24]

Outraged by the Catholic bishops' joint pastoral on 10 October condemning resistance to the Provisional Government, de Valera agreed to participate in the charade of establishing an emergency, republican government that was ratified by a meeting of republican members of the Dáil on 25 October – the same day that the Dáil approved the Constitution of the Irish Free State Bill. 'I do not care what Republican government is set up so long as some one is,' he wrote to Joe McGarrity in language reflecting both his ambivalence and his impotence. 'I will not take responsibility if I do not get the corresponding authority to act in accordance with my judgement. If the Army think I am too moderate, well let them get a better President and go ahead.'[25]

The arrest of Erskine Childers on 10 November marked the beginning of what, for de Valera, was the most distressing phase of the war. 'President very upset and unhappy,' wrote Kathleen O'Connell in her diary on 17 November, the day of the first of the 77 executions of republican prisoners. Childers was tried on the same day for the unlawful possession of a revolver that had been given him by Michael Collins – 'a tiny automatic, little better than a toy and in no sense a war weapon,' wrote de Valera[26] – and he was executed a week later. Worse was to follow: on 8 December Rory O'Connor, Liam Mellows and two other republicans who had been in Mountjoy jail for five months since the attack on the Four Courts were executed without even the pretence of a trial, as a reprisal for the assassination of a pro-Treaty deputy the previous day. De Valera's pleas to Liam Lynch to abandon his policy of reprisals were in vain.

Calls for peace, which became more frequent from January 1923, seemed to offer opportunities for de Valera to reclaim his 'personal freedom' but he remained unable to reassert his authority: 'When he resurrected Document No. 2 as a possible means to achieve compromise, in a letter to the press of 17 February, it became apparent that External Association was no more popular with the IRA than it had been thirteen months earlier.'[27]

On 10 April 1923 Liam Lynch was fatally wounded in a skirmish in the Knockmealdown mountains in County Tipperary. De Valera's reaction, in an address to the 'Soldiers of the Republic,' reeked of that reverence for militarism that made his behaviour so ambivalent throughout the civil war: 'Better to die nobly, as your chief has died, than live a slave. Your cause is immortal.'[28] But Lynch's death and the unanimous election on 20 April of Frank Aiken to succeed him as the IRA's chief of staff removed the last obstacle on de Valera's circuitous path to peace.

Aiken, who had been with Lynch when he was mortally wounded, had always been among those who strove hardest to avoid civil war: he had played a key role in negotiating the Collins–

de Valera pact, had urged Mulcahy to declare a truce after the attack on the Four Courts and had acted as liaison officer in securing the Limerick truce. He had declined all invitations to join the IRA executive until de Valera had formed a republican government in October 1922 and when he attended the next meeting of the executive, in March 1923, he supported de Valera's peace resolution, which was defeated by six votes to five. De Valera's relationship with Aiken, rooted in mutual respect and understanding, was utterly different from his relationships with hard-line republican ideologues such as Rory O'Connor and Liam Lynch.

Aiken acted immediately: he successfully proposed to the same meeting of the IRA executive that had made him chief of staff that de Valera's Republican Government and the IRA's Army Council 'make peace with the FS "Government"'. The ensuing joint meeting of the Republican Government and the Army Council directed the new chief of staff to issue an order suspending all offensive operations and President de Valera was simultaneously directed to issue a proclamation embodying the terms for a negotiated peace. These negotiations were entrusted to de Valera, a decision that, as Michael Hopkinson has pointed out, ensured that 'at that critical juncture the political leadership was allowed to return to the centre of the stage'.[29]

On 27 April 1923 Aiken's order to the IRA to suspend all offensive operations was co-ordinated with de Valera's simultaneous publication of a proclamation of the political principles on which peace could be negotiated, notably: '(1) that the sovereign rights of the nation are indefeasible and inalienable; (2) that all legitimate governmental authority in Ireland . . . is derived exclusively from the people of Ireland; (3) that the ultimate court of appeal deciding disputed questions of national policy and expediency and policy is the people of Ireland'.[30]

Senators Andrew Jameson and James Douglas, who acted as intermediaries between de Valera and the government, reported that 'what he wanted was a peace which would enable his followers to return to constitutional action'. Asked by Douglas if he was in control of the republican movement, de Valera replied that 'he was now in a position to decide on behalf of the whole Republican Party and . . . in a stronger position than he had ever been before'; he then identified the oath of allegiance as 'the only barrier to Republican participation in the Dáil'. Douglas described de Valera's 'whole bearing . . . [as] that of a defeated man' and as a man 'very anxious to explain how much worse things would have been if he had not been with them and seemed extra anxious to apologise for himself . . . He is trying to get his followers to hold together as a constitutional party'.[31] But the government was in no mood to make deals and another joint meeting of the Republican Government and the IRA executive directed Aiken to issue an unconditional order to cease fire and dump arms. The order, published on 24 May 1923, was again coordinated with another grandiloquent proclamation from de Valera to

Soldiers of the Republic, Legion of the Rearguard: The Republic can no longer be defended successfully by your arms. Further sacrifice of life would now be vain . . . Military victory must be allowed to rest for the moment with those who have destroyed the Republic. Other means must be found to safeguard the nation's right.[32]

De Valera now held what Michael Hopkinson has described as 'a superficially dominant position based on the IRA's weakness, his handling of the peace initiatives, and his good relations with Aiken'.[33] He had finally broken through the wall of glass surrounding him since the occupation of the Four Courts and had re-emerged as the unchallenged and once more unchallengeable leader of Irish republicanism. His attitude to the use of military means, symbolised by his re-enlisting as a mere private, to overthrow the Treaty had always been hesitant. 'At no time during the Civil War', his authorised biographers carefully remind us, 'did he rank as a military leader'.[34] Now the way was clear for him to reassert the primacy of politics.

9

The Path Back to Power

'From the beginning, it has been clear to me', wrote Éamon de Valera on 29 May 1923, 'that the utmost we could hope for from such a fight [the civil war] was a negative gain, such as the abolition of the oath and the Governor General. We have definitely failed to attain *this* objective by military action, but we have gained a position in which that objective is possible of attainment by non-military action.' Writing for republicans still licking the wounds inflicted by military defeat, 'non-military' was, of course, de Valera's coy euphemism for 'political'. The prerequisite for political power was a democratic mandate and, although purist republican logic demanded the rejection of the election machinery as well as all the other institutions of the Free State, he accordingly insisted that Sinn Féin must contest the forthcoming general election in August 1923. He was more explicit at the end of June in a memorandum outlining 'the one policy that has a chance of success', which served as a remarkably prescient blueprint for the programme he executed when he achieved power a decade later:

Maintaining that we are a sovereign state & ignoring as far as possible any conditions in the 'Treaty' that are inconsistent with that status – a policy of squeezing England out by a kind of boycott of Gov General [*sic*]. Breaching the 'Treaty' by the Oath, smashing thro' that first and then compelling England to tolerate the breaches or bring her to a revision which will lead to something like the Doc[ument] 2 position.[1]

The Free State government, he acknowledged, was 'not an obviously alien administration, but what appears on the surface to be a home administration set up by and apparently willing to be deposed by a majority vote of the people governed'. They had 'the shield of popular approval and we must get inside it before we can hope to make any real progress'.[2]

What remained of the Sinn Féin party was de Valera's chosen instrument to contest the election. P. J. Ruttledge, the IRA's adjutant-general, supported him and declared that 'it was the duty of every soldier to join and organise Sinn Féin clubs'. The party was duly re-established at a public meeting in the Mansion House on 11 June.[3] De Valera spelled out the new policy in a press statement on 24 July: 'It is not the intention of the republican government or army executive to renew the war in the autumn or after the elections. The war, so far as we are concerned, is finished. Our present purpose is to work through the Sinn Féin organisation.'[4] A Sinn Féin convention in Clare invited de Valera to run as its candidate, an invitation that provoked Desmond FitzGerald, the minister for external affairs, to say that 'as long as we are in power de Valera and every other enemy of the country will have to be on the run' (see plate 12). But de Valera realised that 'by coming out of hiding he would definitely transfer the struggle from the military to the political field' and his published response was immediate. 'Our opponents make a mistake if they imagine that we are going to remain on the run. If the people of Clare select me as their candidate again I will be with them and nothing but a bullet will stop me.' Feeling was running so high after the civil war that de Valera, aware of the risk of assassination, nominated Ruttledge to act as president if it became necessary. He also made his will.

His dramatic reappearance in public at a mass meeting in Ennis on 15 August, revered by Catholics as the feast of the Assumption – commemorating the death of the Blessed Virgin Mary and her assumption into heaven before her body could begin to decay – was carefully choreographed. He thought it less likely that he would be assassinated if the meeting were held in a public place and believed it tactically important that 'if he were arrested, that it should be on the platform. His arrest would prove to all that the election was not a free one. If he were arrested beforehand, it might be claimed that he had no intention of coming out of hiding.'[5] He shaved off his disguise of beard and moustache (see plate 13) and succeeded in evading government troops until reaching the platform. A 'pale and drawn' de Valera, reported *The Times* of London, 'had uttered only a few sentences . . . when an armoured car pushed its way into the crowd and troops began to move towards the hustings'.[6] But his arrest won worldwide publicity and so served its purpose.

The election results abundantly vindicated de Valera's strategy – he topped the poll in Clare with more than twice as many first-preference votes as the next candidate (Eoin MacNeill) and Sinn Féin won 44 of the 155 seats in the Dáil. This was more than double the 20 seats de Valera had targeted two months earlier. Indeed despite, or perhaps because of, the civil war – particularly in Kerry where the atrocities of Free State troops had alienated the electorate – their share of the vote (27 per cent) was 6 per cent higher than that achieved by the anti-Treaty wing of Sinn Féin in the election of June 1922.[7]

The election enhanced de Valera's reputation as a vote-winner and an incomparable political leader; his imprisonment burnished his radical credentials, although the government, more attuned to the dangers than his British jailers, denied him the opportunity to exercise his political talents from prison, as he had done so effectively in 1917–18, by keeping him in solitary confinement at first in Arbour Hill prison and, from October 1923, in Kilmainham jail where he had been court-martialled in 1916. He disapproved of the hunger strike of hundreds of republican prisoners in October–November 1923 and, when 'Ruttledge as Acting President of the Republic issued a message stating that the Chief, on strict orders of the Republican cabinet and in the best interests of the cause, was not on hunger strike', it fizzled out.[8]

Solitude in imprisonment never held any fears for Éamon de Valera. Although the subject matter of his reading had first to be approved by the prison authorities, he had as many books as he wanted, many of them on mathematics. 'I am very lonely of course at times and anxious about Sinéad and the family,' he wrote to Kathleen O'Connell, 'but I have no end of work to do'; and, in January 1924, he even admitted to her that 'Sinéad has grown cynical about my relation to books . . . The privilege of being in jail is that one can ask to be indulged in whims of this sort. I'll be shut off as completely as if I were on another planet and these books, old or new, the only friends at hand.' In spring 1924, when he was sent back to Arbour Hill, the conditions of his imprisonment became more relaxed as the government had by then begun gradually releasing political prisoners. But Sinéad was allowed her first visit to her husband only late in June and he was not finally released until 16 July. Even then the political took priority over the familial: he and Austin Stack went first to Sinn Féin's office in Suffolk Street. They then went to de Valera's home in Sandymount, after which, recorded Stack in his diary, 'de Valera went visiting'.[9]

When de Valera 'had to act the part of the father in his home', as Owen Dudley Edwards has observed, his behaviour was conditioned by the fact that he himself 'had never known a father, and his treatment of his children, while meaning to be kind, had the insistence on discipline which he associated with fatherhood: his will must be supreme'.[10] In that respect it mirrored his attitude to political leadership. So, too, did the attribute identified by one of his sons, Éamon, who later became an eminent gynaecologist and who remembered how 'he resented his [father's] intrusion into our lives' when he returned from prison and from America. 'Looking back, I realise that he has never really appreciated the difficulties and shortcomings of minds less gifted than his own.'[11] This was precisely the failing that underlay de Valera's calamitous errors of judgement in his dealings with the plenipotentiaries during the Treaty negotiations and in his conduct during the Dáil debates on the Treaty. And it now hampered his sinuous efforts to win the support of less sophisticated minds as he tried to wriggle out of what he regarded as 'the straitjacket of the republic'.[12]

Sinn Féin had achieved nothing of moment in de Valera's absence and had failed to capitalise on its gains in the 1923 election. The attempt of some like-minded republican deputies to enter the new Dáil while refusing to take the oath of allegiance was frustrated when the clerk of the Dáil announced that no deputies would be admitted until they had signed the oath.

De Valera's first public appearance after his release from prison – again in Ennis and once more on the Feast of the Assumption on the first anniversary of his imprisonment – was as meticulously stage-managed as his arrest. 'I am afraid', he began, 'I would disappoint a number here if I were not to start by saying, "Well, as I was saying to you when we were interrupted". The key passage in his speech was his rejection of the 'taunt [of] being undemocratic'. Having insisted that the elections of 1922 and 1923 did not constitute a democratic determination of 'the form of government or the freedom that the Irish people wanted', he then stated the circumstances in which his own commitment to democracy would be absolute and unqualified: 'When you are free to determine without any pressure from England or from any outside power, when the form you choose will be the expression truly of your own free will, then we are certainly ready to bow down our heads before it.'[13]

Procedures were now well advanced for the establishment, under Article 12 of the Treaty, of the boundary commission that would determine the border between the Irish Free State and Northern Ireland and de Valera set about milking anti-partitionist sentiment among nationalists, south and north. Yet again he invited one of those periods of imprisonment that he used to punctuate his political career to heighten his leadership profile and to refurbish his radical credentials – decades later Ian Paisley embraced much the same strategy for much the same reasons. Although the minister for home affairs in Belfast had published an order prohibiting de Valera from entering Northern Ireland, he did so in order to campaign in the forthcoming United Kingdom election for the Down constituency for which he was still an elected representative. 'He knew that he was likely to be imprisoned,' his authorised biographers piously inform us, 'but he would do all in his power to speak to his Down constituents.' He was duly arrested when he arrived in Newry on 24 October 1924 and sent back across the border the next day. But he persevered and crossed the border into Derry where he was again arrested and brought to Belfast where he was sentenced to a month's imprisonment; he was released on 28 November.[14] Tim Pat Coogan has calculated that the jail term and his defiant public exchange with the magistrate when he refused to recognise the court 'was worth nearly 1000 votes a day' because in five by-elections in the Free State on 18 November, Sinn Féin polled 29,000 more votes than in the same constituencies in the general election and won two seats, one of which went to Seán Lemass, who became one of de Valera's most important supporters in engineering a breach with the diehard element in Sinn Féin, who continued to resist entering the Dáil.

In the meantime de Valera was mending his fences with the Catholic Church. He had been outraged by the hierarchy's joint pastoral of 10 October 1922 condemning resistance to the Provisional Government and declaring that 'the guerrilla warfare now being carried out by the Irregulars is without moral sanction and therefore the killing of national soldiers in the course of it is murder before God'. From then until the end of the civil war, de Valera, 'in deference to the terms of the October Pastoral, did not receive the sacraments'.[15] But the role of the bishops in 1922 rankled with him until the end of his life. Talking in 1973 to Father Seán Farragher, the chronicler of his days in Blackrock College, he recalled how he had told Pope Pius XI that 'he considered himself as committed a Catholic as any of the Bishops and even the Pope himself but he held the Bishops of Ireland had no right in 1922 to make what was a political judgement as between those for and against the Treaty'; indeed he became so excited that his secretary in Áras an Uachtaráin (the president's residence in the Phoenix

1 De Valera in an open-topped car waving to crowds outside New York City Hall during his American mission of 1919–20.

2 Catherine (Kate) Coll, de Valera's mother, in New York, shortly before her second marriage to Charles Wheelwright.

3 Edward (Ned) Coll, de Valera's uncle, who brought him from New York when he was two years old to live at his grandmother's home near Bruree, Co. Limerick.

4 Edward (although the caption, from a later date, calls him 'Eamonn') de Valera at school in his last year in Charleville in 1898 (back row, second from the left); and (*right*) in 1899 at Blackrock College: the transformation from raw country boy to young gentleman is already apparent.

5 In the company of priests: the teaching staff of Rockwell College in 1903; Edward de Valera is in the back row on the left.

6 Rockwell 1904: de Valera with a hunting rifle.

7 Éamon de Valera and Sinéad Flanagan on their wedding day, 8 January 1910.

8 Commandant de Valera leading the 3rd Battalion of the Dublin Brigade of the Irish Volunteers under escort by British troops to Ballsbridge Barracks after his surrender on 29 April 1916.

9 De Valera with cheering supporters at the East Clare by-election in July 1917 that marked his emergence as the leader of nationalist Ireland.

10 De Valera in Limerick on the morning of 6 December 1921, the day of his catastrophic decision to oppose the Treaty signed in London hours earlier – Richard Mulcahy is in the back row (right) and Cathal Brugha in the front row (right); this is the only photograph in the de Valera archive in a folder headed 'Anglo-Irish Treaty of 1921'.

11 De Valera and Arthur Griffith in Dublin, 13 August 1921.

12 'On the run': a bearded de Valera on 12 August 1923 at Ciamaltha House in north Tipperary, en route to speak at Ennis on 15 August when he was arrested by Irish Free State troops.

13 De Valera with J. W. Dulanty (the Irish High Commissioner in London) on 17 November 1932 in Victoria station en route to a meeting of the Council of the League of Nations in Geneva.

14 De Valera with Malcolm MacDonald (the Secretary of State for Dominion Affairs) outside his house in Hampstead on 24 April 1938, the day before he signed the Anglo-Irish agreements that represented his greatest diplomatic achievement.

15 De Valera with Winston Churchill during a courtesy visit to London in 1953.

16 De Valera in New Delhi in June 1948 with the prime minister, Jawaharlal Nehru, and the wife of the Governor-General, Lady Edwina Mountbatten, of whose subsequently notorious love affair he presumably knew nothing.

17 De Valera during a visit to the Vatican in 1950 with Joseph P. Walshe (the then Irish ambassador and formerly among his closest confidants as Secretary of the Department of External Affairs, 1932–46) and Frank Aiken.

18 President de Valera kissing the ring of the Catholic Archbishop of Dublin, John Charles McQuaid, on the occasion of the cutting of the first sod for the science building in University College Dublin on 7 June 1962.

19 President de Valera with US President John F. Kennedy on 6 June 1963 during his visit to Ireland as part of a tour of Europe.

20 President de Valera with General de Gaulle during his visit to Áras an Uachtaráin on 17–19 June 1969, after his resignation as President of France.

Park) 'had to get him to change the subject'.[16] But he never allowed
his resentment to deter him from seeking powerful allies among
the bishops and in Rome. The rector and vice-rector of the Irish
College in Rome – Monsignor John Hagan and Monsignor Michael
Curran (who had hidden de Valera in his house after his escape
from Lincoln jail) and Father Peter Magennis (the head of the
Carmelite order, who, as president of the Friends of Irish Freedom,
had been de Valera's ally in America in 1919) were his staunchest
supporters in Rome; other supporters were Michael Browne,
professor of moral theology at Maynooth, and – arguably the most
important because he was the most high-ranking in the clerical
corridors of power – Daniel Mannix, formerly president of
Maynooth and then the Archbishop of Melbourne.

'The Government and Army Command have unanimously
decided that the Republican cause can no longer be defended
successfully by military effort,' de Valera advised Hagan as the civil
war drew to an end. 'It has become necessary to transfer the contest
to another plane . . . We are in sore need of the assistance of all our
friends everywhere.'[17] He was just as frank with Mannix in October 1923: 'I am unable to state anything definite with regard to the
republican policy in the immediate future. On the whole I should
be inclined to wish to see them enter the Dáil even at the price of
taking the oath; but any information I have on the subject would
lead me to conclude that such is far from their intention.' But he
had clearly become more interventionist when he was released
from jail: 'I met the President [de Valera] recently,' Browne wrote
to Mannix on 23 July 1924, his use of the title showing how closely
both writer and recipient identified with the republican cause. 'He
is very, very busy gathering up the skeins. He looks forward very
eagerly to the return of the young priests [after the summer vaca-
tion] as a preliminary step on the road to victory.'[18]

In the summer of 1925 Mannix led an Australian pilgrimage to
Rome when en route to Ireland. Disguised as a priest and travelling
on a false passport, de Valera went secretly to Rome where he had

a series of meetings with Mannix, Hagan and Magennis in the Irish College; he was accompanied by Seán MacBride, who acted as his secretary and interpreter.[19] De Valera told MacBride – they were not staying in the Irish College but sharing a bedroom in a hotel in Rome – of his tête-à-têtes with Mannix who had been urging him 'to accept the status quo . . . saying that this was the only way in which de Valera could really place the Irish hierarchy in an indefensible position, if he came out openly, and accepted the status quo, and sought election to the Free State government, so that he could participate in the political development of the country'.[20] Although ostracised by the government and by the Irish bishops, Mannix attracted large crowds as he travelled through Ireland later that summer and his arrival 'offered a glimmer of hope to devout republican Catholics'.[21] More importantly from de Valera's perspective, Hagan and Mannix had prepared a document 'which provided both a theological and historical explanation of how to enter the Dáil'. By then he was also being encouraged by Seán T. O'Kelly, Seán Lemass and Gerry Boland, to try to get the Sinn Féin deputies to abandon their abstentionist policy.[22]

The crisis triggered by the Boundary Commission agreement of 3 December 1925 guaranteeing that there would be no change in the border between Northern Ireland and the Irish Free State signalled the total collapse of the Cosgrave government's Northern Ireland policy and further highlighted the frustrations of those opposed to abstentionism. Denied access to the Dáil, de Valera was reduced to inviting the Sinn Féin deputies to attend a meeting in the Shelbourne Hotel called by the leader of the Labour Party; it came to nothing when there was again no agreement on entering the Dáil. But those who favoured such a course realised, as Michael Browne wrote to Hagan, that 'it was fortunate that the boundary crisis came to give it an impetus . . . The feeling is growing especially among the young and impatient that it would be desirable if a trial of strength came quickly.'[23] That trial of strength was again postponed when the Sinn Féin *ard fheis* on 17 November 1925 evaded the issue, but an IRA convention on 14 November had sharpened the divide. In effect, the IRA members renounced their allegiance to de Valera by adopting a new constitution, freeing them from political control; henceforth the only authority recognised by the IRA was its Army Council. The convention also debated resolutions prohibiting even the further discussion of republican representatives entering the Dáil, notwithstanding the reservations of Frank Aiken, who was dismissed as their chief of staff when he insisted on his right 'to advocate when I think fit, outside Volunteer work, any honourable political policy for strengthening the nation to achieve independence'.[24]

In January 1926 de Valera declared his intention to enter the Dáil if he could do so without taking the oath. He finally grasped the nettle by summoning an extraordinary *ard fheis* of Sinn Féin on 9 March 1926 to discuss his motion that, once the oath of allegiance had been removed, 'it becomes a question not of principle but of policy whether or not republican representatives enter the Dáil'. Robert Brennan, a life-long ally of de Valera, once observed that, although he could be a good listener who encouraged debate, he always wanted his own way in the end. '"You can talk about this as much as you like, the more the better and from every angle," he would say . . . [but] in the last analysis, if you don't agree with me then I quit."'[25] Indeed de Valera felt he had already 'wasted a couple of years' since his opponents in the party had made it plain that, in time-honoured republican fashion, they would not accept a majority verdict against them. 'Under these circumstances, it mattered very little to me whether we had a majority or a minority at the *ard fheis*.'[26] In fact, his resolution was never put but an amendment declaring that it was incompatible with Sinn Féin principles was carried on 10 March by a narrow margin (223 votes to 218); the amendment 'was then in turn defeated (by 179 votes to 177) when it was proposed as a substantive motion'.[27]

The next day Éamon de Valera resigned the presidency of Sinn Féin, a position he had held since the autumn of 1917. He explained why to Joe McGarrity, his closest Irish-American confidant:

I have been convinced that the programme on which we were working would not win the people in the present conditions. It was too high and too sweeping. The oath on the other hand is a definite objective within reasonable striking distance. If I can mass the people to smash it, I shall have put them *on the march* again, and once moving, and having tasted victory, further advances will be possible . . . It is vital that the Free State be shaken at the next general election, for if an opportunity be given it to consolidate itself further as an institution – if the present Free State members are replaced by Farmers and Labourers and other class interests, the national interest as a whole will be submerged in the clashing of the rival economic groups. It seems to be a case of now or never – at least in our time.[28]

This was both a blueprint for de Valera's political programme in the next decade and an explanation of why he believed it imperative that the fundamental party-political divide in Ireland should be based on the Treaty split, rather than on the left–right divide rooted in class differences commonplace elsewhere in Europe. He had said much the same thing to the *ard fheis* that he said to McGarrity: 'We are not going to win back the people of Ireland by the attitude which we are taking up . . . The majority of the people are going to mould the future. They are moulding it every day. Things are settling down. The Free State junta is solidifying itself as an institution.'[29]

Winning a majority of the people and moulding the future demanded a new weapon. The weapon de Valera forged was Fianna Fáil (the Republican Party). The name – traditionally translated as 'Soldiers of Destiny' or, more precisely, as 'Warriors of Fál' (a legendary name for Ireland) – was a compromise. The pragmatic Lemass, indifferent to the Irish language, had favoured the simpler 'Republican Party'. De Valera sought to evoke heroic echoes from both an ancient and a more recent past – appealing to the memory of the mythical warriors of the Fianna and the more prosaic fact that 'FF' had been the initials on the Volunteers' badge and was still used on army uniforms. De Valera got his way. Setting a pattern that endured for nearly thirty years in the new-born party, the will of the Chief prevailed.

On 17 April, a month before the party was publicly launched, de Valera issued a press statement outlining its aims. The first aim was 'securing the political independence of a united Ireland as a republic'; its other objectives were the restoration of the Irish language, a social system of equal opportunity, land redistribution designed to maximise the number of families on the land, and economic self-sufficiency. The inaugural *ard fheis* or general convention of Fianna Fáil took place in Dublin's La Scala theatre on 24 November 1926, the fourth anniversary, as de Valera immediately reminded his audience, 'of the day on which Erskine Childers suffered martyrdom for Ireland . . . I have never said, and am not going to say now, that force is not a legitimate weapon for a nation to use in striving to win its freedom . . . But a nation within itself ought to be able to settle its polity so that all occasions of civil conflict between its members may be obviated.'[30] De Valera's abandonment of physical force as a political weapon, in other words, was pragmatic, not principled. Such unapologetic invocations of their revolutionary past nicely blended with a genuflection to democracy characterised the new party's political rhetoric in opposition between 1926 and 1932; it was most succinctly captured in Seán Lemass's celebrated description in 1928 of Fianna Fáil as 'a slightly constitutional party'.[31]

The task of organising the new party fell largely to Seán Lemass and Gerry Boland, who drove all around the country establishing local branches and recruiting 'the key republican activists in each area . . . in the certain knowledge that each would be followed by a strong cohort of supporters'.[32] They swiftly established the most efficient and dynamic party organisation in Irish politics. The basic unit was the *cumann* (local association) and there was one in almost every parish; old IRA companies, battalions and divisions were used for the party's structural foundations and de Valera himself went on a 1,700-mile countrywide tour. Fianna Fáil also pioneered the system of church-gate collections at Sunday masses, which increased the sense of local participation as well as raising funds. A national executive, on which the front bench of the parliamentary party was dominant, kept in close touch with local *cumainn* which were registered at party headquarters.[33]

The first real test of Fianna Fáil's popular appeal was the general election in June 1927 when the Free State was 'shaken' just as de Valera had hoped. The government party, Cumann na nGaedheal, slumped from 63 seats in 1923 to 47, only just ahead of Fianna Fáil with 44; Sinn Féin collapsed from 25 (of the 44 elected in 1923 who stayed with Sinn Féin after the split at the 1926 *ard fheis*) to 5. If Fianna Fáil had entered the Dáil, the Labour Party and other smaller parties and independents would have held the balance of power. But that became irrelevant when, on the first day of the new Dáil session, de Valera and his followers were refused admission because they would not take the oath. De Valera immediately began preparing a petition that, under Article 48 of the Constitution, if signed by 75,000 voters, would force a referendum on a constitutional amendment abolishing the oath.

But the assassination of Kevin O'Higgins, the vice-president of the Executive Council, as he walked to Mass near his home on Sunday, 10 July, utterly transformed the political climate. De Valera unreservedly denounced it as 'murder and . . . inexcusable from any standpoint . . . It is a crime that cuts at the root of representative government.' But despite his expression of confidence 'that no Republican organisation was responsible',[34] it was generally thought to have been the work of an IRA splinter group and it prompted a draconian reaction from Cosgrave's government. On 20 July they introduced three bills: a Public Safety Bill enabling them to declare associations (such as the IRA) illegal and establishing non-jury courts with military judges; an Electoral Amendment Bill requiring parliamentary candidates to declare before nomination their willingness, if elected, to take the oath of allegiance; and a Constitution Amendment Bill removing the provision for constitutional amendment by a popularly initiated referendum.

These measures effectively spelled the end of de Valera's scheme to remove the oath and he told Fianna Fáil's national executive that it had to make a stark choice: enter the Dáil or give up political action. There was no doubt what he wanted and he devised a characteristically pedantic and self-righteous fudge in the form of a press statement that a meeting of Fianna Fáil deputies dutifully endorsed. It stated that 'the required declaration is not an oath; that the signing of it implies no contractual obligation, and that it has no binding significance in conscience or in law; that, in short, it is merely an empty political formula which deputies could conscientiously sign without . . . obligations of loyalty to the English Crown'.[35]

This, then, was the device that, on 11 August 1927, enabled de Valera and his followers to 'sign the book' as requested by the Clerk of the Dáil and to take their seats without reading, repeating or hearing the actual words of the oath. To de Valera's opponents, as indeed to neutral observers, the episode might have the air of a charade, if not of a farce. Well might they ask why what could be treated as an empty formula in 1927 could not have been so treated in 1922? But de Valera's object, as always, was to sustain his supporters, not placate his opponents. However tortuous his reasoning, it enabled him to save face by rejecting the hated oath, so retaining the mass of republican support Fianna Fáil had won in the election. What mattered was not the ritual of reservation but the reality of participation. De Valera had achieved his aim: mainstream republican opposition was henceforth conducted within parliament; the abstentionism of Sinn Féin and the IRA was no longer significant, and Irish parliamentary democracy was no longer seriously flawed. There followed a tied vote of confidence in the government and, on 15 September, another general election, when Fianna Fáil increased its seats to 57. Although Cumann na nGaedheal, with 61 seats, retained office, it was soon seen as a 'lame duck' government, increasingly under siege after the world-wide economic collapse of 1929.

Economic prosperity was not a priority for Éamon de Valera and he never saw it as an essential element in his bid for power. Ireland, he told the Dáil in July 1928, was 'a comparatively small country' which could not 'afford to carry on our administrative services here on the same scale as if, for instance, we were part of the British administrative system – the centre of an empire'. Independent Ireland must instead

make the sort of choice that might be open, for instance, to a servant of a big mansion. If the servant was displeased with the kicks of the young master and wanted to have his freedom, he had to make up his mind whether or not he was going to have that freedom, and give up the luxuries of a certain kind which were available to him by being in that mansion. He had to give up the idea of having around him the cushions and all the rest that a servant in the mansion might have, and the various things that might come from the table of the Lord . . . If a man makes up his mind to go out into a cottage . . . he has to make up his mind to put up with the frugal fare of that cottage.[36]

This was one of the few speeches de Valera made in the Dáil before the next general election, in 1932. Another, in May 1929, proposed that the land annuities, collected under the Land Acts of 1891 to 1909 and transferred to the British government, should henceforth be retained for the use of the Irish government. The motion was lost but it became a central plank in his next election manifesto.

Now that he had achieved his objective of entering the Dáil and was poised to win power through the democratic process, de Valera was content to bide his time and he devoted much of his energy in opposition to extra-parliamentary activity. Ever since 1922 de Valera had complained that 'the propaganda' against the opponents of the Treaty was 'overwhelming' because not 'a single daily newspaper' was on their side. His efforts in 1926 to buy the titles of the *Freeman's Journal*, formerly the newspaper of the Irish Parliamentary Party, came to nothing when he was outbid by the Murphy family who integrated the title into their *Irish Independent*.[37]

Once Fianna Fáil had been established, de Valera's first priority was to raise money for a national newspaper and, in March–April 1927, even before he entered the Dáil and accompanied by Frank Gallagher, who was to become the first editor of that newspaper, the *Irish Press*, he criss-crossed Irish-America seeking funding for 'both his political campaigns and the founding of the newspaper on which he had set his heart'.[38] He spent two more long tracts of time in the United States on the same mission – from December 1927 until February 1928 and from December 1929 until May 1930. In September 1928, although his American fundraising was not yet complete, he incorporated the Irish Press Ltd. 'It was de Valera himself who drew up the company's carefully drafted articles of association, securing for himself the most powerful position on the board – that of controlling director', a position that 'also incorporated the powerful positions of editor-in-chief and managing director'. This gave de Valera 'complete control of the editorial content of the paper as well as over the appointment of all staff'. He invited Margaret Pearse, the mother of Patrick and William who had both been executed in 1916, to press the button that started the presses rolling for the first issue. 'That early morning of 5 September 1931, when the first copies of the *Irish Press* began to come off the machines, was a memorable one for de Valera', wrote Joseph Connolly, who became of his cabinet ministers, 'probably the most memorable date in his diary next to Easter Monday 1916.'

The date was chosen to coincide with the GAA All-Ireland Hurling Final. Both the sports editor and deputy sports editor were English and their story gave the 'kick-off time', not knowing that both GAA hurling and football began not with a 'kick-off' but with a 'throw-in'. But what mattered was not the consequent complaints but the fact that 'from the very beginning the *Irish Press* gave

Gaelic games more coverage than anyone had ever done and forced everyone else to follow'. The *Irish Independent* and the *Irish Times* then reserved their front pages for advertisements and government notices and another mark of difference was that, from the outset, the *Irish Press* carried 'current affairs news on its front page, an idea spotted by de Valera while in America'.[39]

Another extra-parliamentary initiative entailed the renewal of his claim to the leadership role in the campaign against partition. On 5 February 1929 he yet again succeeded in having himself arrested – at Goraghwood station en route to Belfast in defiance of the order excluding him from entering Northern Ireland. A month in Belfast jail – his final period of imprisonment at forty-six years of age – boosted his revolutionary image. He struck a different populist chord by constantly reiterating his promise to retain the land annuities for the Irish exchequer. This, together with the promise to abolish the oath, took pride of place in Fianna Fáil's 1932 election manifesto that also undertook to re-examine other payments (notably for RIC pensions) negotiated under the Anglo-Irish financial agreements of 1923–6. De Valera, Oliver MacDonagh has argued persuasively, 'had played his hand superbly . . . Promises of larger and more comprehensive doles, of protection and industrialisation, coupled with repudiation of the British debts, constituted a nice amalgam of nationalism and democracy. They clinched the wide and durable support which Fianna Fáil enjoyed among the poorer classes.'[40]

The outcome of the election of February 1932 was not immediately apparent. Fianna Fáil's share of the vote jumped by 9 per cent to 44.5 per cent (72 seats), which was nearly 5 points higher than Cumann na nGaedheal had ever achieved, even in 1923. All the other parties lost ground but the key factor enabling de Valera to take office was the support of the Labour Party.

The Dáil elected Éamon de Valera president of the Executive Council and he formed the first Fianna Fáil government on 9 March 1932.

10

The Attainment of Independence, 1932–8

On 9 March 1932 Éamon de Valera regained the power he had lost ten years earlier. By December 1937, within six tumultuous years, he had torn up those elements of the Treaty of 1921 he had opposed and had rewritten, almost single-handedly, the constitutional relationship between Ireland and Britain. The magnitude of that achievement may be simply stated. The quest for sovereignty was at an end: the 1937 constitution made Ireland an independent republic in all but name.

Yet when the Dáil elected Éamon de Valera head of government (president of the Executive Council until 1937 and Taoiseach thereafter) by 81 votes to 68, his majority was dependent on the support of the Labour Party and of some independents, in addition to the 72 Fianna Fáil deputies. So he moved swiftly to seal Fianna Fáil's understanding with the Labour Party. The decisions at its first cabinet meeting included the introduction of an old-age pensions bill and a savage cut in ministerial salaries from £1,700 to a £1,000 in fulfilment of the election slogan that no man was worth more than a thousand a year; unsurprisingly, de Valera, having been restored as 'president' to the pre-eminence he had enjoyed in 1917–21, was in a place apart: his salary was £1,500.

But from de Valera's perspective, such measures were no more than populist tinsel. Deeply conservative, he had no interest in dismantling the state's power structures and sought only to bend them to his own purposes. Radicals and republicans, craving dismissals from the civil service, army and police to create the vacancies they hoped to fill, waited in vain. De Valera instead instantly reassured those in control of the levers of power. After discussing the apparatus of government decision-making with J. J. McElligott, the secretary of department of finance and, in effect, the head of the civil service, he declared himself content. On 10 March, his first full day in office, he met the heads of all government departments and, as McElligott vividly recalled decades later, 'told them at once that he had no intention of changing any of them'.[1] His 'only immediate appointments . . . were the transfer of Maurice Moynihan, a civil servant in the department of finance, to his office as private secretary, and the reinstatement as a civil servant of his personal secretary, Kathleen O'Connell'.[2]

More than any other incoming head of government in independent Ireland, Éamon de Valera knew exactly what he wanted to do with power: delete the repugnant elements in the Treaty and loosen the British connection so as to win the independence he had argued for since 1922. He became his own minister for external affairs, as well as president of the Executive Council. Rather than entrusting the conduct of foreign policy to any of his ministerial colleagues, the dark legacy of the Treaty split forged his determination to retain the control of the day-to-day detail of Anglo-Irish policy in his own hands. His reliance on administrative continuity found powerful expression in his use of a troika of senior officials in the department of external affairs, which he had inherited from the previous government: Joe Walshe, the secretary of the department from 1922 until 1946; John Hearne, the department's legal adviser, who provided many of the first drafts for what became de Valera's new constitution; and John Dulanty, Ireland's diplomatic representative as high commissioner in London. Hearne recalled that one of de Valera's first actions as minister for external affairs was 'to ask for the files on the Commonwealth conferences of the 1920s. Some time later, he told Hearne he had read them with interest, adding: "I didn't know ye had done so much."'[3]

De Valera's style of chairmanship in cabinet was benevolent but authoritarian. Marathon meetings were more a matter of style than substance, a consequence of his insistence on ministerial unanimity born of the trauma of the Treaty split. He 'relied upon the force of physical exhaustion to get agreement', observed Seán Lemass. 'In other words he'd never let a cabinet debate on any subject end with a vote of ministers.' But liberty to discuss never meant liberty to decide – not, at least, if de Valera wished to decide otherwise. On 14 March his ministers meekly agreed that he would make press statements on policy and 'that no such communication should be made by any member of the Executive Council without previous consultation with the president'.[4] In January 1934 the establishment of the government information bureau in the president's department, under the immediate control of a director nominated by de Valera, gave easier effect to that decision.

The reaction of foreign diplomats in Dublin to de Valera's assumption of power has been well described by Deirdre McMahon: 'Essentially remote and inaccessible . . . to the emotional temperament he is a romantic and glamorous figure, mysterious and inscrutable,' wrote the American minister. 'He dresses habitually in black and so appears with his rather stern countenance to be in perpetual mourning for a nation in bondage.' And he reported that an awe-stricken papal nuncio had told him that 'no cleric lived a more austere life than did de Valera . . . He never smoked, never took a drop of alcoholic drink except in public when as a matter of courtesy he forced himself to gulp down a few swallows of wine . . . For his evening meal, for example, he took nothing except a cup of black tea, while his breakfast and lunch were very meagre repasts.'[5]

The first plank in Fianna Fáil's election manifesto and the first task de Valera now set himself in rewriting the Treaty was the deletion of the oath of allegiance from the constitution. Removing the oath went hand in hand with an onslaught on that other major symbol of the link with Britain, the office of governor general. De Valera and his ministers deliberately degraded the office by humiliating the incumbent, James McNeill, by such measures as refusing to attend any public function where he was expected. On 21 April

Frank Aiken and Seán T. O'Kelly, to the suppressed displeasure of their wives, hastily left a dance at the French Legation when McNeill arrived. McNeill protested in vain to de Valera about the coverage of the incident in the *Irish Press*, a newspaper 'known to be under your personal control [which] can only mean that it is part of a considered policy [of] deliberate discourtesy'. This de Valera denied, pointing out that the story had been given greater prominence in the *Irish Independent* and claiming that the incident had been 'no less embarrassing' for the ministers and that 'the publicity which ensued might have seriously affected the public interest. The whole affair was unfortunate and regrettable, and should never have been allowed to occur. If the governor general's public social engagements are communicated to me in advance, such an incident will certainly not occur in the future.' Such testy exchanges rumbled on for weeks and, when the governor general threatened to publish the correspondence if he did not receive an apology, an emergency meeting of the Executive Council at eleven o'clock at night on 7 July made an order declaring 'the corres- pondence to be confidential State documents' and advising the governor general not to publish it. Although Joe Walshe pro- nounced the governor general's threat 'the purest bluff . . . [which] unless he gets quite out of hand he has no intention of carrying out', McNeill persisted. Reports that he had given the corres- pondence to the Dublin newspapers triggered the decision at another emergency cabinet meeting in the early hours of 11 July approving instructions already issued to the police by the minister for justice: these included cautioning the newspapers 'as to the seriousness of publishing having regard to the Official Secrets Acts and the law relating to confidential state documents' and warning wholesale distributors of newspapers 'that anyone knowingly distributing the newspaper containing the letters would do so at his own responsibility'. The government also directed the minister for justice to tell the police to stop any Northern Ireland newspapers containing the correspondence crossing from the border. But de

Valera retreated from such dramatic actions at another cabinet meeting later that day which instead approved a statement he had prepared in advance authorising the immediate publication of the entire correspondence 'as these letters have today appeared in foreign newspapers' and which withdrew 'the ban on the importation of external newspapers containing the correspondence'.[6]

Although de Valera decided that McNeill had to go because, in Joe Walshe's phrase, he had got 'quite out of hand', he took care to avoid confronting the British government on the issue and instead resorted to the constitutional doctrine that the king must act on the advice of his ministers. He waited until September 1932, when he himself was in Geneva attending the Assembly of the League of Nations, before instructing Dulanty to advise the king of his intentions. When the king asked Dulanty to tell McNeill on his behalf that it would be best if he resigned, de Valera embraced the suggestion and Dulanty went to Balmoral to convey his agreement to the king; he was also instructed to say, if the king asked about the appointment of a new governor general, that the government could 'hardly make an appointment before the New Year'. McNeill reluctantly gave way and his resignation, at an audience with the king on 3 October, took effect on 1 November 1932.[7]

De Valera then used the same constitutional device to secure the appointment of his successor. On 24 November the Executive Council made an order 'advising the King to appoint Mr Donal Buckley to be the Governor General'.[8]

A nondescript veteran of 1916, Donal Ó Buachalla (his preferred Irish variant of his name) was a shopkeeper of modest means in his native town of Maynooth who completed the process of reducing the office of governor general to a joke by refusing to live in the Viceregal Lodge; he instead took up residence in a simple house provided for him in a Dublin suburb. He never appeared in public and his sole function, until the process of abolishing the office was formally completed in 1937, was to sign legislation.

If the understandably irate McNeill had not chosen the course of confrontation with the government in 1932, de Valera might well have been content to leave him in place until 1937. But the episode serves as a template for de Valera's cautious, step-by-step campaign to achieve his objectives across the broader spectrum of British–Irish relations. The key to his strategy was to minimise the prospect of British retaliation. His insistence that he was acting constitutionally was underpinned by the Statute of Westminster, enacted by the Westminster parliament in December 1931; this provided that no law of the United Kingdom should extend to any of the dominions without their consent; he also obtained numerous legal opinions to the effect that the statute 'leaves it open to the Irish Free State to amend the 1922 constitution in any way it pleases'.[9]

A secret and hastily handwritten letter from Joe Walshe to de Valera on 12 March, only three days after the change of government, foreshadowed this strategy. He told de Valera of how a dominions office official while 'being too generously (but deliberately so) entertained by the Irish staff in Geneva in 1931 had remarked, "You fellows have been the cause of all our troubles for the last ten years. We must stop making concessions. Something must be left for de Valera." . . . I fear very much that hurried action by us may put their backs up against us.' Walshe counselled that the proposed introduction of the bill the following week should be postponed until the Dáil reassembled a month later; de Valera ensured his cabinet's concurrence at a meeting the same day.[10] On 18 March, when de Valera met Dulanty for the first time, he told him that he was not to take the initiative in advising the British of his minister's intentions but 'if he were asked what they were he was to state them definitely in his official capacity as high commissioner' and to explain

the main reasons which motivated the Minister's intended action. The Oath was not mandatory in the Treaty. We had an absolute right to modify our Constitution as the people desired. The Constitution was the People's Constitution, and anything affecting it appertained to our internal sovereignty and was purely a domestic matter. But besides these legal and constitutional considerations there was another and paramount consideration more than sufficient in itself to make the Minister's decision final and irrevocable. The people had declared their will without ambiguity. The abolition of the Oath was the principal and the dominating issue before the electors. It had been the cause of all the strife and dissension in this country since the signing of the Treaty. The people – and not merely those who supported the present Government's policy in the past – regarded it as an intolerable burden, a relic of medievalism, a test imposed from outside under threat of 'immediate and terrible war'. The new government had no desire whatever to be on unfriendly relations with Great Britain. Quite the contrary. But the British Government must realise that real peace in Ireland is impossible so long as the full and free representation of the people in their Parliament is rendered impossible by a test of this character.[11]

Dulanty duly conveyed his instructions to the dominions secretary on 22 March and the necessary legislation was introduced on 22 April.

De Valera's strategy of claiming that he was acting constitutionally and that he had the law on his side put the British in something of a quandary, because the last thing they wanted was to allow him to win sympathy among the other dominions. J. H. Thomas, the secretary of state for the dominions, put their dilemma in a nutshell: 'Our policy has always been that, if the Irish Free State intends to secede [from the Commonwealth], it should do so by an overt act about which there can be no possible doubt and that we ought not to allow ourselves to be open to the charge that we have forced the Free State out of the Commonwealth.'[12] De Valera's determination to avoid overt acts that might afford the British such an opportunity underpinned his strategy in 1932–7. His approach was essentially pragmatic. Responding to an opposition motion in the Dáil that his government ought either to 'abandon the profession of republicanism' or to seek an electoral mandate for 'the immediate establishment of a republic', he claimed that Fianna Fáil 'want to see established here a completely free Ireland and they believe that this country is not completely free until its freedom is expressed in the form of a republic'. He denied charges of inconsistency with his 1922 position – de Valera invariably reacted to charges of inconsistency like a bull to a red rag: 'We tried to maintain it [the Republic] in arms and we failed. We are here because we failed then, and because we believe that we could not at the present moment make good our desires, and for no other reason ... We believe that we are real Republicans because we are taking the best means at our disposal to re-establish the Republic'; and he went on to say 'that though we are in the British Commonwealth today we are not of it'.[13]

But the British had no qualms about confronting de Valera on financial as opposed to constitutional issues when he refused to continue transferring the annuities payable under the Land Acts to the British Treasury; they were determined not to reopen the complex financial negotiations of the 1920s which had resulted in the secret agreement of 12 February 1923 and the ultimate financial settlement (provided for in the Treaty and tying up loose ends with regard to the payment of annuities under the Land Acts of 1891–1909 and the arrangements for the payment of Royal Irish Constabulary pensions) of 19 March 1926. That neither agreement had been ratified by the Dáil and that de Valera learned of the former only after taking office made for comparable intransigence in Dublin. The dispute took some months to come to a head because de Valera was determined that any financial negotiations would not become entangled with negotiations over the oath of allegiance, which, he insisted, was 'a purely domestic matter'.[14] But once the Dáil had passed the bill abolishing the oath of allegiance, he was ready to talk about the land annuities. On 6–7 June J. H. Thomas, accompanied by Lord Hailsham, the most hardline and anti-Irish member of the British cabinet's Irish Situation Committee, came to Dublin to meet de Valera, who was accompanied

by Seán T. O'Kelly, the vice-president of the Executive Council.
The meeting came to nothing, as did further talks when de Valera
went to London on 10 June. The Irish Situation Committee, dominated by Tories, shied away from the suggestion that the prime
minister, Ramsay MacDonald, talk directly to de Valera because
they doubted his ability to hold his own with the Irish leader, who
they recognised as 'a notoriously difficult and procrastinating
negotiator'.[15] But de Valera 'was not prepared to come to Downing
Street unless he was to see the Prime Minister alone' and they
'had a conversation alone for about a quarter of an hour' before
MacDonald summoned his colleagues. The British, although
previously reluctant to submit the matter for arbitration, now
proposed arbitration by a Commonwealth tribunal. But de Valera
rejected any such restriction and the talks collapsed. On 1 July he
withheld the £1.5 million payment due for land annuities and the
British imposed a 20 per cent duty on about two-thirds of all Irish
exports to the United Kingdom in order to recoup their losses; the
Irish government responded in kind and the so-called economic
war of 1932–8 had begun. Although an Irish delegation was
already at sea en route to the Imperial Conference in Ottawa, de
Valera telegrammed their leader, Seán T. O'Kelly, that 'in view of
British penal tariffs delegation should not attend opening or any
meeting of conference pending further communication'.[16]

Seldom has a dispute between two countries been so ill named:
although the weapons of the war were economic, the issues were
overwhelmingly political. British obduracy was politically motivated because the British saw de Valera as the man who had tried
to wreck the Treaty and who had caused civil war. Their hope was
– and in this they were encouraged by messages from opposition
leaders in Dublin – that if they presented an unwavering front de
Valera's government might crack or his slender parliamentary
majority disintegrate, with the result that another pro-Treaty
government with which they could resume harmonious relations
would take office. Once the economic war had begun, moreover,

de Valera also saw advantages in obduracy and had no appetite for seeking a financial solution to what he was convinced was a political problem. In this sense the economic war was a godsend to de Valera because it enabled him to tell Irish voters that the 'frugal fare' he had offered in his Dáil speech in 1928 was the price they must pay for political freedom: the British could now be blamed for force-feeding that frugal fare to a people no longer cushioned by the Treaty.

He was in no mood for compromise when he led the Irish delegation at another conference with British ministers on 14–15 October in London. Although the proceedings were amicable, the time was not ripe to achieve what de Valera described as 'the whole purpose of the conference . . . to arrive at a final settlement between the two countries'.[17] 'If the British government should succeed in beating us in this fight,' he told the Fianna Fáil *ard fheis* on 8 November 1932, 'then you could have no freedom, because at every step they could threaten you again and force you again to obey the British. What is involved is whether the Irish nation is going to be free or not.'[18]

British–Irish relations were also a factor in de Valera's snap decision, opposed by most of his ministers, to dissolve the Dáil during the Christmas recess and seek a stronger electoral mandate: the British, he explained to the Labour Party leader, William Norton, would not negotiate for as long as they expected his government to fall. The election, on 24 January 1933, was one of the most bitter, turbulent and colourful in the history of independent Ireland; the record turnout of 80 per cent – despite all the disadvantages of a midwinter campaign – testified to his having created a national mood of excitement. Fianna Fáil yet again pushed up its vote, to 49.7 per cent (76 seats), while Cumann na nGaedheal fell to 30.5 per cent (48 seats); the Centre Party, 9.1 per cent (11 seats), Labour, 5.7 per cent (eight seats) and nine independents made up the balance. This slenderest overall majority of one, consolidated by a by-election victory in 1934, gave de Valera the mandate he wanted to push ahead with his constitutional changes. The abolition of the senate, which had had the temerity to delay his oath bill, was now added to the list of policies approved by the voters. The British now realised that they could no longer hope for the return of a more congenial government in Dublin. De Valera alone 'could deliver the goods', noted a dominions office official in 1934. 'If therefore a settlement with Mr de Valera has to be made, surely the sooner it is made the better.'[19] But the pragmatism of the official mind could make little headway against the political obduracy that still prevailed in London, as in Dublin.

De Valera still hastened slowly. He had outlined his strategy at an Easter Rising commemoration in April 1933:

Let it be made clear that we yield no willing assent to any form or symbol that is out of keeping with Ireland's right as a sovereign nation. Let us remove these forms one by one, so that the state we control may become a republic in fact: and that, when the time comes, the proclaiming of the Republic may involve no more than a ceremony, the formal confirmation of a status already attained.[20]

This was de Valera's programme for 1933–7 and, before the end of 1933, the oath bill and three new constitutional amendments had been enacted – these abolished the right of appeal to the privy council, transferred the governor general's function of recommending money bills to the Executive Council and abolished his right to withhold his assent to bills.

In late April 1935, de Valera instructed John Hearne, the legal adviser in the department of external affairs, to begin drafting the heads of a new constitution and, speaking at Ennis at the end of June, he 'gave his first public intimation of his plans when he announced that before the present government left office they would have an Irish Constitution from top to bottom'.[21] In May 1936 he told the Dáil that he would introduce a new constitution before the end of the year. On 18 August, in a passage that revealed both his authoritarian style in cabinet and his total control of British–

Irish policy, the Executive Council minutes recorded that 'the President and Minister for External Affairs *mentioned* [author's italics]' that he was going to write to the new king, Edward VIII, of his intention to introduce a new constitution in the autumn:

King Edward would be informed
   (a) that the constitution would deal with the internal affairs of Saorstát Éireann [the Irish Free State];
   (b) that amongst the provisions of the new constitution would be the creation of the office of a president elected by the people and the abolition of the office of governor-general.
   It was agreed accordingly.[22]

De Valera now enjoyed a great stroke of luck in the shape of the abdication crisis that broke at the end of November. Edward's determination to marry Mrs Wallis Simpson, an American divorcee, precipitated a major constitutional crisis in Britain and de Valera seized the opportunity to launch a surgical strike advancing his constitutional revolution. On 10 December, the day of the abdication, his cabinet decided not merely to give effect to the abdication as far as the Irish state was concerned, but 'to delete from the constitution all mention of the representative of the Crown whether under that title or under the title of governor general' and 'to make provision by ordinary law for the exercise of certain functions in external matters as and when so advised by the Executive Council'.[23] The first decision was a major step towards ridding the state of forms inconsonant with Irish sovereignty. The second implemented de Valera's concept of external association, first enunciated during the Treaty debates: it provided that for so long as the king was associated with the other member states of the Commonwealth and was recognised as the symbol of their association, he was authorised (when acting on the advice of the Irish government) to make diplomatic appointments and to conclude international agreements. Two bills were hurriedly drafted and rushed through all stages in an emergency session of the Dáil to which deputies were summoned by telegram. The first, the Constitution (Amendment No. 27) Bill had been passed by 11 p.m. on 11 December; it was prepared in such haste that Michael McDunphy, assistant secretary in the department of the president of the Executive Council, complained that it had been introduced 'without even a copy being furnished' to his department 'except for the purpose of handing it to the Dáil, for which purpose it was in [his] hands . . . for about ten minutes. There was no time to even read the Bill nor was any information given regarding it to enable comments to be made on its contents. All action on the Bill was taken by the Department of External Affairs, which in this, as in many other matters, completely ignored the Department of the President.'[24] The other bill, the External Relations Bill, providing for the continuance of all existing diplomatic relations, had gone through all stages in the Dáil by 10.30 p.m. on the following night.

The abdication crisis enabled de Valera to carry out the most delicate manoeuvres in his quest for sovereignty – at least so far as British sensitivities were concerned: taking the king out of the constitution. However irritated British ministers might have been at his initiative, they were unlikely to relish controversy about the relationship between the monarchy and a dominion that might have implications for other dominions; and, as in the case of de Valera's earlier constitutional changes, they chose not to retaliate. British embarrassment was epitomised by Malcolm MacDonald's recollection of the bizarre circumstances under which he had to communicate the highly sensitive news of the abdication to de Valera. MacDonald, a son of Ramsay MacDonald, had succeeded J. H. Thomas as dominions secretary in November 1935, and used to tell the story of sitting in the cabinet room in 10 Downing Street at a crucial point in the abdication crisis, surrounded by his cabinet colleagues, and shouting down a bad telephone line to Dublin: 'THE COOK HAS GIVEN NOTICE, THE COOK HAS GIVEN NOTICE!'[25]

But de Valera's non-confrontational conduct of his relations with British ministers was beginning to pay dividends. 'De Valera is against the monarchy,' observed Stanley Baldwin, the British prime minister who had succeeded Ramsay MacDonald in 1935, 'but he is such a gentleman he won't kick an enemy when he is down.'[26]

The path was now clear for John Hearne to proceed with the detailed drafting of the constitution and 'a complete worked out draft in both English and Irish' was available for de Valera to take with him to Zurich on 11 January 1937,[27] a journey necessitated by his rapidly failing eyesight, which had been causing his wife and family 'great anxiety' since 1933. He had consulted specialists in Harley Street in 1932 and 1933, in Geneva in 1934 and, from 1935, he was under the care of the director of the University Eye Clinic in Zurich, where he had already spent six weeks in the spring of 1936.[28] He was reluctant to give up driving, which he enjoyed. 'The last time he drove was in 1938 after he bought the beautiful seven-seater Dodge,' recollected one of his sons. 'He only drove it for a few hundred yards before saying to Christy Cruise, his senior driver, "Ah, no Christy, I cannot see properly." He never drove again.'[29]

De Valera agreed to Malcolm MacDonald's request for a meeting in London on his way back from Zurich, a meeting that began with MacDonald 'conveying the warm thanks of Mr Baldwin and the other members of the Cabinet' for de Valera's help during the abdication crisis. MacDonald's main concern was the implications of the External Relations Act. De Valera was conciliatory: he emphasised that the act 'did no more than record in a statute the precise extent to which the King at present exercised functions for Saorstát Éireann'. MacDonald, too, was conciliatory in the course of two conversations in one day at de Valera's hotel. He told de Valera that he hoped he could persuade his cabinet colleagues of his own view that the recent Irish legislation and impending constitution were not 'incompatible with full membership of the Commonwealth'. But de Valera was already looking ahead: mindful of the war clouds gathering over Europe, his principal preoccupation was those elements in the Treaty providing that the British would retain the right to harbour and other defence facilities at Berehaven and Queenstown (Cobh) in County Cork and Lough Swilly in County Donegal. British use of these facilities would make it impossible for Ireland to remain neutral in the event of war and de Valera made it clear to MacDonald that what he

really wanted was a position of neutrality. The nearer we approximated to that position the better. In our own interests we would not allow our territory to be used as a base of attack on Britain but obviously we could only be at war when our interests were jeopardised and the Dáil had so decided. It would be fatal he thought even to appear to insist upon occupation of the ports in any circumstances except by our free invitation.[30]

But de Valera's priority was the enactment of his new constitution and the pace quickened after his return to Dublin. He circulated the draft constitution to his cabinet colleagues and to some of the more sympathetic members of the judiciary on 16 March 1937. He also established a small, four-member committee to examine and revise the draft in the light of observations that might be received from ministers or from their departments. Few ministers bothered. Even so energetic and independent-minded a cabinet colleague as Seán Lemass contented himself with some minor and anodyne comments relating to social policy. Indeed, it well illustrated the extraordinary reluctance of Fianna Fáil ministers to question de Valera's authority that the only trenchant criticism of his draft constitution came not from a cabinet colleague but from a civil servant: J. J. McElligott, secretary of the department of finance.[31] But McElligott's objections fell on deaf ears because, as Michael McDunphy minuted in response, 'this is a matter of policy'.

The composition of the drafting committee again demonstrates de Valera's determination to retain control of the drafting process in his own hands. It included no ministers, but consisted exclusively of civil servants: John Hearne, Maurice Moynihan, Michael McDunphy, and Philip O'Donoghue (the legal adviser in the attorney general's department). None of the four worked in an outside department under the direction of any other minister, and all but O'Donoghue answered directly to de Valera, with whom they were in constant communication throughout the drafting process, which was completed by the end of April.

The procedure followed in regard to the religious provisions of the constitution (Article 44) is a particularly striking example of de Valera's determination to control the most sensitive aspects of the process. The religious article was omitted not only from the first draft of the constitution, as circulated on 16 March, but from the first and second revised drafts, circulated on 1 April and on 10 April. Nor was the constitutional committee entrusted with any responsibility for the draft religious article, which he retained in his own possession. Its wording was unveiled only at the last possible moment, in the final text printed on 26 April. De Valera's youngest son remembered him battling with failing eyesight as he worked on the draft in his study at home. 'He could only write by using a pen with a very large nib, which meant that vast amounts of paper often overflowed from his desk . . . I remember going into his study where I was warned not to walk on the many sheets of paper which were scattered on the floor.'[32] There is no evidence whatever that any of de Valera's cabinet colleagues offered, or were invited to offer, any observations on the religious article before that point. They considered its text once – on 27 April – and it went unchanged for final printing on the very next day.

The absolutism of de Valera's control was likewise demonstrated by his reaction to the representations made by some of the leading Catholic churchmen he had consulted. In September 1936 he had responded positively to a statement of Catholic principles sent to him by a Jesuit, Father Edward Cahill, saying that he had found it 'useful as indicating the principles which should inspire all governmental activity, so as to make it conform with Catholic teaching'; he asked Father Cahill to draft a preamble as well as some articles of the draft constitution. De Valera also lent heavily on the advice of Father John Charles McQuaid, the president of his *alma mater*, Blackrock College (who became Archbishop of Dublin in 1940) in connection with the social articles; he also consulted the then archbishop, Dr Edward Byrne, Cardinal MacRory, the Archbishop of Armagh, and the papal nuncio. But he incurred the displeasure of these Catholic prelates by including the heads of the other churches in Ireland in his consultation process.[33] The outcome was the religious article of the constitution (44) providing that:

the State recognises the special position of the Holy Catholic Apostolic and Roman Church as the guardian of the Faith professed by the great majority of the citizens.

The State also recognises the Church of Ireland, the Presbyterian Church in Ireland, the Methodist Church in Ireland, the Religious Society of Friends in Ireland, as well as the Jewish congregations and the other religious denominations existing in Ireland.

So determined was de Valera to resist the Irish bishops' preference for a wording that would exclude all references to other churches and religions that he sent Joe Walshe on a special mission to the Vatican seeking approval of the religious clause. Both the pope, Pius XI, and the secretary of state, Cardinal Pacelli (who was elevated to the papacy as Pius XII in 1939), took the view that the 'special position' accorded the church in de Valera's draft 'had no real value so long as there was not a formal acknowledgement of the Roman Catholic Church as the church founded by Christ'. Walshe reported to de Valera that he was 'very disappointed when [he] received . . . the exact text of the words used by the Holy Father . . . "I do not approve, neither do I not disapprove; we shall maintain silence." I tried to translate the evil out of this double negative but the Cardinal held me to the sense . . . It was an attitude of complete neutrality.'[34]

From the liberal, secularist perspective of the twenty-first century what strikes most observers about Article 44 is the special position it conferred on the Catholic Church: a position that obtained until December 1972 when the clauses in question were deleted by referendum as a gesture towards Protestant suscepti-bilities under the impact of the Northern Ireland crisis. From the perspective of 1937, however, Article 44 was a compromise that denied the Catholic Church the kind of exclusive recognition it wanted.

Nor was this the only respect in which de Valera saw his new constitution as a compromise. This was also why Article 4 declared that 'the name of the state is Éire, or in the English language, Ire-land' – *not* Poblacht na hÉireann or the Republic of Ireland. De Valera's reasoning was based on nationalist Ireland's outstanding cause of contention with Britain and Ireland: the continuance of partition. 'When the name of the State is changed from Éire to Poblacht na hÉireann,' he told the Fianna Fáil *ard fheis* in October 1937, 'we want to see it in operation, not for the twenty-six counties alone, but for the whole thirty-two counties'.[35] Similar reasoning explained his retention of the vestigial link for diplo-matic purposes with the Commonwealth, embodied in his External Relations Act of 1936: 'in order that, when Northern Ireland came in', as he over-optimistically explained, 'the contact with the Crown which they valued so highly should not be entirely severed'.[36]

How, then, did de Valera reconcile this readiness to compromise and his anxiety to assuage the Ulster unionists with other appar-ently intransigent constitutional assertions: the assertion in Article 2, for example, that 'the national territory consists of the whole island of Ireland', and the declaration in Article 8 that 'the Irish language as the national language is the first official language'?

There was a point beyond which de Valera was not prepared to compromise the beliefs of the majority in the interests of concili-ating the minority. He distinguished, too, between the nation and the state. Although he saw the first section of his constitution – on the nation – as the appropriate place in which to lay claim, on behalf of the nation, to 'the whole of the national territory', Article 3 also explicitly stated 'that the area of jurisdiction of the government which is provided by this Constitution shall be of the same extent as that of the State'.

Latterday critics of the state's identification with the Catholic religion and with the Irish language as embodied in de Valera's constitution too easily lose sight of their function as devices for bonding together a deeply divided people. Here again we must ignore the twenty-first-century context and instead look backward to the traumatic impact of what happened in 1921–2. No one was more conscious than Éamon de Valera of the wounds inflicted on the body politic by a civil war for which he was in large part responsible. The amputation of the six northern counties continued to inflame those wounds. Together they had created not merely a divided nation but a state so bitterly split that many citizens paid it no more than a grudging allegiance, while a smaller number continued to claim the right to bear arms against it. In so deeply divided a state there was a real need to find common ground where citizens could gather irrespective of political affiliation, a need that found expression in a search for badges of national identity. Religion and language – identifiably different from those that characterised the British national ethos – were the two most obvious hallmarks of independent Ireland. And it was as such that they were embodied in de Valera's constitution. Catholic triumphalism and language revivalism alike were rooted in the necessity to find something to celebrate in an infant state scarred by political disappointment and economic austerity and by the general disenchantment typical of a post-revolutionary age.

Neither should those who damn the Catholic triumphalism they identify in de Valera's constitution ignore the residual impact of that ingrained anti-Catholicism that had so characterised Britain's dealings with Ireland since the sixteenth century. Nor should they forget that an especially vicious form of anti-Catholic prejudice and discrimination was still a feature of that part of the island of Ireland remaining within the United Kingdom. Such considerations of alienation and allegiance explain the rationale that underpinned de Valera's constitution.

De Valera accepted that his fellow citizens had a right to dispute the legitimacy of the 1922 constitution and, consequently, to withhold their allegiance from the institutions of the state. This had been his own position – certainly from 1922 until 1926 and arguably between 1927 and 1932. His aim was to enact a constitution that would satisfy what he regarded as justifiable republican aspirations and thereby secure the legitimacy of the state.

The legitimisation of the state, in his eyes at least, explains why the constitution was so significant a watershed in the evolution of de Valera's relationship with the IRA. His initial ambivalence about the IRA when he took office had been reflected in the very first decision recorded in the Executive Council minutes: an order releasing under free pardon seventeen IRA prisoners held under the Special Powers Act. And public opinion invariably focuses on what governments do rather than on what they fail to do, which is why the failure of de Valera's government to repeal the Public Safety Act, enacted by the previous government in 1931, ultimately proved of greater historical significance than his effort to placate the IRA by releasing the prisoners in 1932. That de Valera first invoked the powers available under that act, in August 1933, against the Blueshirts (the Army Comrades Association formed in February 1932 and composed of former members of the Irish Free State army) has added to the confusion; indeed the most significant contribution of the Blueshirts to Irish history was to postpone the moment when de Valera came to grips with the IRA. Yet it is in his speech replying to opposition criticisms of this use of the act that the phrase 'rule of order' rang like an ominous refrain for the IRA. His policy, de Valera declared, was to permit every nationalist who had any aspirations for the independence of the country to pursue these aspirations in a peaceable way, in a way in which he could settle his differences with his neighbour by the only *rule of order* that human beings have been able to discover.

I have been attacked for want of consistency. It has been suggested that my devotion to majority rule is quite a new thing. I deny that. There is absolute, positive documentary evidence in the last ten or twelve years since these differences began that I have recognised the fact that every sensible person must recognise, that either we have got to settle political differences by force or settle them by some *rule of order*. I never suggested that there was in majority rule anything more than a *rule of order*, but that it was a precious *rule of order* I have held at all times.[37] [Author's italics.]

By January 1934 de Valera's patience was already wearing thin as this extraordinary outburst in a letter to Joe McGarrity illustrates:

You talk about coming to an understanding with the IRA. You talk of the influence it would have both here and abroad. You talk as if we were fools and didn't realise all this. My God! Do you not know that ever since 1921 the main purpose in everything I have done has been to try to secure a basis for national unity . . . It has taken us ten long years of patient effort to get the Irish nation on the march again after a devastating civil war. Are we to abandon all this in order to satisfy a group who have not given the slightest evidence of any ability to lead people anywhere except back into the morass?[38]

The internal logic of de Valera's position demanded that he strip the state of all those elements that he deemed repugnant to right-minded republicans before he could move ruthlessly against the IRA. But he hinted at what lay ahead in May 1935 when he told the Dáil that if his government introduced a new constitution it would have to include 'certain emergency provisions which would give power to the executive, in case the ordinary courts were set at defiance, to bring those who were acting in an unlawful and illegal manner before courts which could not possibly be intimidated'.[39] Armed murders in the spring of 1936, most notoriously of Vice-Admiral Somerville in County Cork, caused him to move against the IRA even before the enactment of his constitution. On 18 June 1936 his government made an order under the Special Powers Act declaring the IRA to be an unlawful association; the imprisonment of many IRA leaders soon followed. The new constitution duly provided, as he had anticipated, for the establishment of special courts (Article 38 (3)) 'by law but for the trial of offences in cases where it may be determined in accordance with such law that the ordinary courts are inadequate to secure the effective administration of justice, and the preservation of public peace and order'.

But what marked the final turning point in de Valera's relationship with the IRA was the definition of treason in Article 39:

Treason shall consist only in levying war against the state or assisting any state or person or inciting or conspiring with any person to levy war against the state, or attempting by force of arms or other violent means to overthrow the organs of government established by this Constitution, or taking part or being concerned in or inciting or conspiring with any person to make or to take part or to be concerned in any such attempt.

De Valera spelled out the significance of this article when he introduced his Treason Bill in the Dáil in 1939. 'The moment the constitution was enacted by the people,' he argued, 'treason had a new meaning. The constitution was the foundation of a state', and the definition of treason had been definitely limited 'to make it clear that treason must no longer be understood in terms of allegiance to foreign powers . . . Once the constitution was passed, treason was defined as an act of treachery against the state, and nothing else.' Now that the 'the Irish people had established freely a state in accordance with their wishes, those who tried, by violent means, to overthrow that state should be held here, as in other countries, to be guilty of the most terrible crime of a public character which is known in civilised society'.[40]

The baldness of de Valera's words contrasts starkly with the labyrinthine language of so many of his earlier utterances on the IRA. But ambiguities were now at an end. The state was no longer the Irish Free State but de Valera's Ireland.

Independence Affirmed: Neutrality in World War II

'What does independence consist of? It consists fundamentally and basically of foreign relations. That is the test of independence,'[1] Prime Minister Pandit Nehru told the Indian parliament in 1949. So it was for Ireland. And World War II, the greatest international crisis since independence and the only such crisis that has so far threatened to engulf Irish shores, was the supreme test. Irish neutrality, the preferred foreign policy of all Irish governments since 1922, has in this sense been rightly termed 'an expression, one might say the ultimate expression, of independence'.[2] Independence had to be established before it could be expressed and, while that was de Valera's priority between 1933 and 1937, he became increasingly preoccupied during those years with the growing likelihood of war in Europe. Chance decreed that his first appearance on the international stage was in the role of acting president of the Council of the League of Nations in September 1932. He wrote his own speech and used the opportunity to explore criticisms of the League, in particular the criticism that 'the equality of status does not apply here in the things that matter, that the smaller states, whilst being given a voice, have little real influence in the final determination of League action'.[3] His speech received international acclaim. The *Manchester Guardian* said it was 'the best ever yet made by a president of a League Assembly' and the *New York Times* described him as 'the outstanding personality' of the session.[4]

De Valera's foreign policy was based on his perception of the national interest and took no heed of Irish public opinion. In 1934, for example, he cast Ireland's vote in favour of Russia's entry into the League, notwithstanding the virulence of anti-communism among Irish Catholics. In June 1936, after the Italian conquest of Abyssinia (Ethiopia), he began to despair of the League. 'The whole position in Europe is one of uncertainty and of menace,' he told the Dáil. 'We want to be neutral.' But he feared that British occupation of the Treaty ports would, in the event of war, give foreign powers the pretext to ignore Irish neutrality. This led him to resort to the realpolitik initially spelled out in his letter of February 1920 to President Woodrow Wilson: 'We are prepared and any government with which I have been associated has always been prepared to give guarantees . . . [that Britain was] not going to be attacked through foreign states that might attempt to use this country as a base.'[5] His determination to prevent Catholicism shaping the direction of Irish foreign policy was even more apparent after the outbreak of the Spanish Civil War. When he received the French draft of a proposed declaration on non-intervention, he immediately informed the French minister in Dublin that his government agreed in principle with its terms although he had not yet had an opportunity to consult his cabinet colleagues.[6] The episode was a classic instance of his making foreign-policy decisions first and only afterwards seeking retrospective endorsement from his ministers. His determination to resist the widespread support and sympathy for Franco and the Catholic cause was also reflected in the Government Information Bureau's reply to those urging that diplomatic relations be broken off with the Republican government in Spain by pointing out 'that diplomatic relations are primarily between states rather than between governments and that the severance of diplomatic relations . . . would serve no useful purpose at the present time.'[7] This was in stark contrast with the emotive language of Cardinal MacRory, speaking in Drogheda in September 1936:

Poor Spain! So long a great country and a faithful friend of Ireland, now torn and bleeding and fighting for her Christian life. There is no room any longer for any doubt as to the issues at stake in the Spanish conflict.

It is not a question of the army against the people, nor of the aristocracy plus the army and the church against labour. Not at all. It is a question of whether Spain will remain as she has been so long, a Christian and a Catholic land, or a Bolshevist and anti-God land.[8]

De Valera also rejected the appeals of the opposition, voiced by Cosgrave in November 1936, that his government recognise Franco's regime and he pushed the Non-Intervention Act through the Dáil some months later in the face of strident opposition from Cumann na nGaedheal, the Catholic hierarchy and the *Irish Independent*.

Two provisions in de Valera's constitution were fundamental for the conduct of foreign policy and guaranteed that, just as the External Relations Act had been rushed through both houses of the Oireachtas in a single day, the government could make foreign-policy decisions without heed to public opinion and with minimal reference to parliament.

Article 28.2 provided that 'the executive power of the State shall, subject to the provisions of this Constitution, be exercised by or on the authority of the Government'; and Article 29.4(10) provided that 'the executive power of the State in or in connection with its external relations shall in accordance with Article 28 of this Constitution be exercised by or on the authority of the Government'.

Éamon de Valera spelled out the meaning of these provisions in his Dáil speech introducing the constitution on 11 May 1937:

The idea of this Constitution is to put this matter of our external relations in its proper position relatively [*sic*] to the Constitution, *and that is outside it, as a matter of foreign policy,* to be determined from time to time according as the people's interests suggest to them that they should put this government or that government into office *with powers to implement their will.* That is what is done here. It is done by giving to the executive authority, namely, the Government, which is the fundamental executive authority, power to use any organ, instrument or method of procedure which may be used for similar purposes by other nations with whom we may be associated.[9] [Author's italics.]

Near-absolute powers over making foreign-policy decisions would thereby be entrusted by the people to the government at an election and could thereafter be exercised as the government saw fit and without further reference to the houses of the Oireachtas.

Although the 1937 constitution undermined executive power and parliamentary sovereignty in many other respects by inhibiting or, in some notable instances such as divorce, prohibiting the right of the Oireachtas to legislate, de Valera made sure that no such constraints applied to the government's control of foreign policy.

His insistence that there could be no constitutional constraint on the government's conduct of foreign policy explains why de Valera was so opposed to enshrining neutrality in the constitution. For him, neutrality was merely a means to an end; the end was sovereignty and neutrality was simply the expression of a sovereignty that enabled Ireland to pursue a genuinely independent foreign policy. If at any time the protection and preservation of independence could be more effectively pursued through the modification – or even, in unforeseen circumstances, the abandonment – of neutrality, then so be it. Neutrality, if it had been written into the constitution, would have been a straitjacket denying de Valera the flexibility he deemed necessary for the conduct of foreign policy.

There was only one exception to the rule that there must be no constitutional constraints on the conduct of foreign policy and that was Article 28.3, which provided that 'war shall not be declared and the State shall not participate in any war save with the assent of Dáil Éireann', although even in this instance the government was empowered to act as it saw fit 'for the protection of the State' in the event of an invasion (Article 28.2). But, taken as a whole, the 1937 constitution decisively tilted the balance of power in favour of the executive and against the legislature to the point where there was no constitutional requirement to consult the legislature about foreign-policy decisions.

Even before Ireland became independent, Éamon de Valera had understood and enunciated the constraints on Irish foreign policy well summarised by Desmond Williams:

States are never wholly free in relation to the policy which they follow. Policy is limited because no state can act against the general philosophy and moral belief of its people and . . . because a state must observe the limits circumscribing its geographic, economic and ideological situations in the world. What states are really free to do is always subject to some restrictions and constraint. Therefore, two principal points arise for a small state: policy cannot be a single, grand design and freedom of action is limited.[10]

In the case of independent Ireland, as in the case of all small states, those limitations on freedom of action are rooted in *raison d'état*. 'The success of a policy of *raison d'état*', Henry Kissinger has written, 'depends above all on the ability to assess power relationships.'

The seminal text illustrating de Valera's instinctive and remarkably perceptive understanding of the power relationship between Britain and Ireland goes all the way back to his 1920 interview in the *Westminster Gazette* in response to the charge that Irish independence would pose a threat to British security. His Cuban analogy and his asking why the British did not provide for their security as the Americans had done under the Monroe doctrine had then provoked bitter criticism from rabid and Anglophobic Irish-American republicans with no understanding of the realities of foreign policy. His critics failed to comprehend that, although de Valera's commitment to the theory of sovereignty was absolute, he also understood that foreign policy must be conducted on the basis of realpolitik if and when Ireland achieved in practice the independence that it was then claiming in theory. Although the term interdependence was not in vogue in 1920, the significance of de Valera's Cuban declaration is that it contains in embryo the theory of British–Irish interdependence that he elaborated during the negotiations of 1938 and that he was to put into effect by his benevolent neutrality towards the Allies during World War II.

On 23 November 1937, his constitutional revolution complete, de Valera had submitted a dispatch to the British government arguing that such negotiations begin as soon as possible. He set his proposals in the context of the rapidly deteriorating international situation and the inherent dangers of 'a continuance of the existing strained relations between the two countries' in the event of an outbreak of war.[11] De Valera's initiative struck an immediate chord with a British government increasingly preoccupied by the menace of Hitler and, since May 1937, led by Neville Chamberlain who, although one of the more hawkish British ministers on the annuities dispute when he had been chancellor of the exchequer, was now as disposed to appease de Valera's Ireland as he was to appease Hitler's Germany.

The British had been relatively indifferent to Irish affirmations of their right to pursue an independent foreign policy for as long as they posed no threat to vital British interests. But that changed when the prospect of another European war with an Atlantic dimension focused British as well as Irish attention on the strategic interdependence of the two islands. The nightmare of an unfriendly Ireland on her western flank in the event of war with Hitler's Germany had already persuaded the British military establishment that using the Treaty ports in such a war would be fraught with danger and that British strategic assets in Ireland were 'not vital and cannot be set against the grave disadvantage of curtailing the status of Ireland and thus making her people feel unsatisfied'. In May 1936, a year before Chamberlain became prime minister and unknown to de Valera, the Committee of Imperial Defence had unanimously endorsed a memorandum from the chiefs of staff stating that, 'provided improved relations are assured, and despite the risks involved, it would be desirable to offer to hand over the complete responsibility of the defence of the reserved ports to the Irish Free State'.[12]

Such was the background to the circumstances in which the Irish delegation led by de Valera began negotiations in London on 17 January 1938. Three months later, on 25 April 1938, and after the German invasion of Austria in March had further darkened the war clouds, three separate agreements were concluded: on finance, trade and defence.

The financial agreement provided that, in return for an Irish lump-sum payment of £10 million, Britain would drop its claim to the land annuities and to all other disputed financial claims. The trade agreement, which was detailed and complex, provided that British–Irish trade should be freer, if not fully free in the sense in which it had been in the 1920s. Taken together, they brought the economic war to an end: that the British Treasury had privately concluded as early as July 1936 that £10 million was as much as any Irish government might reasonably be expected to raise was confirmation that the obstacles to its resolution had always been political rather than economic.

But, from de Valera's perspective, the defence agreement was incomparably the most important. It provided that the defence facilities retained by the British under the Treaty – the dockyard port at Berehaven and the harbour defences and aviation facilities near Berehaven, Queenstown (Cobh) and Lough Swilly – should be handed over to the Irish government. What Winston Churchill and Chamberlain's other critics subsequently denounced as his foolhardy generosity is best explained by the response of his chiefs of staff to another request for an estimate of the strategic significance of the ports in the event of war. The chief of the imperial general staff, Lord Gort, advised that it would be 'an almost intolerable situation if Ireland were hostile' and that it would take at least one British Army division to defend each port, and the chief of the air staff concluded that the loss of the Irish ports 'would be a nuisance but their importance was not sufficient to warrant the extensive effort necessary to hold them against a hostile Ireland'.[13]

De Valera always regarded the defence agreement as his outstanding diplomatic achievement. And so it was. Its effect, as he explained to the Dáil, was 'to hand over to the Irish state complete control of those defences, and it recognises and finally establishes Irish sovereignty over the twenty-six counties and the territorial seas'.[14] The key to his triumph was that, after six years in power, he had won the trust of the British government, in the sense that Chamberlain and his colleagues believed that he meant what he said: that he would resist the British use of the ports just as he had resisted the implementation of the Treaty of 1921, but also that he would never allow Ireland to be used as a base for an attack on Britain.

De Valera was as good as his word. On 31 August 1938, six weeks after the Cork harbour defences had been transferred to the Irish government and more than a year before the Second World War began, Joe Walshe and John Dulanty met an officer of the British Security Service (then MI5) in London. Walshe spoke of the concern of de Valera's government about German activities in Ireland and requested assistance in setting up a counter espionage department 'similar to the Security Service'. Further such meetings with Colonel Liam Archer, the head of G2 (Irish Military Intelligence) took place in London in October and by late 1938 G2 had also begun establishing a Coast Watching Service based on a chain of coastal observation posts to monitor belligerent activity close to Ireland. Before the Second World War began, G2 and MI5 were already corresponding regularly through the Irish high commissioner's diplomatic bag as it went to and from the department of external affairs in Dublin. 'From the outset the personal relations between the British and Irish intelligence officers immediately concerned were extremely friendly,' records the official history of MI5 and Ireland, 'and this mutual confidence was maintained and developed during the war.'[15]

But this intelligence co-operation was shrouded in secrecy. Publicly, de Valera continued to insist that Ireland would be neutral in the event of war. 'If we can help it, we will not be in that war at all,' he told the Dáil in February 1939. He also spoke of 'the possibility of Britain trying to make use of our territory . . . In so far as we are not naked here, in so far as we have some defence forces here, we may also limit the possibilities of attack and cause to hesitate those who might otherwise think that it would be to their interest to try to use this country for their own purposes.' On 2 September 1939, the day after Germany had invaded Poland, he reaffirmed his commitment to Irish neutrality and introduced an Emergency Powers Bill that gave his government what he admitted were 'very extensive powers, powers which a representative government of a democratic state could ask for only in times of emergency'.[16] By then de Valera was armed with a new popular mandate achieved when Fianna Fáil won a decisive overall majority in the general election on 17 June. The Irish aim, he had said in April 1938, 'was to preserve for the parliament the sovereign right of determining, in the circumstances of the moment, what action is best in the national interest. That is the freedom we wanted to preserve and that is the freedom we have preserved.'[17]

The need to preserve that freedom explains the extraordinary additional powers taken by his government under the Emergency Powers Act that came into effect on 3 September 1939, the day the British declared war on Germany. In what for Ireland was never the war but always 'the Emergency', the act conferred powers in some respects even more drastic than the British draft legislation on which it had been consciously modelled during the Munich crisis a year before. The key section provided that:

The government may, whenever and so often as they think fit, make by order (in this act referred to as an emergency order) such provisions as, in the opinion of the government, are necessary or expedient for securing the public safety or the preservation of the state or for the maintenance of public order, or for the provision and control of supplies and services essential to the life of the community.

Throughout the war de Valera thereby effectively suspended the normal legislative processes of parliamentary democracy. Government was instead conducted by emergency powers orders, hundreds of which were made on a multiplicity of subjects ranging from the freezing of wages to restrictions on the possession and use of pigeons (which spies might use and so threaten neutrality). On 8 September he reshuffled his cabinet and created two new government departments. The department of supplies, based on the emergency-supplies branch set up in the department of industry and commerce the year before, and run by the former minister and the secretary of that department – Seán Lemass and John Leydon – was responsible for keeping the populace fed, fuelled and supplied with the essentials of life. The other change was the enhanced role given to Frank Aiken, minister for defence since 1932, who now became defence supremo with the title of minister for the co-ordination of defensive measures. His remit included a censorship so drastic that it prohibited the publication of a press photograph of a government minister ice-skating in the Phoenix Park lest it convey meteorological information to the Germans.

A cautious but amicable correspondence between de Valera and Neville Chamberlain – 'I would like you to know how much I sympathise with you in your present anxieties,' wrote de Valera on 22 September – resulted in his government's approving the appointment of Sir John Maffey as British diplomatic representative in Ireland on the same day. De Valera established a warm if sometimes inevitably fraught relationship with Maffey from their first meeting when he 'gratefully accepted' Maffey's offer to read a letter from Chamberlain aloud, explaining that his eyesight was so bad that he could not read it himself. And, as Maffey reported to Anthony Eden, the British foreign secretary, de Valera also assured him that he did 'not want Irish freedom to become a source of British insecurity'.[18]

There was no real threat to Irish neutrality until France fell to the Germans in June 1940. The threat then was twofold. Germany, aware of Ireland's lack of air cover and tiny army, might invade as a back door into Britain. The British, on the other hand, isolated during the Battle of Britain and the first phase of the Battle of the Atlantic in 1940–41 and now led by Winston Churchill, who had passionately resisted and continued to resent the return of the ports, wanted Irish bases and might be tempted to invade to get them. But Ireland was a lucky neutral – lucky in that the geographical accident of being an offshore island behind the larger offshore island of Britain made her the least vulnerable of European neutrals to the onslaught of the triumphant German war machine of 1940. Lucky, too, because, as Desmond Williams observed, 'the occupation of Irish territory never became absolutely vital or was thought to become vital to the security of any of the belligerents. The advantages to be derived from any attempted occupation were not greater than the costs, moral and military, involved in such an operation.' That said, de Valera's consummate diplomatic skill 'in convincing all parties that he would oppose by force the first power which tried to interfere with Irish neutrality' was a critical factor in the belligerents' determination of this balance of advantage.[19]

After the fall of France, however, the danger that Britain might soon suffer the same fate threatened the survival of that Irish independence of which neutrality was the visible expression. 'An independent Ireland that is interested in maintaining its own independence', de Valera had declared in his speech on the 1938 agreement, 'is interested in seeing a strong shield between her and the dangers of the Continent.' The fall of France exposed the frailty of de Valera's British shield. Thereafter he set about secretly ensuring that Ireland do all in its power to ensure that Britain was not defeated.

The result, as the British dominions secretary Lord Cranborne acknowledged in February 1945 as the war in Europe was drawing to a close, was that de Valera's government 'have been willing to accord us *any* facilities which would not be regarded as *overtly* prejudicing their attitude to neutrality' (author's italics); and he appended a remarkable 14-point list for the British war cabinet. These included:

- close liaison between Irish and British military authorities to plan against a possible German invasion of Ireland;
- exchange of information between British and Irish intelligence services;
- the use by British aircraft based on Lough Erne of a corridor over Irish territory and territorial waters for flying out over the Atlantic;
- 'the immediate transmission to the United Kingdom Representative's Office in Dublin of reports of submarine activity received from their coast watching service';
- transmission of meteorological reports and of reports of aircraft sightings over or approaching Irish territory;
- supplying particulars of German crashed aircraft and personnel crashed or washed ashore or arrested on land;
- the internment of all German fighting personnel reaching Ireland while Allied service personnel were 'allowed to depart freely and full assistance is given in recovering damaged aircraft';
- de Valera's government's silent acquiescence in the wishes of the thousands of Irish citizens who fought in the Allied forces; and
- the establishment in February 1945 of a radar station on Irish territory for use against the latest form of German submarine warfare. (This was a radio navigation station sited on Malin Head in County Donegal and, although the war ended before it came into operation, it is the only example of de Valera agreeing to the establishment of a British military facility on Irish territory.)[20]

The Americans were even warmer than the British in their praise of the secret contribution of de Valera's government to the Allied cause. The wartime history of the OSS, the American intelligence service that pre-dated the CIA, recorded the 'substantial results in intelligence' produced by their 'clear cooperation'; the Pentagon even recommended that three of the highest-ranking officers in the Irish defence forces (the chief of staff, deputy chief of staff and the chief of the army air corps) be awarded the American Legion of Merit for 'exceptionally meritorious and outstanding services to the US', although the recommendation was never implemented because the state department realised how it would embarrass the Irish government.[21]

There were two reasons, both rooted in *raison d'état*, why it was necessary that Irish support for the Allies had to remain buried in secrecy. First, because any public departure from neutrality would expose Irish cities to German air-raids or other retaliation. Second, because for de Valera to have publicly abandoned neutrality would have outraged the philosophy of foreign policy that he himself had created and cultivated so successfully since 1920. There was an intrinsic merit, moreover, in 'the secrecy with which de Valera shrouded his ultimate intentions and wishes', because, as Desmond Williams has pointed out, it enabled both belligerent blocs to interpret his statements 'according to their desires and in a sense favourable to themselves. De Valera in fact appears never to have told anyone, even in his cabinet, everything that was in his mind.'[22]

Éamon de Valera never received, nor would he have ever wanted or expected, gratitude for his comprehensive secret support for the Allies throughout the war. Ireland's neutrality instead attracted virulent British abuse not only during the war but for decades afterwards, in some quarters even to the present day. The explanation lies in what the Austrian historian Gerald Stourzh, has identified as twin paradoxes peculiar to the foreign policy of neutral states: the affinity paradox and the credibility paradox. The affinity paradox rests on Machiavelli's axiom in *The Prince* that

your friends want you to be allies, [but] your enemies want you to be neutral. In other words, neutrality will satisfy a potentially more hostile power or power bloc more than a potentially friendlier power or power bloc. Powers with whom for whatever reasons close ties of sympathy exist may be disappointed or even irritated that the neutral state pursues merely a neutral policy . . . The credibility paradox consists in the fact that permanent neutrality strictly speaking is but a means to secure the end [of] independence. As a means, it may, like all other means, be abandoned in favour of other means better able to secure the end, independence.[23]

The British response to Irish neutrality in World War II offers a classic illustration of the affinity paradox: in particular, the response of one man, Winston Churchill, whose influence was paramount in disseminating an overwhelmingly negative perception of Irish neutrality and of Éamon de Valera throughout the English-speaking world. 'Of all the neutrals Switzerland has the greatest right to distinction,' wrote Churchill in his history of the Second World War, for which he won the Nobel Prize for Literature in 1953. 'She has been a democratic state, standing for freedom in self-defence among her mountains, and in thought, in spite of race, largely on our side.' Of Sweden, another of Germany's neutral neighbours, Churchill likewise wrote that 'the choice was a profitable neutrality or subjugation' and that she was blameless if she did not share British perceptions.[24] But in Churchill's eyes, Ireland, as a dominion and as Britain's nearest neutral neighbour, had no right to be neutral. Legally, Churchill declared in October 1939, Ireland was 'at war but skulking'; Irish neutrality was incompatible 'with her position under the Crown unlike other dominions which were separated from us by thousands of miles, Eire was an integral part of the British Isles'.[25]

The Irish public knew nothing of de Valera's secret support for the Allies. Cocooned by the censor's cloak, it saw only what the government wanted it to see: a lonely stand in defence of neutrality against the combined might of British and American pressure. De Valera's notorious visit on 2 May 1945 to the German minister, Dr Edouard Hempel, to sign the book of condolences opened on the news of Hitler's death reinforced the public perception that neutrality was being impartially administered between the two belligerent blocs. Although it must be placed in the context of de Valera's sense of outrage at what he saw as the unprofessional conduct of the American minister, David Gray, with whom he had had a stormy meeting that morning arising from the American demand that the German legation should be handed over to the Allies before the cessation of hostilities, even his senior officials in the department of external affairs regarded the gesture as grotesquely ill judged. At a time when the world was becoming aware of the horrors of Auschwitz and Belsen, it provoked international outrage. The 'incident has attracted more attention than anything else arising from our neutrality', reported Robert Brennan, the Irish minister in Washington, and there was 'considerable adverse criticism' even among Irish-Americans.[26]

De Valera was unrepentant. His explanation, in a personal and revealing 'Dear Bob' letter to Brennan (a fellow prisoner with him in Dartmoor in 1916 whom he had appointed as the first head of the Dáil Éireann department of foreign affairs in 1921), was utterly unapologetic:

I acted very deliberately in this matter. So long as we retained our diplomatic relations with Germany to have failed to call upon the German representative would have been an act of unpardonable discourtesy to the German nation and to Dr Hempel himself. During the whole of the war Dr Hempel's conduct was irreproachable. He was always friendly and invariably correct – in marked contrast with Gray. I certainly was not going to add to his humiliation in the hour of defeat . . . I am anxious that you should know my mind on all this. I have carefully refrained from attempting to give any explanation in public. An explanation would have been interpreted as an excuse, and an excuse as consciousness of having acted wrongly. I acted correctly and I feel certain wisely.[27]

Never explain, never apologise. 'I acted correctly and I feel certain wisely': there is no better epigram for that impregnable sense of self-righteousness that characterised de Valera's behaviour throughout his political career.

Although there were many Irish as well as international critics of his paying condolences on Hitler's death, that neutrality commanded the support of the opposition parties and of all the leading politicians in the state – James Dillon, the son of John Dillon (the last leader of the Irish Parliamentary Party), a renowned orator who resigned from Fine Gael in 1942 because it supported neutrality, was an exception – immeasurably strengthened de Valera's authority.

While his political opponents never forgot or forgave his role in 1921–2, he could again lay claim, at least in part, to the kind of national leadership he had then lost. De Valera, in Oliver Mac-Donagh's phrase, 'reigned as the man "who kept us out of the war"' and, in 1943, Fianna Fáil electioneered on the slogan 'Don't change horses while crossing the stream'. Although he was then returned only as the head of a minority government, his adroit use of a sense of national solidarity engendered by his rejection of the so-called 'American note' (a virtual ultimatum demanding that Ireland sever diplomatic relations with Germany and Japan) contributed to his regaining an overall majority when he called another snap election in 1944.

The final, decisive episode in determining popular perceptions of neutrality was his celebrated exchange of radio broadcasts with Winston Churchill when the war in Europe ended in May 1945. Churchill's self-congratulation at his government's having refrained from seizing the Irish ports when her national interest demanded it and his sneering references to the Irish government's being left 'to frolic with the Germans and later with the Japanese diplomatic representative to their hearts' content' incensed Irish opinion. De Valera's dignified rebuke to Churchill – pointing out that if Britain's necessity were admitted as a moral code 'no small nation adjoining a great power could ever hope to . . . go its way in peace' and even praising him for having resisted the temptation to add 'another horrid chapter to the already bloodstained record' of British–Irish relations – caught the public imagination and irrevocably identified neutrality with Irish independence.

Other historians have focused unduly on the negative aspects of neutrality. F. S. L. Lyons, for example, in an eloquent and oft-quoted passage on its alleged psychological consequences, has written of Ireland's 'almost total isolation from the rest of mankind . . . The tensions – and deliberations – of war, the shared experience, the comradeship in suffering, the new thinking about the future, all these things had passed her by.'[28] The elegance of expression is seductive but misplaced. 'Tensions', 'shared experience', 'comradeship in suffering' – Irish perception associated these things not with the experience of war but with the experience of neutrality. One might question, too, the 'liberating' value of war for a people who had so recently emerged from the war of independence followed by the civil war and in whose midst the IRA were still practitioners of violence, to say nothing of a 'fire of life' that had incinerated the dead of Coventry, Dresden, Hiroshima and Nagasaki, to mention but a few of the most spectacular instances of carnage. Éamon de Valera succeeded in protecting Ireland's citizens from such horrors while at the same time doing nothing to prevent the 50,000 or so Irish volunteers who so wished from enlisting in the Allied forces. That war was the great shared experience of Europe and beyond in these years is indisputable, just as it is indisputable that Irish neutrality seemed singularly unheroic in Whitehall and in Washington. But de Valera understood a phenomenon well described by John A. Murphy: 'When a small nation has been placed by the facts of geography and history in uncomfortable proximity to a great power, the people of that small nation, scarred by such a history, crave not only material progress, not only political sovereignty but the psychological independence as well so that their dignity and self-respect can be asserted against the superiority, contempt and disdain of the great power.'[29] Elizabeth Bowen, the novelist and journalist who reported on Irish opinion to the British ministry of information during the war, likewise explained how as early as 1942 neutrality had taken on 'an almost religious flavour; it has become a question of honour; and it is something which Ireland is not ashamed of, but tremendously proud'.[30] Honour and pride demanded of most Irish citizens that they resist Britain's will, not that they fight Britain's war. Isolation was not so much a fate to which they had been condemned as a choice that they had freely made and, in many instances, enthusiastically embraced. Understanding why they made that choice demands a closer examination of the distinguishing characteristics of de Valera's Ireland.

12

De Valera's Ireland

'The Irish genius', Éamon de Valera had declared when he opened Radio Éireann's Athlone station in 1933,

has always stressed spiritual and intellectual rather than material values. That is the characteristic that fits the Irish people in a special manner for the task, now a vital one, of helping to save Western civilisation. The great material progress of recent times, coming in a world where false philosophies already reigned, has distorted men's sense of proportion: the material has usurped the sovereignty that is the right of the spiritual.[1]

He returned to the theme repeatedly. The most notorious example is his St Patrick's Day broadcast of 1943 when he described his ideal Ireland as

the home of people who valued material wealth only as the basis of right living, of a people who were satisfied with frugal comfort and devoted their leisure to the things of the spirit – a land whose countryside would be bright with cosy homesteads, whose fields and villages would be joyous with the sounds of industry, with the romping of sturdy children, the contests of athletic youths and the laughter of comely maidens, whose firesides would be forums for the wisdom of serene old age . . . The home of people living the life that God desires that man should live.[2]

Although later generations have mercilessly lampooned and satirised de Valera's rural idyll, it is the other side of the coin of his indifference to national prosperity and economic progress. Nor does such a pastoral utopia remotely resemble the life in rural Ireland he himself had experienced in Bruree, from which he had sought only to escape. Instead, as Joe Lee has observed, 'Reared in an agricultural labourer's cottage, by an uncle with Labour loyalties, he sublimated the bitter social resentments of rural Limerick in a bland Arcadian image of an ideal Ireland.'[3]

Ireland's isolation during the Second World War and a certain smugness characteristic of neutral states fortunate enough to avoid its contagious horrors of death and destruction reinforced the tendency to contrast Irish other-worldliness with Anglo-Saxon materialism. 'As a community which has been mercifully spared from all the major sufferings, as well as from the blinding hates and rancours engendered by the present war', said de Valera in his broadcast response to Churchill, 'we shall endeavour to render thanks to God by playing a Christian part in helping, so far as a small nation can, to bind up some of the wounds of suffering humanity.'[4] The preservation of the Catholic faith in the face of long persecution and its diffusion through Irish missionary efforts and the restoration of the Irish language were recurring motifs in de Valera's enunciations of a vision that was as dogmatic about Irish identity as it was flattering to national pride. These themes were not peculiar to de Valera. Cosgrave's government had also sought the common ground of a national identity fostered by the state where the bitter differences of civil war would be no barrier to consensus and of which religion and language were the distinguishing marks. John A. Costello, who succeeded de Valera as taoiseach in 1948, likewise described Ireland as 'a spiritual Dominion which more than compensates for her lack of size and material wealth'.[5]

But the pace had quickened when Fianna Fáil came to power in 1932 because de Valera set about ridding the party of any taint of the 'red scare' with which its opponents had smeared it during elections. A cabinet meeting in April 1932 favoured suspending sittings of the Oireachtas on church holidays, opening sittings 'with an appropriate form of prayer' and displaying a crucifix in the Dáil chamber; in October 1933, the minister for justice was instructed to inquire 'into the possibility of altering the dates of public holidays so that they should coincide as far as possible with church holidays'.[6] This had been foreshadowed in a Dáil debate in March 1929 on a Fianna Fáil motion to the same effect. 'From my point of view as a Catholic,' de Valera had then proclaimed, 'I think we ought not to distinguish between holidays that are instituted by the Church and the Sabbath.'[7] The Eucharistic Congress of June 1932 gave de Valera a golden opportunity to expunge any remaining doubts about Fianna Fáil's fidelity to the Church in the greatest international celebration of Catholicism in the history of independent Ireland. Although continuity with the previous government was symbolised by Cosgrave's serving side by side with de Valera and Seán T. O'Kelly as canopy-bearers for the papal legate, Cardinal Lauri, de Valera seized every opportunity to take pride of place. 'I have had considerable trouble with the President,' complained Edward Byrne, the Archbishop of Dublin, to Cardinal MacRory in regard to the arrangements for the reception of Cardinal Lauri when he arrived at Dun Laoghaire. The suggestion that the archbishop, 'as sponsor of the Congress and the Legate's host', should accompany him travelling to Dublin', wrote Byrne, was 'superseded by the extraordinary proposal that the President alone should accompany the Legate . . . His claim amounted to excluding me altogether from the Legate's car' – the compromise ultimately negotiated with the department of external affairs was that both men should accompany Cardinal Lauri.[8] De Valera also drew on his close friendship with John Charles McQuaid, then the president of Blackrock College and subsequently Archbishop of Dublin, to hold a state garden party in the college grounds 'to avoid the embarrassment of the state function being associated with the Viceregal Lodge or with the representative of King George V'.[9]

The *Irish Press* used the occasion as a vindication of de Valera's unrelenting quest for sovereignty: one editorial described the congress as 'the august resurrection of a nation'; another, taking up the theme of Irish missionary activity, asserted that 'if we can get ourselves to realise all that has gone out to other nations from this land we shall find it easy to stand stoutly before the nations we have so gifted for the rights that are still withheld from us'.[10] Unprecedented and frequent joint appearances under circumstances of grandeur and devotion by leaders of church and state in front of vast crowds stamped de Valera's government with the Catholic Church's seal of approval. But the 1937 constitution, as we have seen, was the outer limit of de Valera's readiness to recognise what he then described as 'the special position' of the Catholic Church because, as Conor Cruise O'Brien has written, 'Mr de Valera did stand up to the Church, where he thought the Church was wrong – about the Irish Republic. But on issues like divorce, contraception, obscene literature, there was no question of standing up to the Church because Mr de Valera – a Catholic, in the traditional sense, from rural Ireland – agreed with the Church on such matters.'[11]

The embodiment of Catholicism in the constitution was mirrored by de Valera's treatment of the Irish language. The relevant article (8) declared that 'the Irish language as the national language is the first official language', although it also recognised English as 'a second official language' and laid down that provision might 'be made by law for the exclusive use of either of the said languages for any one or more official purposes, either throughout the state or in any part thereof'. Here again de Valera was pragmatic rather than pre-emptive in seeking to extend and develop the policy of the Cosgrave administration. In fact, English remained the working language of his government – both of public servants and of his ministers, whether in the Dáil debates or in the Executive Council and cabinet minutes. The first, isolated instance of Irish being used in the cabinet minutes occurs in April 1932 when condolences were recorded in Irish on the death of Patrick Pearse's mother; the purpose was merely ceremonial and honorific.

This gulf between principle and practice was exposed in an exchange between H. P. Boland and Seán Moynihan in 1934. Moynihan (whom de Valera had appointed, when he entered government, to the sensitive post of secretary to the Executive Council, whose own Irish was fluent and who, in 1936, was made chairman of a permanent commission on Irish in the civil service) was replying to a communication from Boland (the department of finance official with overall responsibility for the civil service) on the recommendation of a cabinet committee that a senior official should be appointed in every government department to liaise with Boland on gaelicisation policy and that, as a start, at least one section in every department should do all its work through Irish. The president's department, replied Moynihan dismissively, was small and principally concerned with matters for decision by the Executive Council. 'The prior submissions, the decisions based thereon and the subsequent correspondence with departments are inevitably in English, and as long as this condition continues, the internal work of the Department must necessarily be conducted in the same language.'[12] Another of many examples was de Valera's rejection of the proposal that Irish should be the 'ordinary language' of the Institute for Advanced Studies that he established through his personal initiative in 1940. Indeed, de Valera's pragmatism irritated some Irish-language enthusiasts when he temporarily added the education portfolio to his own ministerial responsibilities in 1940; he expressed scepticism about the policy initiated in the 1920s of teaching other subjects through Irish to children who lacked a grounding in the language and instead argued in favour of giving teachers latitude in teaching through English. In 1943, he also rejected the extremism of Thomas Derrig, his minister for education for all but nine months of Fianna Fáil's first sixteen years in government, who claimed that Irish could not be saved 'without waging a most intense war against English, and against human nature itself for the life of the language';[13] the episode was another illustration of his distaste for Anglophobia.

De Valera's personal contribution to the advancement of the Irish language was constructive and of a higher order. He moved Derrig from the department of education to the department of lands when he reorganised his cabinet on the outbreak of war. On 27 September 1939 de Valera told the Dáil that he was assuming ministerial responsibility for the education portfolio. He then steered through the Oireachtas a pet project that linked his passion for Irish with his passion for mathematics: the Institute for Advanced Studies Bill that had been prepared under his direction and introduced before the summer recess of 1939. De Valera's initial focus was on mathematics and his institute in Dublin was modelled on the Institute for Advanced Study in Princeton University where Einstein was a professor. Conscious of the deterioration of Dublin's Dunsink Observatory, where William Rowan Hamilton, the most eminent of all Irish mathematicians, had once served as Astronomer Royal, he consulted two of his former professors of mathematics – Professor Thrift, then the provost of Trinity College Dublin, and Professor Whittaker of Edinburgh University.

In March 1938 Whittaker told de Valera that Erwin Schrödinger (formerly professor of theoretical physics at the University of Berlin, where Einstein had been a colleague, and later a professor at the University of Graz in his native Austria, from where he had fled to Rome after the German annexation) was interested in coming to Dublin. De Valera told Maurice Moynihan, the secretary to the government, to draft a letter to Schrödinger and to ask the department of justice if there would be any problem about his admission to Ireland. Schrödinger accepted de Valera's provisional offer of a professorship in an institute that did not yet exist and on 19 November 1938 attended a luncheon in the taoiseach's room in Leinster House when the offer was confirmed. Moynihan arranged for Schrödinger to have an interview with an official of the department of justice that afternoon about obtaining visas not only for himself and his wife but for another woman, Frau Hilde March, the wife of an Austrian colleague with whom Schrödinger had fathered a daughter in 1934. Schrödinger foresaw no difficulty with the visas for himself and his wife but, as he wrote to de Valera, 'In the case of our friend, Frau Heldegrund March from Innsbruck,

you advised me, Sir, to apply to yourself . . . Mrs March is holding
an ordinary open (non-Jewish) German (not ex-Austrian) passport. She does, of course, not intend to go in for any work of any
kind and I take personal responsibility for her entertainment as
well as for her never causing any trouble to you, Sir, or to your
country.'[14] The taoiseach's wishes that no obstacle should be placed
in the way of Schrödinger's coming to Dublin prevailed over whatever Catholic mores might have informed the attitudes of officials
in the department of justice. In October 1939, a year before the
establishment of the institute, this *ménage à trois* duly took up
residence in Kincora Road, Clontarf; Schrödinger fathered two
other daughters by two different women during his time in Dublin.
He and his wife became Irish citizens in 1948 but they retained
Austrian nationality and returned to Austria in 1955 after the end
of the occupation by the Soviet Union.[15]

None of this was in the public domain; indeed Schrödinger
was never mentioned by name during the parliamentary debates
on the Institute for Advanced Studies Bill. A historian, Helena
Concannon, captured the surreal atmosphere in which the second-
stage debate took place in the senate on 15 May 1940 – the day the
Dutch forces surrendered before the German blitzkrieg – when
she told her colleagues that

It would be only fitting if we should bring to our consideration of this
Bill a prayer of gratitude to God, because in the midst of the terrible
tempest which has set almost the whole world reeling on its foundations,
and strewn its seven seas with shipwrecks and corpses, we can have peace
enough, tranquillity and leisure of mind enough to take thought for other
things besides war and its havoc, for construction rather than destruction, for the things of the mind and the spirit rather than for the cult of
that brutal materialism which has before our eyes sent its own shrines
crashing, and carried its own appalling retribution.

De Valera made no mention of war in a lengthy speech[16] in
which the School of Celtic Studies was centre stage and the School

of Theoretical Physics disingenuously presented almost as an after-thought. But he correctly anticipated that the opposition would concede that he had made a case for Celtic studies and ask why he did not stop there. 'It was a mischievous and silly thing for the Taoiseach to inject into this initial proposal mathematical physics,' argued James Dillon, who claimed that it had only 'one . . . silly, childish purpose, and that is to lend verisimilitude to the myth that the Taoiseach is a great mathematician, which he never was and never will be. He is a man who takes an interest in mathematics, but there are thousands of decent secondary teachers who were his colleagues before he entered politics and who are as good mathematicians as he is . . . But the myth has to be created in the world that in Ireland we have a scholar Prime Minister.' De Valera was undaunted. Having insisted that he did 'not pretend to be a Celtic scholar any more than . . . to be a mathematician', he went to the heart of the matter. Theoretical physics had been chosen because the war had made available the services of 'the greatest mathematical physicist in the world'.[17]

The bill was duly enacted on 19 June 1940, establishing the institute with two constituent schools – the School of Celtic Studies and the School of Theoretical Physics (a School of Cosmic Physics was added in 1947). The inaugural meeting of its governing board, on 21 November, unanimously appointed Schrödinger director of the School of Theoretical Physics. It provided a neutral meeting ground that had not previously existed for scholars from University College Dublin and Trinity College. This had been one of de Valera's objectives for, just as he had never been Anglophobic, neither had he ever shown the faintest antipathy to Trinity, with many of whose leading mathematicians he enjoyed close personal relations.

Nor, especially in later life, did he identify with the ban against foreign games promulgated by the GAA. 'For my part I have always preferred rugby,' he confided to a newly appointed British ambassador, who, accompanied by Frank Aiken, in his capacity as minister for external affairs, called on him in Áras an Uachtaráin in 1967. Aiken, offended by the ambassador's asking whether 'Gaelic football was really a made-up sort of game, not really native', disagreed. 'Gaelic football is *not* a made-up game', he retorted, but 'a *splendid* game', which, he claimed, had been 'played a thousand years ago and more', a remark that prompted President de Valera to jest: 'I know my position – I must not argue with a Minister!!!'[18] Ten years earlier, when he was still taoiseach, he had explained his attitude more comprehensively in a letter he wrote to the general secretary of the GAA, Pádraig Ó Caoimh, when his remarks in praise of rugby at a Blackrock College past-pupils dinner had been reported in the press. Having first warmly welcomed all the work the GAA 'has done and is doing', he took issue with their maintaining their ban on 'foreign' games. 'The supremacy of the GAA is so well established that the protection it might have needed in its infancy is no longer required . . . Anything that tends to restrict individuals from playing games for which they feel themselves specially fitted or which they like particularly should, if possible, be avoided and such a thing as bans taboo.' He then reiterated his theme at the Blackrock dinner: that there was no international competition in hurling – which he acknowledged as 'distinctively our national game' – or Gaelic football. 'If Ireland is to match herself in football and play with the national teams from England, Wales, Scotland and from France, it must be in rugby or soccer.' Rugby, clearly, was foremost in his mind since these were the four other teams in what was then the annual international championship. Ireland, he pointed out, had a much smaller selection pool than those countries with much larger populations 'and we ought not to do anything which tends to restrict the field. Many who play Gaelic football would, if the ban did not prevent them, be inclined to play rugby also. And I have not the slightest doubt that if this were permitted our successes in the international field would be outstanding, and our prestige abroad enhanced.' And so it proved, after the ban was abolished in 1971. But de Valera, as always, was pragmatic and acknowledged in a revealing postscript that, despite his own preference and 'enthusiasm for rugby' from his days at Rockwell and Blackrock, he had refrained from attending rugby matches because 'I did not think my assertion of my personal right to do so would be worth the fuss, the misrepresentation, and the necessary explanation to which it would give rise'.[19]

Publicly, he said nothing that might dilute his commitment to Patrick Pearse's vision of an Ireland free, Gaelic and united: 'That is the objective of the Irish people today', he proclaimed in a radio broadcast after his victory in the 1933 election, 'and it will remain their unshakeable resolve until it has been finally attained.' Ten years later, in his St Patrick's Day broadcast of 1943, he reaffirmed that 'the restoration of the unity of the national territory and the restoration of the language are the greatest of our uncompleted national tasks'.[20] However, his campaign against partition was as pragmatic as his pursuit of the restoration of the language.

De Valera's approach to the issue of Ulster, like his formulation of foreign policy, was remarkably consistent. 'The difficulty is not the Ulster question,' he had told the Dáil during the Treaty debates. 'As far as we are concerned this is a fight between Ireland and England. I want to eliminate the Ulster question out of it.'[21] Hence the fact that the treatment of Ulster in his Document No. 2 does not differ significantly from the terms of the Treaty. Leaving Ulster out of it remained de Valera's policy until he had completed his constitutional revolution. Some of his followers, notably Seán MacEntee, disagreed with him. MacEntee, a Belfast man by birth, had opposed the Treaty because he believed that it had made Irish unity impossible. In 1924, at a meeting of abstentionist Sinn Féin deputies after de Valera's release from jail, he was even more out-spoken in his criticism, describing Document No. 2 as 'no better' than the Treaty and demanding 'a strong unequivocal declaration that republicans would not accept any solution based on partition'. De Valera took refuge in the response that 'the two fundamentals were the unity and sovereignty of the nation and these he would always endeavour to get'. That order was disingenuous because, for de Valera, sovereignty was the first goal to which unity was always subordinated and with which, indeed, unity could not be readily reconciled.

De Valera was always conscious, moreover, of his own inability to end partition. 'Personally,' he had told the inaugural meeting of Fianna Fáil in May 1926, 'I knew there is no clear . . . way of solving the problem. That is a fact.' And he returned to the same theme at the inaugural Fianna Fáil *ard fheis* in November 1926, admitting that Irish unity could not be solved overnight.[22] This acceptance of the reality of partition was again spelled out in a Fianna Fáil advertisement during the September 1927 election: 'What Fianna Fáil does not stand for: Attacking the North East: Fianna Fáil does not stand for attacking "Ulster". It will accept EXISTING REALITIES, but will work resolutely to bring Partition to an end.'[23]

His opposition to the use of force to achieve that end was also remarkably consistent. 'They had not the power, and some of them had not the inclination to use force with Ulster,' he had told the Dáil as early as August 1921. 'He did not think that policy would be successful. They would be making the same mistake with that section [Ulster] as England had made with Ireland. He would not be responsible for such a policy.'[24] He force-fed the final Fianna Fáil *ard fheis* before the party entered government with another dose of realism:

With regard to partition, I see no solution of that problem. Force is out of the question. Were it feasible, it could not be desirable. The only hope that I can see now for the reunion of our country is good government in the twenty-six counties, and such social and economic conditions here as will attract the majority in the six counties to throw in their lot with us.[25]

Partition continued to take a back seat to his quest for sovereignty in 1932–7. 'We have no plan', he again admitted in the Dáil in May 1935, that could 'inevitably bring about the union of this country'.[26] He made the same admission privately to Maurice

Moynihan, then the secretary to the government, in January 1938 in the context of his forthcoming negotiations with British ministers.

Those negotiations laid bare the scale of de Valera's impotence on the partition issue. 'On his return to Dublin on board the Holyhead to Dun Laoghaire mail-boat . . . he could not hide his genuine disappointment [at] having failed to secure any concessions on partition.' Despite, or perhaps because of, that disappointment he immediately initiated 'a new Fianna Fáil anti-partition campaign in Great Britain and Northern Ireland' because 'he would at the very least give the impression that Fianna Fáil offered the best chance of ending partition. Propaganda, therefore, became his preferred policy.' In effect this was what Stephen Kelly has described as 'the pre-emptive strike to curtail any anticipated backlash, both within Fianna Fáil and from the wider nationalist community, concerning his inability to secure concessions on partition'. His main ally in this campaign was Frank Aiken, his minister for defence, whom he appointed as chairman of the party's publicity sub-committee.[27] Aiken's republican credentials as the former chief of staff of the IRA who had called off its armed offensive at the end of the civil war were impeccable and his South Armagh background seemed initially reassuring to Northern nationalists. From de Valera's perspective, moreover, Aiken's unquestioning personal loyalty was an added bonus – something that could not be said of Seán MacEntee, who came from Belfast and who contemplated resignation during the 1938 negotiations because he disagreed with de Valera's handling of the issue of Northern Ireland.

Alarmed by the resolutions from party members that 'poured into his office' during the negotiations 'denouncing any settlement which failed to solve the problem of partition',[28] de Valera initially assumed 'responsibility for co-ordinating the campaign' and 'devised the constitution, rules and regulations for the Anti-Partition of Ireland League of Great Britain'.[29] This was in keeping with his determination to retain absolute control of Northern Ireland policy in his own hands while keeping Northern nationalists at arm's length and resisting all proposals that Fianna Fáil should organise branches in Northern Ireland.

Éamon de Valera's attitude towards Northern Ireland found its most significant expression in February 1939 in a senate debate on a motion moved by an Anglophile and independent senator, Frank MacDermot, that Northern policy pay more heed to unionist 'sentiments and interests':

I would not tomorrow, for the sake of a united Ireland, give up the policy of trying to make this a really Irish Ireland – not by any means . . . I believe that as long as the language remains you have a distinguishing characteristic of nationality which will enable the nation to persist. If you lose the language, the danger is that there would be absorption . . . There is another price I would not pay. Suppose we were to get unity in the country provided we were to give up the principles that are here in this first article of the constitution – 'the sovereign right of the nation to choose its own form of government to determine its relations with other nations and to develop its life, political, economic and cultural, in accordance with its own genius and traditions' – I would not sacrifice that right, because without that right you have not freedom at all. Although freedom for a part of this island is not the freedom we want – the freedom we would like to have, this freedom for a portion of it, freedom to develop and to keep the kernel of the Irish nation is something and something that I would not sacrifice, if by sacrificing it we were to get a united Ireland and that united Ireland was not free to determine its own form of government, to determine its relations with other countries. Our people have the same right as any other people to determine these vital matters for themselves and they ought not to surrender them in advance to anybody or for any consideration . . . even the consideration of a united Ireland.[30]

De Valera instructed that 2,000 copies of this speech be printed and distributed as a government white paper. There could be no clearer proof that he intended the speech as official policy and as a definitive statement of his views on the relationship between independence and unity.[31] It was also designed for international consumption: in August 1940, in an interview for the *Christian Science Monitor* published in Boston, he explained that 'he had laid out the basis of his war-time policy some seven months before the outbreak of war. He had stated in the Senate that unity could not be purchased at a price which would indicate taking from the Irish nation the right to decide for itself whether or not it would participate in a war.'[32]

His argument that unity must always be subordinate to independence likewise explains why de Valera did not respond positively to the British offer, made in their darkest days of June 1940, of their immediate support for the principle of a 'United Ireland' in return for that united Ireland immediately entering the war as a British ally. The offer was conveyed by Malcolm Mac-Donald who came to Dublin three times – on 17, 21 and 26 June. MacDonald reported that de Valera had spelled out the constraints on his freedom of manoeuvre with remarkable frankness in their initial conversation:

Too many Irishmen actually thought that the Germans would make them more free. Prejudice against Britain was still strong, it would still take a long time to remove such an old sentiment. Indeed, his countrymen would actually fight with greater zeal if we were the first to violate Eire's neutrality than they would if the Germans were the first aggressors. He was only able to keep national unity at its present unprecedented level by making it clear that the government would resist whichever belligerent invaded the country.[33]

The discussions were lengthy, courteous and amicable but went nowhere. Independence so hard won and so recently achieved would not be so soon surrendered in return for a promise that, in the face of unionist opposition, the British might well be unable (or even, if and when the crisis passed, unwilling) to overcome: and this at a moment when, as John Bowman has pointed out, 'the Irish political élite was convinced that Britain was unlikely to win the war.'[34] Joe Walshe was a case in point: 'Britain's Inevitable

Defeat' was the heading of a memorandum he sent to de Valera on 21 June that began, 'Britain's defeat has been placed beyond all doubt.' De Valera reaffirmed his readiness 'to go as far as he could' in co-operating 'short of publicly compromising the country's neutrality' but told MacDonald that 'his countrymen would not believe that if they came into the war there would be a united Ireland at the end of it. On the contrary, they would feel that at the end we [the British] should say that Ulster must still maintain her independence of the rest of Ireland because she had entered the war at the very beginning.'[35] Another factor was de Valera's fear, of which he had spoken to Neville Chamberlain some months before the war began, that 'his position might rapidly come to resemble that of Mr Redmond in the Great War when the latter lost the support of the *majority* in Ireland through his loyalty to the Empire'.[36] 'MacDonald's report of his visit is discouraging,' wrote Chamberlain in his diary. 'The de Valera people are afraid we are going to lose, and don't want to be involved with us.'[37]

Sovereignty, as always, was the real sticking point, as de Valera explained to Chamberlain in his formal reply on 4 July:

The plan would involve our entry into the war. That is a course for which we could not accept responsibility. Our people would be quite un-prepared for it, and Dáil Éireann would certainly reject it.

We are, of course, aware that the policy of neutrality has its dangers, but, on the other hand, departure from it would involve us in dangers greater still.

The plan would commit us definitely to an immediate abandonment of our neutrality . . . it gives no guarantee that in the end we would have a united Ireland, unless indeed concessions were made to Lord Craigavon, opposed to the sentiments and aspirations of the great majority of the Irish people.

Our present Constitution represents the limits to which we believe our people are prepared to go to meet the sentiments of the Northern Unionists.

The terms of de Valera's reply 'were not unexpected', admitted Chamberlain when Dulanty handed him the letter next day, but he took some comfort from the assurance that de Valera 'would fight' if the Germans invaded Ireland – Dulanty reminded him of de Valera's 'unequivocal statements long before the war that he would not allow our territory to be made the base of attack on Britain'. Chamberlain's closing remark, that 'he supposed we must continue on our present lines and hope for the best', serves as an epigram for the conduct of Irish–British relations for the rest of the war.[38]

Winston Churchill's melodramatic telegram to de Valera when the Americans entered the war after Pearl Harbor – 'Now is your chance. Now or never. "A Nation once again". Am very ready to meet you at any time' – fell on still stonier ground because while de Valera had liked and admired Chamberlain, he neither liked nor trusted Churchill. 'Our opinion', recalled Joe Walshe who had to arrange for Sir John Maffey to deliver the message to de Valera at his home at four o'clock in the morning, 'was that Churchill had been imbibing heavily that night after the news of Pearl Harbor . . . and that his effusion flowed into the message.' Maffey explained that 'it was an invitation to go over to see him [Churchill]', a suggestion that de Valera described as 'unwise; that it would probably be misunderstood by our people . . . [who] were determined on their attitude of neutrality'; he saw 'no opportunity at the moment of securing unity'. De Valera subsequently suggested that a visit to Dublin by Lord Cranborne, secretary of state for the dominions, 'would be the best way towards a fuller understanding of our position'. But that, too, proved fruitless. De Valera's scepticism was justified for, as Cranborne pompously explained to Maffey on 9 December, Churchill's use of the phrase 'a nation once again' 'certainly contemplated no deal over partition' but meant that 'by coming into the war Ireland would regain her soul'.[39]

The Second World War, then, affirmed rather than altered the order of priorities in de Valera's Ireland: independence first, unity a poor second. As the war wore on, it became ever more apparent that, independence achieved, partition would increasingly assume the aspect in Irish nationalist eyes of the last cause of contention with the British. In October 1944, after the successful Allied invasion of Europe, the Fianna Fáil *ard fheis* resolved that the abolition of partition should be the first plank of the party's post-war programme.

The lack of any progress on the anti-partitionist front since 1938 reinforced de Valera's determination to keep personal control of his government's Northern policy for fear of being outflanked by more radical republicans. This fear had been exacerbated by the threat posed by the IRA's declaration of war on the United Kingdom and its bombing campaign in British cities between January 1939 and March 1940 – one IRA bomb, in Coventry, killed five and wounded 70. De Valera responded with the Treason Act (providing for the death penalty for treason as defined in Article 39 of the constitution) and with the Offences Against the State Act; this gave a broader definition of unlawful association and the government promptly declared the IRA an illegal organisation; it also provided for a special criminal court, composed of five military officers, which functioned from 1939 until 1946.

De Valera suffered his greatest humiliation at the hands of the IRA on Christmas Eve 1939 when it seized over a million rounds of ammunition in a raid on the Magazine Fort in the Phoenix Park. The Dáil met in special session in the first days of 1940 and passed an amendment to the Emergency Powers Act empowering the government to intern alleged subversives on suspicion and without trial in detention camps at the army's headquarters in the Curragh. Such a stringent measure was necessary, claimed de Valera, because the IRA was ready to use armed force 'against the organised forces in the state. They are prepared to embroil the state, if they think it accords with their purposes, with neighbouring states.'[40] De Valera's real concern was that Churchill's government might use the IRA's establishing links with Germany as an excuse to infringe Irish neutrality, and his apprehensions were aggravated at the end of January by a report from Dulanty that the British police had received information 'of the possibility of an attack by the IRA on Sir John Maffey'.[41] A gunfight in the centre of Dublin between the IRA and armed detectives thought to be taking dispatches from Maffey to the department of external affairs brought matters to a head. The government's 'policy of patience has failed and is over', warned de Valera in a special radio broadcast on 8 May 1940. He also warned that the IRA would not be allowed to continue 'their policy of sabotage. They have set the law at defiance. The law will be enforced against them. If the present law is not sufficient, it will be strengthened; and in the last resort, if no other law will suffice, then the government will invoke the ultimate law – the safety of the people'.[42] The outcome of the ensuing trial of strength between de Valera and the IRA was predictable. Ultimate law – the policy of executions carried out after a trial by military tribunal and of internment without trial in the Curragh – prevailed.

In November 1939 de Valera's response to an IRA hunger strike had been unyielding. 'We are in a time of great peril,' he told the Dáil. What was at stake was whether or not the IRA would succeed in destroying Irish independence and 'the fruits of all the efforts that have been made for the last twenty-five years . . . The government had been faced with the alternative of two evils. We have had to choose the lesser, and the lesser evil is to see men die rather than that the safety of the whole community should be in danger'.[43] He was compassionate, however, when told that one hunger striker, Patrick McGrath, was dying in great pain and instructed that he should be removed from Mountjoy prison to hospital, where he subsequently recovered and was released. But when nine IRA prisoners began another hunger strike in February 1940, de Valera's patience was exhausted and two died before the hunger strike ended on 16 April. In August two detectives were shot dead when they entered a house occupied by McGrath and another IRA suspect, both of whom were arrested, convicted of murder and executed. Appeals for clemency fell on deaf ears; de Valera believed that his act of clemency in November 1939 had resulted in six deaths rather than one. There were no more IRA hunger strikes during the war.

A shrewd unionist, Wilfrid Spender, looking at Dublin from Stormont in 1938, remarked that 'that the Southern Irish voter is always "agin the government" and it suits de Valera that they should be against the British government rather than against himself'.[44] That he was so persistently represented by the British government as *its* enemy, whether in opposition in the 1920s or during the economic war or in his confrontations with Churchill during and after the Second World War, explains the IRA's inability to undermine him as he and other republicans had undermined John Redmond during the Great War.

The end of the war left Ireland isolated: an outsider, if not a pariah, from the perspective of the victorious powers. The sense of isolation, coupled with de Valera's innate conservatism, explains why his government moved only slowly to dismantle the apparatus of emergency powers. A cabinet meeting on 8 May 1945 (VE Day, marking the end of the war in Europe) decided that all emergency-power orders should be referred to the relevant departments for examination rather than revoked. It was agreed, however, that press, postal, telegraph and telephone censorship should end immediately; orders prohibiting the photography of military installations and the use of carrier pigeons were also revoked.[45]

Allied alienation, of which Churchill's attack on Irish neutrality in his radio broadcast was but the most vehement British expression, was mirrored by anti-Irish sentiment in Washington. In March 1945 the department of state advised David Gray, the American minister in Dublin, that Ireland would not be invited to participate in the inaugural conference of the United Nations in San Francisco. If Gray were asked to explain why, he should 'reply orally' that only those countries that had declared war on the Axis powers by 1 March had been invited and that 'Ireland's adherence to a policy inconsistent with its historic bonds of blood and friendship with this and other United Nations has made necessary this decision'. But de Valera was determined not to curry favour with the Allies and was, in any event, sceptical about the value of establishing a new world organisation in the post-war triumphalist atmosphere. His views, voiced in the rarefied forum of the College Historical Society at Trinity College Dublin, where he was proposing the vote of thanks to Michael Yeats's auditorial address on 'The Small Nations', were duly publicised in the *Irish Press*. He questioned whether what was being proposed to replace the League of Nations was an improvement. While he recognised that 'the democratic character of the League' had inhibited 'its ability to take action when action should have been taken', he felt that the proposals represented 'a swing round from the democratic to the dictatorial form of organisation. What is being substituted now is a dictatorship of the great powers'. He accordingly instructed Robert Brennan, the Irish minister in Washington, to reply to any questions about whether Ireland would attend the San Francisco conference, if invited, by saying that '"Ireland's position as a neutral state is well known. In any case [the] question is purely hypothetical and there is nothing to be gained by such speculation." Since we are not one of the United Nations, we do not expect [an] invitation and it would be [a] bad thing to give the remotest impression that we want one'.[46] The Americans responded in kind: Joseph Grew, the acting head of the state department, told David Gray to adopt an attitude towards Ireland 'as frigidly indifferent as its government has seen fit to adopt towards the aspirations of the United Nations' – and this was even before de Valera's provocative visit to the German legation to offer condolences on the news of Hitler's death infuriated the Americans to the point where the state department came close to advising President Truman to break off diplomatic relations with Ireland. One American immune to the hostile resentment in Washington towards de Valera was Joseph P. Kennedy, the father of the future president, John Fitzgerald Kennedy, who had become acquainted with the Irish leader while ambassador in London from 1938 to 1940. In a letter in August

1945 thanking Gray for his hospitality to his son during a post-war holiday in Ireland, Joe Kennedy wrote of his 'great confidence in de Valera's honesty of purpose. He seems to me to be one of the very few heads of government today who isn't an opportunist. This policy may be wrong, but I am sure he is honest in what he thinks.'[47]

Speaking in the Dáil on 26 June 1946, de Valera reiterated his conviction that Ireland was losing nothing by not applying to join the United Nations. But all changed in a matter of weeks because the British and Americans, alarmed at the Russian campaign for the admission of constituent Soviet republics and their other satellite states as the cold war deepened, decided that their own best interests lay in encouraging neutral European states such as Sweden, Portugal and Ireland to apply. On 5 July 1946 the British government duly authorised the dominions secretary to arrange for the Irish government to be informed that, if it applied to join the United Nations, the British would back the application.

Although de Valera had consistently refused even to explore the possibility of applying until he knew that the British and Americans would support an Irish application, he acted decisively once he knew their support was assured. On 11 July he circulated a six-page memorandum to government that again illustrates his penchant for taking major foreign-policy decisions without prior discussion with his cabinet colleagues; the memorandum was also noteworthy for what it omitted rather than for what it contained. It merely noted the Potsdam declaration of August 1945 when the British, Americans and Russians had indicated their readiness to support applications from neutral states. It questioned whether any former neutral could rely on the support of all three powers and suggested that applications would be considered less on their merits and more with regard to 'their probable effect on the distribution of political forces and voting power'. Otherwise the memorandum was little more than a potted guide to the United Nations, stressing what distinguished it from the League of

Nations. It said nothing of the supportive communication of 4 July that de Valera had received from the dominions office.

On 19 July the government obediently approved his wording of the resolution 'that Dáil Éireann, being willing to assent to acceptance of the obligations contained in the Charter signed at San Francisco on the 26th June 1945, recommends the government to take steps with a view to Ireland's admission to membership of the United Nations Organisation as soon as they consider it opportune to do so'. For de Valera, sovereignty was, as always, the yardstick: 'The decision as to whether we should or should not enter into this organisation ultimately resolves itself into the one question,' he told the Dáil. 'Is the independence and freedom which we have achieved and the independence and freedom to which we aspire for the whole country likely to be better guaranteed by our being a member of this organisation or by our not being a member of it?'[48] The unpreparedness of political and public opinion to discuss a subject that the government had until then resolutely avoided explains the bizarre character of the debate on the resolution on 24 and 25 July. Speakers criticised the UN Charter 'in the light of what might be called Catholic social principles and Catholic international principles'; one deputy argued that Ireland's role should be 'to impregnate these counsels with something of the Christian spirit which is so lacking today'; another, Liam Cosgrave, the future minister for external affairs (1954–7) and taoiseach (1973–7), was critical of the fact that 'the Vatican has not been invited to participate in the framing of the Charter'. Partition, inevitably, was also a favoured theme; here debate centred on the perils of what Dr T. F. O'Higgins described as 'asking dagoes and blacks and yellow men and all kinds of foreigners to settle an Irish question'. But the most interesting aspect of the debate was de Valera's reaction to the accusation from Deputy Oliver J. Flanagan that he had changed his mind about Ireland applying to join the UN because the British had told him to do so. Although he admitted in closing the debate that he had received a communication from the British, he refused to read it to the Dáil, saying only that it intimated that the Potsdam declaration applied to Ireland and 'that in line with that declaration they would naturally support our application'. He instead insisted that it was the changed attitudes of other neutral states that had caused him to change his mind, making much of the fact that he 'knew a number of other nations were applying because that appeared in the public press about the 9th or 10th July'. He made no reference to his meeting on 5 July with the British chargé d'affaires when he was given the dominions office memorandum.

De Valera's explanation, understandable in terms of his determination not to be thought to be acting at the behest of the British, was at best disingenuous. But his insistence that it was 'impossible to be enthusiastic' about the deficiencies of the United Nations in Irish circumstances was genuine. The Irish application, he told the Dáil, was no more than a pragmatic decision weighed in 'the balance of the pros and cons' and based on a lukewarm belief that 'we might be able to protect our own interests better inside the organisation than outside it'. Such apathy accounts for the indifference with which de Valera reacted when the application was rejected by Russian veto in the security council. 'Comment is unnecessary; the position is self-explanatory,' responded de Valera when asked for his reaction. 'All I wish to do is to express thanks to the representatives of the nations who supported our application.' Freddie Boland, who had succeeded Joe Walshe as secretary of the department of external affairs in May 1946, wrote in similar terms to the heads of all Irish missions abroad. 'Just as there was very little enthusiasm for our application, there was little heart-burning when the application failed.' It had 'occasioned neither surprise nor disappointment'. Ireland then had diplomatic relations with only nine of the fifty-one members of the United Nations and had no immediate plans for extending diplomatic representation to the Soviet Union despite that being the reason they had given for their veto. A senior British minister, Herbert Morrison, who paid a courtesy call on de Valera while returning from an Irish holiday in September 1946, told his own cabinet colleagues of how he had been struck by his 'shrug of the shoulders attitude' when he had commiserated with him on the fate of the Irish application. He told Morrison that he had 'thought it right to make the application but he did not appear to be unduly disturbed at its rejection . . . It was not likely to cause him any embarrassment among his people.'[49]

Nor did it and partition now reassumed what had become its primacy of place among Éamon de Valera's preoccupations. Stephen Kelly has shown how he manipulated the procedures of the Fianna Fáil *ard fheis* in 1945 and in 1946 to 'ensure that the number one partition resolution at both party conferences called for the commencement of a worldwide anti-partition campaign. This was a preemptive strike . . . to ensure that an anti-partition propaganda campaign was to form the nucleus of Fianna Fáil's official Northern Ireland policy in the post-war era.' In October 1946 he also established a new sub-committee of the party's national executive on partition. But the sub-committee met only rarely and was merely 'a tactical ploy . . . to create the impression that the Fianna Fáil hierarchy were listening to party supporters' concerns on the lack of progress on partition.' The reality, Stephen Kelly argues persuasively, was that 'the committee had no authority to decide the party's partition strategy; this always remained the sole responsibility of de Valera. This episode highlighted the degree of control that de Valera held over his party colleagues and emphasised his obsession with maintaining absolute control over Northern Ireland policy.'[50]

In July 1946 this obsession was sharpened by the establishment of a new political party, Clann na Poblachta: a radical, republican party dedicated, according to its inaugural declaration, 'to work for the achievement of republican ideals by purely political means'. That commitment to purely political means was necessary because, as had been the case with Fianna Fáil in 1926, the party was composed largely of former members of the IRA. Its leader was Seán MacBride, son of Major John MacBride (executed in 1916) and

Maud Gonne, the inspiration for many of William Butler Yeats's greatest love poems. Briefly their chief of staff in 1936, MacBride had broken with the IRA when he accepted the 1937 constitution and opposed their bombing campaign in Britain in 1938–9. He then became a barrister who defended many of his former IRA comrades and he appeared at inquests for the next of kin of IRA hunger-strikers who died in 1940 and in 1946. That was a crucial factor enabling him to become leader of the new party, which had its origins in committees formed to help released republican prisoners who had been interned during World War II.

MacBride posed a serious threat to de Valera on his republican flank: the new party wanted to repeal the External Relations Act of 1936 (the sole remaining link with the British Commonwealth) and to pursue a more vigorous campaign against partition. Its programme also stressed social issues and the evils of emigration, unemployment and rising prices. Above all the Clann sought to take advantage of the post-war disillusion with a joyless government and to capitalise on the sense of boredom born of Fianna Fáil's having been continuously in office since 1932. The new party spread quickly, establishing branches countrywide. Austerity; food and fuel shortages during the bitterly cold winter of 1946–7; a rash of strikes and other industrial disputes, most notably a prolonged strike of primary-school teachers between March and October 1946 – these were but some of the factors contributing to the government's growing unpopularity. The Clann won over many former Fianna Fáil voters, especially from the ranks of embittered teachers who played a key role in its organisation. Its first electoral success came on 30 October 1947 when it defeated Fianna Fáil in two out of three by-elections, enabling MacBride to enter the Dáil. But de Valera pre-empted the prospect of its building on those gains and further heightening its public profile by calling a snap election in February 1948.

Although Fianna Fáil then lost ground to Clann na Poblachta, its percentage share of the vote was the same as in the 1943 election and its number of seats (67) one higher; so initially it seemed likely that de Valera would again retain his grip on power. But in 1948 there was a will to power among the opposition parties without parallel since 1932. Parties as disparate as the pro-Commonwealth Fine Gael, the republican Clann na Poblachta, two separate Labour parties and an agrarian party (Clann na Talmhan) united behind a common election slogan, PUT THEM OUT, and one observer of the election in Mayo described how 'the big message was: put Dev out anyway and give us – and yourselves – a chance'.

And put Dev out they did: an inter-party government with John A. Costello of Fine Gael as taoiseach, William Norton (the leader of the Labour Party) as tánaiste and Seán MacBride as minister for external affairs took office on 18 February 1948.

13

Marking Time, 1948–59

'I am bored,' Bismarck once said. 'The great things are done. The German Reich is made.' Although de Valera never became bored with the exercise of power, much the same might be said of him at the end of the Second World War. The great things were done. The Irish state was made. For de Valera, as for Bismarck, all policy was foreign policy and by 1945 his foreign policy objectives had been achieved. Even his most ardent apologists effectively acknowledge that he did little thereafter; his authorised biography by Lord Longford and T. P. O'Neill devotes a mere 21 of its 500 pages to the years between 1945 and 1959 – and many of those are given over to a recital of his health problems and his travels abroad.

De Valera had no appetite for playing the role of leader of the opposition in the Dáil when he lost power in 1948. 'He'll not get my left flank,' he said of Seán MacBride to his son on the day the Dáil reassembled.[1] De Valera's response to Clann na Poblachta's criticisms of Fianna Fáil for having no plan to end partition was immediately to launch a spectacular worldwide propaganda campaign grandiloquently described as putting an anti-partition girdle round the earth. Accompanied by Frank Aiken, he left Ireland on 8 March and, after a month in the United States, moved on to Australia and New Zealand (27 April–11 June) and then to India (14–16 June, see plate 16); there followed anti-partition tours of Britain in October and November.

MacBride's reaction vindicated de Valera's suspicion that their respective parties were bent on outdoing one another in anti-partitionist posturing. 'He sought to expunge all references to de Valera-inspired literature in the government's promotion of

Ireland's foreign policy, including anti-partition publicity, and personally forbade the provision of Irish diplomatic facilities and support to de Valera and other members of the opposition on visits abroad.'²

Some of the most senior Irish diplomats, whose attitudes towards their former minister, under whom they had served for the previous sixteen years, ranged from the admiring to the adulatory, were outraged by such pettiness. 'Dear Chief, I want to let you know how upset I am at the news – that for the time being anyhow – you are not the Taoiseach and my Minister,' began a handwritten letter of 20 February from Seán Nunan, the Irish minister in Washington. 'The result was a great disappointment and shock to me, as well as to your many friends here who were looking forward to your coming to give the necessary drive to the anti-partition movement.' Nunan's shock and disappointment can only have been exacerbated by an eight-point list of instructions telegrammed on 3 March by Freddie Boland, who had succeeded Joe Walshe as secretary of the department, spelling out in humiliating detail how he and Ireland's consular representatives in the United States should behave during the forthcoming visit. The reaction of Walshe, who as the secretary of the department had worked hand in glove with de Valera from 1932 until 1946, and who now had to prepare for a two-day visit of de Valera and Aiken to Rome in his capacity as the Irish ambassador to the Vatican, was scathing. 'I must, first of all, make sure that the Government suffers no loss of prestige in the eyes of the Holy See by any apparent – even remotely apparent – lack of generosity towards a beaten foe,' he wrote to Boland on 3 June. 'I shall be asked by the Vatican if they are staying here, and if [I] have to reply they are staying in a hotel there will be no concealment of their surprise.' Apart from the likelihood of a bad reaction in the Vatican and in Rome, added Walshe, 'the Minister would, perhaps, consider another important factor, namely that of the extent to which I can control the situation in the alternative circumstances.'³

The commonest criticism of de Valera's propagandist campaign, whether in the United States, Australia or the United Kingdom, was that he was preaching only to the converted. Hugh Delargy, the British Labour politician who was chairman of the AntiPartition of Ireland League of Great Britain, remembered 'enormous and enthusiastic meetings . . . in the biggest cities' but he thought that 'they were all flops. They were not political meetings at all. They were tribal rallies: tribesmen met to greet the Old Chieftain.' In such circumstances it was, perhaps, unsurprising that some of de Valera's speeches – notably a speech in Manchester in late November 1948 – were inflammatory and seemed to contemplate the use of force if all else failed; indeed some felt his campaign ultimately 'provoked the younger generation in Ireland to sympathise with IRA violence'. One such was Seán MacEntee, his cabinet colleague from Belfast; another was Archbishop John Charles McQuaid, who privately believed 'that de Valera's speeches were "all humbug"'.[4]

Anti-partitionism was temporarily forced into the background, however, when John A. Costello made the utterly unexpected announcement in Ottawa on 7 September 1948 that the inter-party government was going to repeal the External Relations Act of 1936. De Valera had contemplated repealing the Act before the election when he told the British representative in Dublin, Lord Rugby (formerly Sir John Maffey) that it had caused him 'constant criticism and humiliation' and had not served the hoped-for purpose of bringing about some sort of association with Northern Ireland.[5] On 21 October his attorney general, Cearbhall Ó Dalaigh, had drawn up a draft bill, 'The Presidential (International Powers and Functions) Bill, 1947' and an accompanying memorandum that also referred to the possible repeal of the External Relations Act.[6] But there the matter rested and, although Clann na Poblachta had been the only party to campaign on the repeal of the Act in the election, MacBride had not made it a condition of his party's entering government and he was as surprised as the British by Costello's speech in Ottawa. During a Dáil debate on 6 August

1948, however, when William Norton, the tánaiste and Labour Party leader, had said, 'It would do our national self-respect good both at home and abroad if we were to proceed without delay to abolish the External Relations Act', de Valera had retorted, 'Go ahead . . . You will get no opposition from us.' He was true to his word when the Republic of Ireland Bill was introduced in the Dáil in November 1948: he acknowledged that he had already concluded that the Act 'would have to be repealed because of the purely mischievous misrepresentation which surrounded it and because it was misunderstood accordingly'. He also explained that he had hesitated about repeal only 'because one of the purposes which that Act was intended to serve was to form, if possible, a bridge by which the separated counties might come to union with the rest of Ireland'.[7] Publicly, de Valera welcomed the end of controversy about Ireland's constitutional status, but privately he questioned the wisdom of the inter-party government's interpretation that the Act marked a final breach with the Commonwealth. Asked by Churchill in 1953 (see plate 15) if he would have taken Ireland out of the Commonwealth as Costello and MacBride then had done, de Valera replied 'no': 'He had no objection ever to Ireland being a member of the commonwealth. What he had an objection to was an oath of allegiance to the king as king of the commonwealth . . . He had come to the conclusion that the commonwealth was a very useful association for us because the commonwealth countries (especially Canada, Australia, and New Zealand) had a strong interest in Ireland.'[8] Again, de Valera reverted to partition and challenged Churchill to explain its continuance. Churchill – who had already tried to explain that a British government 'could never put people out of the United Kingdom so long as the majority in the Six Counties wished to remain part of it' – dismissively replied, 'Politics, my dear fellow, politics.'[9]

The fantasy of reunification loomed larger once the appetite for unambiguous sovereignty was satiated by the Republic of Ireland Act, which came into effect on Easter Monday 1949. In the meantime, the inter-party government's rejection of the invitation to join the North Atlantic Treaty Organisation (NATO) in January 1949, like the Republic of Ireland Act, affirmed its inability to escape from de Valera's agenda. He endorsed MacBride's explicit linkage of partition with neutrality when he told a press conference in March 1949 that, if he were in power and 'if the partition business were out of the way', he, too, 'would advocate entrance into the pact if Ireland was united'.[10] The unanimous if futile nationalist demand for reunification had also led to the formation of an all-party, anti-partitionist Mansion House committee on 27 January, and two of de Valera's future biographers, Frank Gallagher and T. P. O'Neill, were among the civil servants seconded to participate in what proved to be no more than a propaganda exercise churning out anti-unionist bombast. But shortly after he had returned as taoiseach in June 1951, de Valera publicly revealed in the Dáil that he had no illusions about the prospects of reunification: 'If I am asked, "Have you a solution for [partition]?" in the sense "Is there a line of policy which you propose to pursue which you think can, within a reasonable time, be effective?", I have to say that I have not and neither has anybody else.'[11]

Éamon de Valera's last years in office as taoiseach – from June 1951 until June 1954 and from March 1957 until June 1959 – are notable less for what he did than for what he did not do. Now that he had achieved his foreign-policy objectives and had nothing left to prove with regard to sovereignty, he appointed Frank Aiken, the most absolutist of his ministerial colleagues on neutrality, in his place as minister for external affairs in both governments. Ireland had finally been admitted to the United Nations in 1955 and although de Valera made no attempt to become personally involved, he supported Aiken's identification with a policy of non-alignment and vigorously rejected criticisms of that policy, most notably with regard to the recognition of communist China. Criticism was most vociferous in the United States where it was endorsed by Cardinal Spellman and other Catholic prelates.

'Dev would drive you mad,' recalled the unfailingly equable Jack Lynch of his first ministerial appointment as a parliamentary secretary in 1951 when one of his responsibilities was liaising with de Valera in drafting answers to parliamentary questions. 'He'd keep on drafting and redrafting the answers for ever. In the end I gave up dealing with the PQs as a bad job.'[12] The ever pedantic taoiseach had too little to do but his diminished interest in the course of domestic politics in the 1950s did not extend to church–state relations, where he retained a close personal control. The most notable example was his micro-management of health legislation in the aftermath of the mother-and-child crisis of 1951, which had precipitated the collapse of the coalition government.[13] The bishops had been slow to react to Fianna Fáil's earlier Health Act of August 1947; not until two months later did they privately communicate their reservations to de Valera in a statement that defined the position to which they adhered throughout the next six years of controversy over health legislation. It objected to the assumption by 'the Minister in the Health Act' of 'certain absolute, unlimited powers where, according to Catholic principles, his powers are derivative and subsidiary' and qualified by 'certain fundamental rights which the State must respect' – the rights of the individual person, of the family, of the medical profession and of the voluntary hospitals. Four months passed before de Valera replied, on 16 February 1948, twelve days after the general election that, two days later, put Fianna Fáil out of office. Although the delay denied the hierarchy the opportunity of taking de Valera to task for the 1947 Act, the issues remained unresolved when he returned to power in June 1951 with a declared policy of extending health services, including a mother-and-child service, in accordance with the 1947 Act. Another year passed before the minister for health, Dr James Ryan, published a white paper outlining his plans. Shortly afterwards, in August 1952, de Valera's eyesight further deteriorated when he suffered a detached retina; it was only after six operations in Utrecht that the retina was reattached and he did not return to

Dublin until December; thereafter he had only peripheral vision, restricting all his movements except in places he knew well. In September, Ryan, at the request of Archbishop John Charles McQuaid, called at the archbishop's palace in Drumcondra to discuss his forthcoming legislation. There followed other meetings between Ryan and an episcopal committee on which the Bishop of Galway, Dr Michael Browne, was the most outspoken member. His most 'far-fetched and ridiculous' objection, in Ryan's words, was to the powers enabling medical officers of health to detain persons suffering from infectious diseases, to which he reacted by painting a picture that might have been drawn from the pages of Orwell or Kafka 'of an unscrupulous and vindictive medical officer of health who had power under this section to kidnap his enemy and then detain him against his will in hospital'. De Valera was alerted as the controversy rumbled on and kept in close touch with Seán Lemass, who was acting as taoiseach in his absence, and he was sufficiently concerned to telephone from Utrecht on 11 November looking for Ryan's report on his discussion with the bishops. But he had already been back in the taoiseach's office for two months when the bill was finally circulated on 6 February 1953.

All the evidence suggests, however, that de Valera and his cabinet colleagues were satisfied that the bill as published took sufficient account of the bishops' representations to prevent another confrontation between church and state. But that belief was shattered on 16 April 1953 when the hierarchy sent the taoiseach, for his information, a copy of a statement signed by their chairman, Cardinal D'Alton, Archbishop of Armagh, 'which they are addressing to the faithful and releasing to the press' for publication on Saturday, 18 April. Although the statement began by welcoming the proposed repeal of aspects of the 1947 Act they had found repugnant, it then listed a series of the points at which 'the bill is not in harmony with Catholic teaching' and concluded that 'all these measures constitute a big step towards the complete socialisation of medicine'.

It was less the substance of the statement than the fact that it had already been released to the press that burst like a bombshell over Government Buildings. Uninhibited by the fact that he was now virtually blind – 'I hate to be a lame duck like this,' he had written to Lemass in September 1952[14] – de Valera's reaction was instantaneous and dramatic. As soon as he received the statement, at about eleven o'clock on Friday, 17 April, he telephoned Seán T. O'Kelly, his former tánaiste and then the president of Ireland, and asked him to arrange an immediate meeting between himself – de Valera – and Cardinal D'Alton. This proved impossible, so the president instead arranged for the taoiseach to meet the cardinal in Drogheda that afternoon in a parish presbytery after he had attended a confirmation ceremony.

Éamon de Valera had known John D'Alton for over fifty years, since 1899 when they had been classmates in Blackrock College – Archbishop John Charles McQuaid, his erstwhile confidant among the bishops, was then out of the country at a eucharistic congress in Australia. De Valera was accompanied by a reluctant Dr Ryan 'whose own instinct was to fight'.[15] The taoiseach, too, was also ready for confrontation if his attempt at conciliation failed and he had already instructed that a selection of documents be sent to Joe Walshe, the Irish ambassador to the Holy See, via the diplomatic bag on the next Aer Lingus flight to Rome. Walshe, who had been de Valera's interlocutor with the Vatican over the religious articles in the 1937 constitution, was instructed to be ready 'to interpret rapidly and accurately' any further instructions he might be sent so that he might try to swing Vatican opinion against the Irish bishops if the need arose.

But de Valera wanted peace, not war. Having first expressed his astonishment at the bishops' statement, he told Cardinal D'Alton that the public would interpret it as meaning 'that there had been a breakdown in the discussions between the bishops and the government'. His assumption that the public would expect such discussions to precede the introduction of health legislation speaks volumes about his attitude to church–state relations. De Valera achieved his first objective when the cardinal agreed that the *Irish Independent* and the *Irish Press* should be immediately told on his authority to stop publication the next morning – the *Irish Times* had not been favoured with a copy of the statement since the bishops had clearly neither forgotten nor forgiven its role in publishing their correspondence with Dr Noel Browne, the minister for health, during the mother-and-child crisis of 1951. But the cardinal's concession came only after de Valera had agreed that there should be another meeting of ministers with the episcopal committee to resolve their differences.

As soon as he had returned from Drogheda that night, the taoiseach telephoned the president, Seán T. O'Kelly, and asked him if he would host such a meeting in Áras an Uachtaráin. The president agreed and it was arranged that the meeting would take place on the following Tuesday, 21 April, when the president also volunteered to host a luncheon. There are few more striking monuments to the special position of the Catholic Church in the 1937 constitution than that meeting in the official residence of the president of Ireland when the taoiseach headed a government delegation to meet a committee of bishops to rewrite those sections of the health bill to which the hierarchy took exception. Given that the president might be – and in the event was – called on to refer the bill to the supreme court for a decision on whether its provisions were constitutionally repugnant, it seems extraordinary that the constitutional impropriety of ministers and bishops meeting secretly to haggle over the terms of the bill under the president's roof seem to have occurred to no one. The explanation might be that, in de Valera's Ireland, the partnership between the authorities of church and state had become so intimate that the choice of the meeting place reflects no more than a desire, on the part of ministers, to avoid again going cap in hand to an archbishop's palace or a presbytery and, on the part of bishops, a wish to avoid the publicity and attendant criticism of interfering in government business that would have attached to their being seen trooping into Government Buildings.

The taoiseach opened the discussion by saying that he regarded the bishops 'as the authoritative teachers of faith and morals'. So explicit and sweeping an expression of obedience was as shrewd as it was deferential, given that his objective was to defuse the crisis. It worked. An additional sub-section of the bill was tabled under Ryan's name at the committee stage and he accepted the bishops' other amendments in principle. On 25 June, after the bishops' summer meeting in Maynooth and after Archbishop McQuaid's return from Australia, de Valera was advised that they had agreed not to publish their statement and the episode seemed at an end. But, after his return from Australia, Archbishop McQuaid won another amendment after yet another meeting in Áras an Uachtaráin on 7 July, tightening clinical teaching in Catholic medical schools and hospitals. Catholic doctors also mounted a last, unsuccessful challenge to the bill after it had completed all its stages and was awaiting the president's signature. But President O'Kelly took only twenty-four hours to reject their petition to refer it to the supreme court and on 25 October 1953 signed the bill into law without further delay.

The episode illustrates the continuing predominance of Éamon de Valera over his cabinet colleagues – including his former tánaiste, albeit that he was now the president of Ireland. The Drogheda meeting, in particular, showed that his capacity for swift capitulation if he sensed a threat to the authority of his government was unimpaired. The key to de Valera's handling of the crisis, as Eamonn McKee has observed, was that he 'understood the complexity and subtleties of the bishops' position' and believed 'that the best interests of church–state relations were served in private. The easy resolution of the issues at the meetings held in 1953 belied the notion of a conflict of interest and testified as much to de Valera's astuteness as to the political gaucheness of the bishops.'[16] On this, as on so many other occasions in the 1930s and

1940s, de Valera shaped government policy single-handedly and without prior discussion with his ministers; the cabinet merely endorsed what he had done after he had done it. Patrick Lynch, who was an assistant secretary in the taoiseach's department in 1951, concluded that the source of 'de Valera's maintenance of power was the fact that "he never told his colleagues anything"'.[17]

Nor should the episode be seen simply as a triumph of church over state. In political terms, the defeat de Valera was determined to avoid was the public denunciation of his government's health legislation by the Catholic bishops and he was prepared to amend the bill to that end. In so far as the 1953 Health Act was a product of consensus politics in church–state relations and in so far as it was enacted without any of the public controversy that had surrounded the coalition government's mother-and-child scheme in 1951, de Valera construed the outcome as a victory, not as a defeat, despite the fact that, unbeknownst to the public, he had chosen to dance to the bishops' tune.

De Valera's response to the boycott in Fethard-on-Sea in County Wexford in May 1957 – when a number of Catholic priests and bishops supported an economic boycott of Protestants caused by a local Protestant woman, Sheila Cloney, who was married to a Catholic farmer, refusing to send her children to the local Catholic school – reflects much the same modus operandi. The boycott immediately became international news and even featured in *Time* magazine. It occurred in the aftermath of a successful tour of the United States by the Jewish Fianna Fáil Lord Mayor of Dublin, Robert Briscoe, which had won praise as an example of Ireland's religious toleration when contrasted with the sectarian treatment of Catholics in Northern Ireland. Kevin McCarthy has shown how the prospect of the partition of Palestine 'bound de Valera to Briscoe in a unique way': he saw Briscoe's involvement in the New Zionist Organisation's mission to America 'as a unique opportunity to further highlight the continuing injustice of Irish partition'. British support for the Zionist cause also ensured that Briscoe shared de Valera's immunity to Anglophobia best illustrated by a vignette from the late 1920s when he asked two of his sons what they were playing in a corner of the room where he was having tea. '"Soldiers, Dad," was the reply. "We are attacking the English." Father replied: "Not the English, Ruairi; just say they're the enemy."'[18] His attitude was poles apart from many in Fianna Fáil, notably Dan Breen, one of the most rabidly Anglophobic Fianna Fáil deputies, who upbraided Briscoe for consorting with British contacts. Briscoe's response – 'it is a matter for your own conscience . . . that you are friendly and on visiting terms with the German and Italian Legations' – informing Breen that de Valera was 'fully aware of [his] activities', prompted a perfect expression of Anglophobia in its most virulent form: 'I hold the old Irish view . . . "You can't serve Ireland well without a hatred for England".'[19]

This was the wider context explaining de Valera's sense of outrage at the Fethard-on-Sea boycott. He 'was incensed at the damage being done to the national reputation and that a vicious little sectarian dispute was undermining the anti-partition campaign'. He brought the issue to cabinet on 31 May 1957 and said he was thinking of writing to Bishop Staunton, the local bishop, and of raising the issue with Archbishop McQuaid – Fethard was within his archiepiscopal province. His ministers responded with their customary docility and it was agreed that it should be left to the taoiseach to take 'such action as he might think best'. He went to see McQuaid in Drumcondra a fortnight later and while 'the Archbishop expressed a desire that the discussion between the Taoiseach and himself on the matter should be treated as strictly confidential', de Valera emerged from the meeting 'satisfied that he was now in a position to intervene in the dispute without McQuaid's opposing him'. He also took the precaution of sending McQuaid an advance, courtesy copy of his answer to a Dáil question on 4 July. It was his first public statement on the subject and an unequivocal condemnation of the boycott.

As Head of Government, I must speak . . . I regard this boycott as ill-conceived, ill-considered and futile . . . I regard it as unjust and cruel . . . I repudiate any suggestion that this boycott is typical of the attitude or conduct of our people . . . I beg of all who have regard for the fair name, good repute and well-being of our nation to use their influence to bring this deplorable affair to a speedy end.[20]

De Valera then did what he here urged others to do and used his influence to bring the boycott to an end. But he did so surreptitiously, again preferring to avoid anything in the nature of a public confrontation with the Catholic hierarchy, by working through Dr Jim Ryan, the minister for finance in his last government and a deputy for County Wexford who knew the Cloney family and who had briefed him from the beginning of the boycott. A secret deal was brokered in Ryan's house in Delgany, County Wicklow, by Anthony Hederman, a young barrister and a member of the Fianna Fáil national executive, who later became attorney general (1977–81). The essence of the deal was that Hederman agreed with members of the vigilance committee enforcing the boycott that it would end on the understanding that the Cloney children would come home by Christmas and that there would 'be no more talk of the boycott in the press by the Protestants'; Hederman duly persuaded George Simms, the Church of Ireland Archbishop of Dublin, 'never to mention Fethard-on-Sea again'. When the Cloneys' daughters, Eileen and Mary, returned, they were educated at home, despite renewed pressure on their father by the local priest.[21]

Éamon de Valera had single-handedly determined the course of Irish politics in the 1930s and throughout the Second World War – indeed, there is a sense in which he had determined the course of politics since he had rejected the Treaty in 1922. But he was powerless to determine the course of politics in the 1950s. The election of 1951 was 'the first pork-barrel election in Ireland';[22] hereafter bread-and-butter issues such as prices, wages and inflation mattered more and more; the old, indigenously Irish issues revolving around the civil war mattered less and less, even if their mythic power could never be discounted. Political discourse gradually veered from the meaning of independence to the uses of independence. There was an increasingly unwavering focus on economics. 'One of the most striking features of Irish politics in recent years', wrote Desmond Williams in 1953, 'has been the frequency with which politicians employ economic phraseology . . . It is probably only since 1948 that ordinary people have appeared to take an interest in economic debate.'[23]

Éamon de Valera was never comfortable with the politics of economics that increasingly characterised party politics; he was now in his seventies and he never learned the new political vocabulary it demanded. His near-total blindness – all documents had to be read to him by his officials – well symbolised a lack of economic vision for which he was unapologetic. How firmly his own blinkered vision of remedies for Ireland's economic ills was rooted in the past is best illustrated by an extraordinary speech he made in the Dáil in July 1956. As leader of the opposition he was responding to the coalition government's imposition of import levies to arrest a growing balance-of-payments deficit:

As the national interest is at stake, there is no other thing for us to do but to try to help the people to realise that the hardships have to be faced and that, as a nation, we have to tighten our belts and face up to the situation as we would face up to any national emergency. I have great belief in our people. They have faced emergencies before. I am against external loans. I would rather go short of the things that have to be got by external loans than have an external loan. The policy of self-reliance is the one policy that will enable our nation to continue to exist. Back in 1917, we had to face the people who were telling us what we would lose by not being incorporated in the British Empire. I remember well that we had to tell people down in Kilkenny: 'We have a choice. It may be that we have the choice of the humble cottage instead of [sic] as lackeys partaking of the sops in the big man's house.'[24]

That de Valera should see nothing incongruous in repeating his message of 1917 in 1956, that he should yet again commend 'the choice of the humble cottage' to men and women already abandoning their homes in their hundreds of thousands for the bright lights of London and New York, was a measure of how out of joint with the times he had become. But de Valera neither had nor pretended to have any remedy for the haemorrhage of emigration. Those seeking a speech on the subject in Maurice Moynihan's voluminous *Speeches and Statements by Éamon de Valera* will look in vain; indeed the index reveals only four isolated instances when the word 'emigration' occurs in over 400 pages on the years after he assumed power in 1932 – and one of those was when an opposition deputy threw it at him across the Dáil chamber when he was in full flight during a debate on the 1937 constitution.[25]

De Valera 'regarded economic matters as an inferior discipline', remarked Kenneth Whitaker, the secretary of the department of finance, who was to become the icon of the new Ireland inaugurated by the publication of *Economic Development* under his name in 1958. 'Other things mattered more'; he had become 'a symbol of Éire passé'.[26] For it is beyond dispute that 'when Éamon de Valera departed from active politics in 1959 he left Irish society very much as he had found it . . . The structure of Irish society remained virtually unchanged.'[27] Nor can one disagree with Tom Garvin's endorsement of what Seán O'Faoláin had written in 1945: 'On our present static position, the best one could say for Mr de Valera would be that his policy may be to give Ireland twenty years of undisturbed peace in order to stabilise and reconstruct.'[28]

But in June 1954 what had by then become thirty years of stability again came under threat when an IRA raid on a military barracks in Armagh marked the beginning of a cross-border campaign that intensified in December 1956 and continued until 1962. The initial response of Costello's second inter-party government, which entered office after the election of May 1954, was tentative – unsurprisingly, perhaps, given that it needed the support of

Clann na Poblachta deputies for its Dáil majority – although in December 1955 it did apply the provisions of the 1939 Offences Against the State Act prohibiting the media from even mentioning the name of the IRA, which could be described only as 'an illegal organisation'.

The greatest threat to stability was the impact of the IRA campaign on the Fianna Fáil party as a result of the deaths of two members of an IRA raiding party, Seán South and Fergal O'Hanlon, in an ambush on an RUC police station in Brooke-borough, County Fermanagh, on 1 January 1957. 'We were encouraged to regard the history of Ireland as unfinished business, a great story that lacked only a noble resolution,' Denis Donoghue has written in a memoir of his early education by the Christian Brothers in Warrenpoint, County Down.[29] The relentless pounding of the anti-partitionist drums by politicians such as Éamon de Valera and Seán MacBride, especially since 1945, nourished that same sense of unfinished business in young men such as South and O'Hanlon. Photographs in the *Irish Press* showed thousands in Dublin's O'Connell Street paying their respects to Seán South when his cortège was en route to an enormous funeral in Limerick on 4 January. The dead men acquired 'the status of popular martyrs and were viewed by many as being part of the purer, unsullied republican tradition which was contrasted with politicians caught up in the materialist world'.[30] Although de Valera used his platform in the *Irish Press* on 7 January unhesitatingly to support John A. Costello's radio broadcast as taoiseach denouncing the IRA as an illegal force, and rejecting the use of violence as a means to end partition, he could not easily contain the sympathy for South and O'Hanlon that spread like wildfire through Fianna Fáil. When a young Limerick deputy and future cabinet minister, Donogh O'Malley, wrote to him saying that since many party members had been 'making goats of themselves' and showing the party 'in a bad light', he should convene a meeting to spell out official policy, de Valera agreed.

The turbulence of the Fianna Fáil party meeting on 15 January 1957, attended by 'over eighty deputies . . . including all senators', was unprecedented. It went on for eight hours, from 3 p.m. until 11 p.m. But this time de Valera's well-tried strategy as chairman, of letting people talk and talk until they were so exhausted that they agreed with him, was in vain. After a majority of those present had spoken about the IRA raids it was decided that 'there could be no armed force here except under the control and direction of the government' and that the 'employment of force at any time in the foreseeable future would be undesirable and likely to be futile'. But the minutes also record that in regard to 'the feasibility of the use of force by any future government as a means of solving partition . . . no definite decision was taken'. Although de Valera and his front bench interpreted the result as a rejection of the use of force – when the Northern Ireland crisis erupted twenty years later, Paddy Hillery, then the minister for external affairs, argued in retrospect that it had been agreed that 'whatever happens in the North we're not going in there' – there was an ambiguity about the outcome that threatened to split the party in 1969–71. That ambiguity was compounded during the general election campaign of February 1957 when 'Fianna Fáil deputies propagated the well-trodden claim that only a Fianna Fáil government could eventually secure Irish unity' – de Valera insisted 'that there had not been a day when he was in office that he "did not keep the idea of a united Ireland fully before his mind"'.[31]

The 1957 election was Éamon de Valera's last great electoral triumph. Although Sinn Féin won four seats in the Dáil (which they refused to attend), all the other parties lost seats except Fianna Fáil, which won an overall majority of 10 – its first overall majority since 1944 – inaugurating what proved to be de Valera's legacy of another uninterrupted sixteen years in government. A second legacy was his unflinching action against the IRA. On 5 July he brought into force Part II of the Offences Against the State (Amendment) Act of 1940, providing once more for the internment of IRA suspects without trial. There 'was no clear way which would

241

inevitably end partition', he told the Fianna Fáil *ard fheis* in November 1957. 'He did not think that force would be successful.'
When some delegates said they hoped that he would live to see the
ending of partition, de Valera took refuge in prayer: 'I pray to
heaven that I will see this problem solved before I die. I don't want
any of you to think that it is more than a prayer to the Almighty
. . . But I cannot promise it to you and nobody else in this country
can.' It was also on this occasion that de Valera spoke publicly of
rumours of his impending resignation – he was seventy-five years
old: 'I do not feel ill. I know I'm hampered by the fact that I cannot
read . . . But as long as this organisation wants me (if they do not want
me, they can get rid of me very easily) and as long as Dáil Éireann
thinks I am doing my work and can do my work, then I stay.'[32]

A year later, he spoke of his wish to bequeath another legacy: the
abolition of the proportional representation (PR) system of voting
that had been used in all Irish elections since independence. 'Single-
member constituencies and straight voting tend to build up an
opposition, since every opposition knows that sooner or later under
that particular system it will come into office', and Fianna Fáil knew,
he told the Dáil in his speech in November 1958 introducing the bill
to abolish PR, that, 'as a result of the passing of this Bill, an opposition will be built up which will almost certainly replace the existing
government as an alternative government'. But 'those countries
which have most successfully built up democratic institutions are
the countries in which there is a single non-transferable vote. The
single non-transferable vote has an integrating tendency; the
proportional-representation system has a disintegrating tendency
. . . It leads to a multiplicity of parties.'[33] He did not say so explicitly
but his thinking was obviously prompted by the rise of Sinn Féin.

The major historical landmark in 1958, Éamon de Valera's last
full year as taoiseach, was the publication in December of *Economic
Development*, the revolutionary policy document outlining the
challenges and opportunities for economic progress that emanated
from the department of finance and that, unprecedentedly, bore the

signature of the department's secretary, T. K. Whitaker. Just as Ireland in the 1930s, 1940s and 1950s is seen as de Valera's Ireland, so Ireland in the 1960s and 1970s came to be seen as Whitaker's Ireland. That *Economic Development* was the foundation document of a new age explains why the fact that de Valera was still taoiseach when it was approved by the government tends to be either forgotten or studiously ignored. This is not to suggest that he had any personal input into the change of course but it should be remembered that his appointment of Dr Jim Ryan, rather than the innately conservative Seán MacEntee, as minister for finance in his last government was an essential prerequisite for what was in effect a U-turn in economic policy. De Valera's increasing reliance on Ryan as a ministerial confidant in matters of sensitivity was demonstrated in their working together on the Health Act of 1953 and in bringing an end to the Fethard-on-Sea boycott in 1957; it was now an important factor in immunising Whitaker's dramatic new departure to criticism within the cabinet or within the wider Fianna Fáil party. Ryan's unobtrusive style has denied him the recognition he deserves but he was very popular in the party and 'regarded as an acute student of personality . . . and skilful handler of men'.[34] 'You look after the administration,' he told Whitaker when he first met his new secretary. 'I'll look after the politics'.[35] Although Seán Lemass has rightly been accorded most of the credit for implementing the Programme for Economic Expansion born of *Economic Development*, it would never have got off the ground without Ryan's unwavering support. 'The continuing presence of de Valera', moreover, as Brian Farrell has pointed out, also 'provided Lemass with a convenient cloak of seeming changelessness under which new policies, concerns and choices could be exchanged for old.'[36]

It was also Jim Ryan who first belled the cat and asked a still hesitant de Valera if he intended to stand down as taoiseach and run as the Fianna Fáil candidate in the presidential election impending when Seán T. O'Kelly's term of office came to an end. On 14 January 1959 Oscar Traynor, then the minister for justice, and who had been the officer commanding the republican garrison in the Gresham Hotel that de Valera had joined when the civil war began, pushed the issue to a conclusion when he suggested that he allow his name to go forward. 'Nevertheless, de Valera's own announcement of his intention to resign the leadership of the Party and of the Government came . . . as a bombshell' when he made it known at a meeting of the parliamentary party the next day.[37]

On the very same day the sustained efforts of an Independent deputy, Noel Browne, publicly to challenge the compatibility of de Valera's acting as controlling director of the Irish Press Group, while serving as taoiseach, on the grounds that it was a corrupt and nepotistic conflict of interest came to a head. Elaine Byrne has explained how the revolutionary generation, whether pro- or anti-Treaty, 'believed that integrity did not need to be legislatively defined' but did not believe 'that those in authority could be capable of moral transgression' and were reluctant 'to intervene in the absence of concrete evidence of corruption'. De Valera's weak and evasive answer when questioned in the Dáil about the existence of conflict-of-interest rules in 1947 was a case in point: 'To lay down precise rules as to the private activities [by ministers] . . . is obviously a matter of considerable difficulty.' He defended the self-evident conflict of interest in his own case, arising from his phenomenal power in the Irish media as controlling director of the Irish Press Group – 'Ireland's second largest chain of national newspapers . . . comprised of the influential *Evening Press, Irish Press* and *Sunday Press*' – by declaring that 'he was not financially remunerated as controlling director and that the day-to-day business of the newspaper [*sic*] was delegated to board members'. Noel Browne riposted that he was 'remunerated by having his speeches reported at great length; his photograph appears on page one, page three or page five – everything he does from the time he gets up in the morning until the time he goes to bed at night'. Elaine Byrne has also pointed out that, while 'debates on conflict of interest were not new . . . the attention they received was'.[38]

On 12 December 1958 Browne had moved a private member's motion in the Dáil stating that de Valera occupied 'a position which could be reasonably regarded as interfering or being incompatible with the full and proper discharge by him of the duties of his office'. The ensuing debate exposed how both de Valera and his eldest son, Vivion, had benefited financially from their control of the newspaper group; Browne revealed that since 1929 they had bought up close to 150,000 shares in the company, which was worth nearly £1 million. The debate was adjourned and the vote on Browne's motion was postponed until 14 January 1959 when the government's majority ensured its defeat but the squalid story was pushed into the background when on the same day de Valera announced his intention to stand down as taoiseach.[39]

Yet he refused to do so until after the presidential election and clung to the appurtenances of power in the taoiseach's department like a limpet to a rock. 'I'm not President yet,' he replied when one of the civil servants closest to him had the temerity to ask about the arrangements for his resignation.[40] The election took place on 17 June and was held in tandem with the referendum on proportional representation. But de Valera was divisive to the end and, while he defeated the Fine Gael candidate, Seán MacEoin, by 538,000 votes to 417,636, his proposal to abolish PR was rejected. Until the last moment he shrank from leaving the office he had occupied for the best part of a quarter of a century. His private secretary, Padraig Ó hAnnracháin, recalled how, when the photographers were waiting to record his leaving Government Buildings for the last time, de Valera asked for a moment alone. After some time had passed Ó hAnnracháin re-entered his office and found the taoiseach with his arms wrapped around the switchboard through which he could 'communicate with ministers, heads of departments, the Army and Gardaí at the flick of a switch . . . There were tears in his eyes. "Oh, Padraig," he exclaimed. "It's awfully hard to leave the levers of power."'[41]

14

Last Laps, 1959–75

'Whatever restrictions which rules and regulations may impose, headship does give opportunity and it gives the power too, if one has the will and the energy.' So said Éamon de Valera on 19 November 1921 on the occasion of his inauguration as the chancellor of the National University of Ireland. 'The chieftaincy of this nation's university at this time', he continued, 'certainly presents a field for endeavour and achievement, wide enough to satisfy the deedfull lust of an Alexander.'[1] The timing was hubristic: less than a month later what many of those who opposed him in the Dáil might well have seen as de Valera's 'deedfull lust' for political power precipitated the Treaty split; indeed, it was when he was fulfilling one of his earliest engagements as chancellor in the Mansion House on 6 December 1921 that he had been first given a copy of the Treaty.

Éamon de Valera's tenure as chancellor, from 1919 until 1975, lasted far longer than his tenure as taoiseach and he clung to the office with even greater tenacity. When the first chancellor, Archbishop William Walsh, had died in April 1921, de Valera's subsequent election was 'essentially a political act. He was a graduate of the university and also held a degree from its predecessor, the Royal University, but he was not nominated on the basis of his academic qualifications . . . In selecting de Valera, the Convocation of the NUI was not simply electing a new chancellor, but affirming its commitment to the cause of nationalist Ireland.' De Valera had hesitated before accepting but, at the height of the war of independence, decided that his 'election at the time might be of public value and of help to our Cause'.[2] But he first took the precaution of ensuring that he would be elected unopposed – just as he had ensured that his election as president of Sinn Féin in the autumn of 1917 had been unopposed.

His place at the apex of the university power structure soothed his self-esteem and erased the memory of earlier academic disappointments, such as his failure to secure an honours degree or to obtain an appointment on the teaching staff of any of the NUI's constituent colleges. The honour was also gratifying because, 'although he had left the teaching profession behind him in 1916, teaching never left him; he was never to lose the teacher's instincts and characteristics; nor his genuine respect for scholarship nor his concern for the advancement of higher learning'. Indeed de Valera, as Donal McCartney has observed, 'remained all his life what one might call a "crypto-academic". This accounted for much of his style of politics.'[3]

The statutory declaration of his appointment as chancellor took place in the senate room of the NUI in Dublin's Merrion Square during the Treaty debates, on 19 December 1921. The civil war then intervened and

that special meeting in December 1921 was the only one that de Valera attended until he reappeared three years later in December 1924 for his first ordinary meeting of the Senate. From then until his death, more than fifty years later, his attendance was exemplary. He missed no meeting during 1925 or 1926, except the one in March in the latter year because of his attendance at the critical Sinn Féin *ard fheis* . . . In 1955, 1958, 1961, 1964, 1969 and 1972, the year of his ninetieth birthday, de Valera had a hundred-per-cent Senate attendance record.

Although some of those who had engineered his election as chancellor – such as Patrick McGilligan and Michael Hayes – were now among his leading political adversaries, they were unable to oust him, even when the pro-Treaty government had jailed him, because the NUI charter decreed that he held office either for life or until his resignation.[4] This meant that, in the NUI at least, even in his darkest days in the political wilderness, he was never deprived of that primacy of place to which he always believed himself entitled.

He never contemplated resigning the chancellorship when he became head of government in 1932, in 1951 and in 1957, or when he became head of state in 1959. Just as issues of a potential conflict of interest clearly apparent in more politically correct times never seem to have occurred to him with regard to his simultaneously serving as taoiseach and as the controlling director of the Irish Press Group, neither did he regard holding the office of taoiseach or of president as a barrier to his continuing to occupy the position of titular head of the largest university in Ireland. Nor does the fact that its senate, whose meetings he chaired in his capacity as chancellor, appointed three of his children to professorships in the National University of Ireland ever seem to have been an issue, either for him or for the senate. The senate minutes show, however, that the chancellor sent his regrets for his inability to attend all three meetings at which these appointments were made. On 24 October 1957, Ruairi was appointed professor of Celtic archae-ology in University College Dublin when he defeated another can-didate by 23 votes to 10. Dr Éamon de Valera was ranked lowest of the three candidates for appointment as professor of midwifery and gynaecology whose names had been forwarded by UCD's governing body to the senate meeting on 27 October 1960, but he was duly appointed when he received 16 votes, as opposed to 11 and 4 votes for his rivals. The case of Máirín de Valera, who was appointed as professor of botany in University College Galway on 29 March 1962, was more clear-cut: the only other candidate had neither presented himself for interview nor sat the examination in Irish designed to establish his competence to teach through the medium of Irish, as was required in UCG; UCG's governing body accordingly reported to the senate that 'the Faculty could only state that from his application he seems academically suitable' and he was duly defeated by 21 votes to 0. De Valera's attendance record at the senate was so phenomenal during this period – he did not

miss a single meeting, for example, in 1955, 1958, 1961 and 1964
– that it seems inconceivable that these absences in 1957, 1960 and
1962 were coincidental. But he did chair another meeting of the
senate in 1960, on 7 July, when Brian Ó Cuív (his son-in-law,
married to de Valera's daughter, Emer) was appointed professor of
classical Irish and literature in UCD; that appointment was unanimous and non-contentious, however, because there were no other
candidates. Ó Cuív subsequently became a senior professor in the
school of Celtic studies in the Dublin Institute for Advanced
Studies, de Valera's brainchild, and he later served as the director
of the school from 1968 until 1973.

The NUI's role in sustaining de Valera's self-image of eminence
in the 1920s might explain why he always interpreted his role as
chancellor as honorific and why his style of academic leadership
was so different from his hands-on style of political leadership on
issues he regarded as important. For the most part 'he approved
as a matter of course the recommendations made by the Registrar',
the senior administrative officer of the university. 'He regarded
the position of Chancellor as a formal and ceremonial office: he
presided over the activity of the National University, but rarely
intervened directly to influence its decisions or to shape its academic policies.'[5]

In this he was unlike his predecessor, Archbishop William
Walsh, and not the least of the innumerable services Éamon de
Valera performed for the National University by his prolonged
retention of the chancellorship was to deny another Catholic Archbishop of Dublin with even more highly interventionist instincts,
John Charles McQuaid, the opportunity of succeeding him. There
had been speculative newspaper stories to that effect in 1959 when
it was rumoured that de Valera would relinquish the chancellorship as well as his position as taoiseach and a copy of the most
detailed report to that effect, in the *Sunday Dispatch* on 18 January
1959, has been retained in the de Valera papers.[6] There is no doubt
that McQuaid had powerful supporters on the senate of the

National University – he was a particularly close ally of Michael Tierney, the president of UCD, on such issues as moving the college campus from Earlsfort Terrace in the city centre to a green-field site at Belfield on the southern outskirts of the city. Nor is it unlikely, given the claustrophobically Catholic temper of the times, that in the event of de Valera's standing down, McQuaid's succession would have been unopposed. But de Valera instantly squashed that prospect when, on 21 January, the *Irish Press* carried the taoiseach's comment that there was 'no foundation' for the report; in the event, he outlived McQuaid. But while de Valera was determined to retain the office, he was less interested than ever in investing it with any power. He 'did not initiate any further correspondence as Chancellor after 1961, nor did he make any comments of his own on letters or documentation which he received through the NUI office'. He had always regarded the chancellorship as 'primarily honorary and ceremonial in character 'and it became 'an exclusively ceremonial position during his final decade in office'.[7]

In 1972 a retired *New York Times* journalist living in Dublin who wanted to profile Éamon de Valera on the occasion of his ninetieth birthday asked for a schedule of a typical day in his life as president. The one-page response laid bare the cloistered character of his existence in Áras an Uachtarain.

DAY IN THE LIFE OF THE PRESIDENT

Early breakfast; listens to radio news bulletins.

Mail and correspondence – that on private matters dealt with in conjunction with Personal Secretary; correspondence of unofficial nature referred to the Secretary to the President.

Daily Mass in Áras oratory. This is also attended by Mrs de Valera, members of the family when in residence, the Aide de Camp on duty, and members of household staff.

Necessary time given daily to deal with the official correspondence and matters in consultation with Secretary to the President. Usually a number of documents to be signed – warrants of appointment, army commissions and bills as they are presented from the Taoiseach's

Department; messages to and from other Heads of State; other official correspondence and matters arising from powers and functions conferred on President by Constitution or law; invitations and arrangements for public engagements – personal attendance or representation at public ceremonies and functions; reception of State or other distinguished visitors; presentation of Letters of Credence etc. as occasion arises.

Luncheon (private or an official as the case may be).

Afternoon
Receives overseas and other visitors, at their direct request and by appointment (Visitors, from time to time, include representatives of international bodies and of Irish organisations with which President is connected as Patron or in whose work or aims he has a special interest). Receives Taoiseach, at least once a month, who keeps him generally informed on matters of domestic and international policy.

Tea; listens to radio, television; readings.

Occasional walks in grounds.

Receives personal friends.

Official dinners occasionally; formal attendance at opera or other cultural event periodically.

Usually in his study until 10 p.m.[8]

Terry de Valera paints a more human picture of his parents' life in Áras an Uachtaráin. The innumerable surviving images from this period – both official, formal photographs and informal, family photographs – reflect the irony that it was only in old age that Éamon and Sinéad have anything approximating to a domestic life together albeit against the stateliest of backdrops. Terry's mother 'disliked the move. She was lonely in these strange surroundings but determined to make the best of it.' But she liked walking alone in 'a lonely wooded area' in the grounds where she would say her prayers. Once she went missing and one of the aides-de-camp 'found her deep "in conversation" with a buck deer' that had strayed from the herd inhabiting the Phoenix Park. Terry, who had an interest in the occult, thought the oldest part of the house where the oratory had been built and near what had been Queen Victoria's bedroom 'quite eerie'. Whenever his father visited the oratory 'the door leading to the corridor was left open; if not, it seemed to close of its own accord. No rational explanation was ever found.'[9]

The oratory meant much to Éamon de Valera. Long a daily communicant, he usually went there five times a day and one of his first acts when he had become president was 'to obtain permission for the Blessed Sacrament to be reserved. He was characteristically scrupulous about its custody' and his official biographers piously record that 'he felt strong personal satisfaction when it was decided that his desk was the safest place for the key of the Tabernacle.'[10]

Much of de Valera's time as president was devoted to what Patrick Murray, in a masterly essay, has described as his policing of his historical reputation. Professional historians, collectively and individually, figured prominently among his visitors 'in whose work or aims he has a special interest'. F. S. L. Lyons, one of a group of historians invited to Áras an Uachtaráin in 1964 to ask de Valera questions about his political career, later wrote of how he had thought it remarkable that at the age of eighty-two the president, who submitted himself 'unweariedly to six or seven hours of interrogation, not only possessed a phenomenal memory, but also revealed an obsessive concern to set the record straight as he saw it'. He did not seem to realise, observed Lyons, that his 'transparent anxiety might be seen as evidence of a very different kind than that which he sought to press upon them'.[11]

For de Valera's anxiety focused almost exclusively on the great catastrophe in his life and on his consequent years in the political wilderness: the six years between the truce of July 1921 and his leading his republican followers back into the Dáil in 1927. The emphasis is apparent in Longford's and O'Neill's authorised biography, which was published in 1970 and which, in John Bowman's phrase, de Valera brought into the world as midwife during his years in Áras an Uachtaráin. This is indeed 'its central virtue' because, 'given his intimate participation in the production of the book', it is as close as we can get to 'an autobiography, his preferred rationalisation at the end of his career, his final self-justification'.[12] Another of his authorised biographers, Pádraig Ó Fiannachta, felt de Valera was 'compulsively interested' in the years before he came to power in 1932 but not in anything that followed it. He wanted the first Irish-language volume 'dealing with the 1920s read and reread to him slowly, and he made innumerable comments on its contents, confirming or questioning at every turn'. Yet as Patrick Murray has concluded, and as this book contends, 'his finest achievements belong to the period between 1932 and 1948 – a period in which, as his official biographers found, he showed comparatively little interest'.[13]

Yet de Valera's perspective during his fourteen years in Áras an Uachtaráin on the interpretation of his place in history makes a certain historical sense. His achievements between 1932 and 1948 speak for themselves and cannot be gainsaid; they need neither defending nor excusing. The same can never be said about his behaviour in 1921–2, whatever about his behaviour after the end of the civil war, when he eventually succeeded in inducing most republicans to return to the democratic fold.

De Valera's most notable visitors in Áras an Uachtaráin were other heads of states. They included Prince Rainier and Princess Grace of Monaco (1961); US presidents John F. Kennedy (1963), whose funeral in Washington later in the same year he also attended, and Richard Nixon (1970); the presidents of Pakistan, India and Zambia (all in 1964); the king and queen of the Belgians (1968); and former French president Charles de Gaulle (1969). He also attended the coronation of Pope Paul VI in 1963 and paid a presidential state visit to the US in 1964.

Terry de Valera, watching the presidents of Ireland and of France walking alone in the garden, later wrote that 'it was seldom, if ever, that I saw someone walking with Father who was considerably taller' (see plate 20). De Gaulle paid de Valera the uncharacteristic compliment of speaking to him in English – a practice he almost invariably eschewed in his dealings with heads of other states – because de Valera's French could not sustain 'a detailed conversation. The two men got on splendidly and developed a deep mutual respect. Father said that the more he knew de Gaulle, the more he admired him.'[14] Before he had met de Gaulle, de Valera said, 'He was France to me. I believed that, without him, France would have been pushed aside and regarded as a second-rate nation in Europe. His great work was to make sure that would not be so. Meeting him confirmed me in all my previous views.'[15]

But it was the visit of John F. Kennedy in the summer of 1963 that resonated most dramatically with the Irish public, who idolised the US president with a 'quasi-religious fervour made manifest after his assassination in the garish triptychs available in gift shops in which his photograph and that of his other murdered brother, Robert, flanked a photograph of Pope John XXIII'.[16] Kennedy liked and enjoyed Ireland and was particularly taken with Sinéad de Valera; 'he was fascinated by her knowledge of poetry which she could recall so freely' and wrote her a warm personal letter after his return to Washington which he hoped she would not dismiss 'as mere flattery even though a wise old Irish lady once told me "a kind word never broke a tooth"'.[17] Éamon de Valera's presence at Kennedy's funeral personified the grief of the Irish people and has been memorably described by Tim Pat Coogan. 'He scorned to take a car to follow the cavalcade to Arlington Cemetery and presented an unforgettable picture on Irish television as he strode along sightlessly, arms swinging, lurching slightly, like a huge heron in a high wind, going at a pace that would have left a man twenty years younger gasping.'[18]

A year later, at the invitation of Kennedy's successor, President Lyndon B. Johnson, de Valera paid an official visit to the United States. The high point was his address to a joint session of both Houses of Congress on 28 May 1964. 'I came here some forty-five years ago, and I toured through this great country,' he began, before going on to speak of the importance of President Wilson's doctrine of self-determination in the Irish struggle for independence. This was the context in which he placed the warmth of the reception accorded to President Kennedy on his visit to Ireland.

He was welcomed not merely because he was of Irish blood, not merely because of his personal charm and his great qualities of heart and mind, not even because of the great leadership which he was giving to the world in critical moments; but he was honoured because he was regarded by our people as the symbol of this great nation, because he was the elected president of this great people. In honouring him they felt they were in some small measure expressing their gratitude to the people of the United States for the aid that had been given to them.

But de Valera could not resist the temptation once more to beat the anti-partitionist drum and yet again refused to acknowledge that Ulster's unionists also had a right to self-determination. 'While I was addressing you here in 1919 and 1920, our ancient nation, our ancient Ireland, was undivided. And since then it has been divided by a cruel partition.'[19]

Another highlight towards the end of the first term of his presidency was Harold Wilson's government agreeing to the exhumation and return to Ireland of the remains of Roger Casement, who had been buried in Pentonville prison after his execution in 1916. De Valera, acting against medical advice, rose from his sickbed and, standing bare-headed in sleet and snow, delivered the oration at the graveside in Glasnevin cemetery.

Seán T. O'Kelly, de Valera's immediate predecessor as president, had been unopposed in 1952 for his second term in Áras an Uachtaráin. But de Valera, as his authorised biographers admit, 'was still too controversial figure to be allowed this honour'.[20] Although de Valera was now in his eighty-fourth year, Seán Lemass, who was to stand down as taoiseach in November 1966 because of his ill-health, persuaded him to stand for a second term. You are 'surely as tough as teak' he had written in response to a congratulatory message from de Valera on the occasion of his own sixtieth birthday in 1965.[21] The Fine Gael candidate was Tom

O'Higgins, a nephew of Kevin O'Higgins, minister for health in the second inter-party government, and subsequently chief justice and a member of the European Courts of Justice. O'Higgins was a strong candidate: 'an articulate, forceful speaker . . . far younger and better able to get around the country than de Valera. Fianna Fáil nullified these advantages by having the President Who Was Above Politics simply not campaign. His age and blindness were thus turned to advantages' because, in the interests of balance, RTE (the Irish broadcasting service), 'which was heavily influenced by the government, gave little coverage to the candidate who was campaigning'.[22] Meanwhile de Valera capitalised on a multitude of televisual opportunities arising from the coincidence of the election with his starring role in the many commemorative celebrations marking the fiftieth anniversary of the Easter Rising in 1966. Nevertheless, O'Higgins came much closer to defeating him than Seán MacEoin had done in 1959 and de Valera was re-elected by only the slenderest of margins: a majority of about 10,000 out of more than a million votes cast.

In his second presidential term, as in his first, Éamon de Valera scrupulously avoided all public comment on party politics. But, behind the scenes, he played a significant role when the Northern Ireland crisis erupted in 1969 and threatened to tear the Fianna Fáil party asunder. From the outset he was strongly supportive of Jack Lynch as taoiseach and he talked Kevin Boland out of resigning from Lynch's cabinet in the summer of 1969. In April 1970 Peter Berry, the secretary of the department of justice, was informed that two senior ministers in Lynch's government (Charles Haughey, the minister for finance, and Neil Blaney, the minister for agriculture) were involved in a plot illegally to import arms through Dublin Airport to the IRA. When Berry was unable to get his minister, Micheal Ó Moráin, to act on his information, he agonised about whether he could bypass Ó Moráin and go straight to the taoiseach. He decided to seek the advice of President de Valera whom he greatly admired because of his firm line with the

IRA during World War II and during the border campaign in the 1950s.

Berry phoned the Áras and told the President that information of a very serious nature had come into his possession, information perhaps of national significance. He did not reveal specific details nor did the President ask any question about the nature of the information. Berry asked for advice on whether his loyalty ended with informing the Minister or whether he was justified in speaking directly to the Taoiseach.

The President asked if he was certain of his facts. When Berry said he was absolutely sure, de Valera told him that he owed his duty to the government as a whole and not just to his own minister and that he should talk to the Taoiseach, which he [Berry] duly did on 20 April.

On 5 May Ó Moráin's resignation was announced in the Dáil and Lynch appointed Desmond O'Malley to succeed him. O'Malley's appointment was not approved by the Dáil until just before 3 a.m. on the morning of 7 May, after the dramatic debate that followed Lynch's dismissal of Haughey and Blaney from his government when they refused to resign and denied any involvement in the illegal importation of arms. 'These are terrible times', said President de Valera, when O'Malley accompanied the taoiseach to Áras an Uachtaráin to receive his seal of office at nine o'clock that morning. The president told them that 'he had been keeping in touch with the overnight drama in Leinster House' and that he had stayed up until 4 a.m. because he thought they would come to the Áras once the debate was over.

Protocol required that the minister for justice accompany judges of the supreme court or high court to Áras an Uachtaráin to receive their seals of office on appointment. This happened twice in 1970, in the summer and in the autumn, and on both occasions de Valera's aide-de-camp asked O'Malley to stay behind for a private tête-à-tête. On both occasions, after O'Malley had described the political situation for the president, de Valera's replies were similar. He clearly expressed the view that Haughey would inflict great damage on the party and that the bitterness and division would last for years ... He was extremely sympathetic to Lynch, whom he thought had been treated very unfairly. With the precarious security situation and violence in the North, de Valera said that Lynch was deserving of total support and full loyalty, particularly from his government. He told me that there had been rows in his own governments, with ministers arguing with him on matters of policy, but, he said, he had been lucky as Taoiseach in that his ministers had always remained loyal and acted loyally. He said Lynch was the first Fianna Fáil Taoiseach who had to suffer that lack of loyalty which made his difficult job even harder.[23]

Northern Ireland was also the subject of another 'private and highly sensitive meeting' at Áras an Uachtaráin in April 1972 when de Valera met Terence O'Neill, the former prime minister of Northern Ireland, at the latter's request. Ken Whitaker, who accompanied O'Neill, recalled that the meeting began on a note of grotesque, if gracious, sentimentality when de Valera stated that 'one of his dearest dreams would be fulfilled if an O'Neill were to sit in his chair as a President of a united Ireland' – a statement he repeated twice in the course of the meeting. He also harped on his perennial complaint that partition was all the fault of the British; that Winston Churchill had tricked Michael Collins into believing that 'no oath of allegiance to the King would be required'. But there was one note of realism when de Valera acknowledged that 'he had totally underestimated the depth of the religious antagonism of the Northern Protestants to Irish unity'.[24] That, for de Valera, was a rare admission. His more well-worn and plaintive theme was British culpability. 'You could not beat us in war but you defeated us in negotiation,' he told one British historian who visited him shortly after he became president. 'Those three men, Lloyd George and Churchill and Smith [Birkenhead], made dupes of Griffith and Collins. I can never forgive the ruthless, pitiless way in which they pushed them over the edge, without a thought as to what would happen to them or to Ireland afterwards.'[25] But he said not a word of how such an outcome might have been avoided if he himself had agreed to participate in the Treaty negotiations.

Publicly Éamon de Valera silently acquiesced in Ireland's entry into the European Economic Community when it was approved by a huge 83 per cent majority in the 1972 referendum. He told his youngest son, Terry, that 'he acknowledged that entry was inevitable', but 'he accepted this with very strong reservations regarding the loss of sovereignty. He agreed fully with the concept of the development of trade and commerce and the more desirable aspects of culture from the continent of Europe. Political union or the diminution or loss of sovereignty was quite a different matter in which he felt the smaller nations would fare worst.'[26] Another son, Ruairí, a colleague of mine at University College Dublin, would not be drawn on how his father had voted in the referendum but smiled and did not dissent when I suggested he would have voted against entry.

When Éamon de Valera and his wife left Áras an Uachtaráin for the last time on 24 June 1973, they took up residence in Talbot Lodge, Linden Convalescent Home in Blackrock, where de Valera had visited the patients when a student at Blackrock College. Such was his personal lack of interest in material wealth (he had refused to accept an increase in his allowance as president when ministerial salaries had been last increased) that in January 1973 his doctor advised the taoiseach, Jack Lynch, that de Valera was suffering from depression because of fears that his pension would be inadequate to cover the constant nursing care his wife now required, and his allowance was subsequently adjusted.[27]

Sinéad de Valera died on 7 January 1975 on the eve of their sixty-fifth wedding anniversary. Éamon de Valera died aged ninety-two, after a brief illness, on 29 August 1975, only a month after he had last presided at a meeting of the senate of the National University. After a state funeral at which his grandson (an tAthair Shan Ó Cuív) celebrated mass, he was buried on 2 September in a simple grave adjoining the republican plot in Glasnevin cemetery.

Conclusion

Edward de Valera had no interest in political power. The story of the first two decades of his life is a story of personal empowerment: a story of his struggle to flee the soul-destroying poverty of an agricultural labourer's life in rural Limerick, a life from which his mother had escaped by emigrating to New York. He was only thirteen when Elizabeth Coll, his grandmother and surrogate mother, who had hoped he might become a priest – a time-honoured escape route for the intelligent poor in Ireland – died in 1895. She had been his only ally in his hunt for a way out of their cottage in Knockmore: going to the Christian Brothers school at Charleville to try to win a scholarship. His mother refused to send him the passage money to join her in New York but yielded to his request to go to Charleville. 'First Victory for E. de V.,' he wrote triumphantly in his diary. And so it was because it opened the door to Blackrock College.

Becoming a student in Blackrock was the great watershed in de Valera's long life. From the moment he stayed there for Christmas in 1898, rather than returning to Bruree, it became the focal point around which all else revolved: his academic life, his religious life and his teaching career. He continued to live in the college until 1908, six years after he left the school and when he was already twenty-five years old. Later, even his family life remained focused on Blackrock, for he chose always to live as close as possible to the college where his sons and grandsons were also educated. When he first arrived at Blackrock he was a raw, poor but bright country boy; when he left Blackrock he was a fully fledged member of the

Catholic bourgeoisie, poised to take its place as the ruling class in independent Ireland. His years at Blackrock and at Rockwell also acclimatised him to being thoroughly at ease in the company of priests, an asset he used to great effect throughout his political career.

There is another respect in which the early decades of de Valera's life shaped that career. For it was then that he acquired an extraordinary composure, self-sufficiency and strength of will: the personality traits that served him so well in his later pursuit of political power. 'A real feeling of piety, a close attachment to one of the most aesthetic of the modern French religious congregations . . . left their mark on him,' wrote Robert Dudley Edwards in 1957. 'The religious training has not merely provided a valuable instrument for the control of emotions, it has also strengthened the tendency of the teacher to see his work as a vocation, to regard himself as inspired by a mission.'[1]

The emergence of this sense of mission in respect of his new-found enthusiasm for the Irish language was delayed until 1908; just as Edward de Valera had disregarded politics while at Blackrock, so had he disregarded the Irish language despite the college offering voluntary classes to anyone interested. But he then decided that learning Irish was necessary for the advancement of his teaching career, which in turn coincided with his falling in love with and marrying Sinéad Ní Fhlannagáin, his Irish-language teacher, in 1909. So 'Edward' became 'Éamon' – such was the exoticism of his father's name that not even the most fanatical language enthusiasts in the Gaelic League ever attempted to translate it into Irish. The zeal of the convert that he brought to learning the Irish language was inextricably interwoven with the sexual passion of the first years of a married life, which produced their first three children – Vivion, Mairín and Éamon – in four years. Momentarily, for four years are no more than a moment in so long a life, the pursuit of domestic felicity held centre stage. But in November 1913, Éamon de Valera joined the Irish Volunteers and marital passion was displaced by a passion for soldiering. Thereafter what little time he spent in the bosom of his family is of scant interest to a political biographer because he so ruthlessly subordinated private life to public necessities – military imperatives prevailed from 1914 to 1916 and political imperatives thereafter. He consigned the care of his children and all other domestic matters almost exclusively to Sinéad, who played that role with great kindness and extraordinary competence, and without ever impinging on her husband's pursuit of power.

Yet in 1913–14 the pursuit of power still did not extend to an interest in politics, from which he continued to remain aloof. He was equally resolute in his refusal to join either Sinn Féin or the Irish Republican Brotherhood, although in the latter case he agreed to become a non-participating member on the grounds that he would otherwise be deprived of information he needed as a battalion commandant in the Volunteers. 'I never expect a soldier to think,' wrote George Bernard Shaw in 1901.[2] But Éamon de Valera was a thoughtful soldier. Soldiering also taught him that he had a talent and a liking for military leadership but it does not seem to have awoken any appetite for political leadership. He played no part whatever in the political planning of the 1916 rising and, immediately afterwards, made a virtue of his having simply been a soldier who obeyed orders.

All that changed utterly when Éamon de Valera became a prisoner in Dartmoor jail in May–June 1916. Martyrdom, Shaw also wrote, was 'the only way in which a man can become famous without ability'.[3] Unlike Patrick Pearse, de Valera, although willing to risk his life, never cast himself in the role of a martyr. The catalyst for his acquisition of power was the fate of those who were martyrs: the power vacuum created by the execution of the political leaders in the aftermath of the rising. He was best placed to fill it by virtue of his age, education and understanding of the requirements of leadership in the closed confines of an environment that in some respects was similar to the environment of a boarding school, with which he was so familiar. Unknown when he was first imprisoned, but armoured with the aura of the most senior surviving Volunteer officer of the rising, Éamon de Valera returned to Dublin in June 1917 as the unquestioned leader of the prisoners.

His victory at the East Clare by-election, in July, swiftly followed; the scale of that victory made de Valera a household name and set the seal on his emergence as the leader of Ireland's revolutionary nationalists.

His success in the Clare election was perhaps inevitable: qualities which appealed to fellow prisoners were equally attractive on the public platform – his height, his ascetic appearance, his evident sincerity, his detachment, his ability to sound magical in speech without expressing any particularly original ideas, above all his 'Irishness with a difference'. In some ways these are but the qualities of the slightly unusual resourceful student: he could turn his mind sufficiently to convincing people of his capacity to grapple with politics because of the high sense of mission about the teacher. That his ideas were very recently acquired, his political studies being limited to the available literature of his prison library, would hardly occur to any but the politically mature. And in the Ireland of 1917 political maturity was at a discount.[4]

The unanimous election of Éamon de Valera as president of Sinn Féin (a position he retained until 1926) on 25 October 1917 and, two days later, as president of the Irish Volunteers set the seal on his ascendancy. This consolidation of a united political and military leadership in his person, while significant for the absolutism of his authority, was somewhat misleading. Henceforth what mattered for Éamon de Valera was political leadership and, in practice, his nominal military leadership of the IRA tended to fall into abeyance.

What Seán O'Faoláin wrote of de Valera in 1939 was already apparent in 1917: 'One of his greatest qualities – and it contributes greatly to his influence – is dignity.'[5] Dignity, a sense of his being above the herd, was an essential component of a style of leadership in 1918–20 that was absentee as well as authoritarian. He was in jail in England from mid-May 1918 until February 1919 – a prolonged period of imprisonment that he willingly entertained and might even have invited. He stayed grudgingly in Dublin for less than four months and then departed for the United States in mid-June where he remained for eighteen months. Neither de Valera nor his senior colleagues behaved as if these prolonged absences detracted from his authority in any way. He expected, and received, deference, loyalty and obedience. 'It is our business to be perfectly loyal to him,' insisted Arthur Griffith, when de Valera sought and received the support of the Dáil cabinet for his Cuban declaration in his interview for the *Westminster Gazette* in February 1920.

The controversy over the Cuban declaration was not only the acid test of de Valera's leadership *in absentia*; it was also the earliest example of his tendency independently to formulate sophisticated policy positions that, while they ultimately made perfect sense, were not readily explicable in the short term to less intellectual minds and less subtle and sinuous intelligences. Sometimes he staked out these positions in formulaic, mathematical terms: his theory of external association, first enunciated in 1921 and put into practice in the External Relations Act in 1936, is the classic example.

A recent suggestive, if problematic, analysis of de Valera's qualities has argued that he bore 'all the hallmarks of an Asperger genius: . . . the penetrating intellect, intense focus and passion, the deep concentration, the prodigious memory, the absolute conviction, and rigid discipline and repetition, the industry, the precision and exactitude'. Like all such geniuses, it argues, he was 'unmistakably flawed. He could be both innovative and archly conservative, sincere and devious, sensitive yet lacking in empathy, erratic and consistent, pontifical and provincial, pragmatic and absolutist. His innate dignity was matched with toughness; asceticism with materialism; charisma with coldness.'[6]

Many of these characteristics were apparent during de Valera's American mission in 1919–20. The supporters of Justice Cohalan, his most formidable Irish-American antagonist, thought 'de Valera's attitude was not so much one of dignity as of infallibility. "He was right. Everybody else was wrong, and he couldn't be wrong." They said that de Valera became so excited at one stage that he blurted out that he had not been in America a month when he concluded that there was not enough room in the country for Justice Cohalan and himself.' When de Valera claimed that the Irish-American leaders had not yet learned the ABC of democracy, John Devoy responded by saying that he personified 'the whole alphabet of autocracy'. Another of Cohalan's supporters suggested that he was 'labouring under some psychopathic condition . . . Whatever President de Valera's qualities might be, his leadership was an accident . . . I thought the man was crazy.'[7] Such condemnation eerily foreshadowed the criticisms of de Valera's reaction when the plenipotentiaries signed the Treaty without his first having approved its terms.

In the eyes of his adversaries and in the eyes of all those who until the present day regard him as a bitterly divisive figure, de Valera's cardinal sin was his rejection of the Treaty and his consequent culpability for the civil war. That charge is incontrovertible. If de Valera had been prepared to swallow his pride, and with it his legitimate complaint that the plenipotentiaries had broken their word not to sign the Treaty without first referring it back to Dublin, the Treaty split could have been contained and might even have been averted. He opposed the Treaty not because it was *a* compromise but because it was not *his* compromise – not, that is, a compromise that he had authorised in advance of its conclusion. Would there have been a civil war if de Valera had denied his support to those who fought against the Treaty? Perhaps there would have been violence from IRA extremists not susceptible to his control, but there was a fair chance that what turned out to be such a bloody split might instead have been only a splinter. De Valera, in other words, was largely responsible for the dimensions, if not for the fact, of the civil war. By allowing those who took up arms against the Treaty to draw on his authority, he conferred a respectability on their cause it could never have otherwise attained. His behaviour in the immediate aftermath of the Treaty, in sum, was petulant, inflammatory, ill judged, and profoundly undemocratic. Part of the explanation for his intemperate reaction lies in the depths of the deference accorded him since 1916. Although there is no evidence that de Valera demanded such unquestioning compliance, he accepted it as a matter of course. 'An Irish immigrant mother – a Spanish-American father dying while he was very small – a return to Ireland, his mother remaining in America – an upbringing by an uncle in what he himself has called a labourer's cottage', even his authorised biographers acknowledged that 'no psychiatrist could forecast the outcome of such an inheritance and early environment'.[8] Add to that an amalgam of his separation from his senior colleagues during his many months in jail and his eighteen-month absence in America, an aloof and ascetic temperament, a sense of distance reinforced by his profession as a schoolmaster and by his elevation (on the eve of the Treaty split) to the chancellorship of the NUI (an honour from which he was separated only by death), even perhaps by his height – 6 feet 1 inch – hence his sobriquet 'the Long Fellow': the result was a carapace of extraordinary self-sufficiency and self-confidence that also later served him well in enduring the affliction of blindness.

But however lamentable de Valera's failure in 1921–2, it must be reconciled with his subsequent greatness. The case for ascribing greatness to de Valera rests on his conduct of foreign policy, which gives him a larger claim than any other twentieth-century Irish politician to the title of statesman. He was the kind of statesman who, like Churchill and de Gaulle, portrays 'his country's inner image of itself and of its character and history' and who 'has no doubts or hesitations and by concentration of will-power, direction, and strength . . . is able to ignore a great deal of what goes on outside him. This very blindness and stubborn self-absorption

266

occasionally, in certain situations, enables him to bend events and men to his own fixed pattern.'[9] De Valera, as one of his earliest biographers observed, 'always remained a man of thought and never ceased from mental adventures and searchings even as he weigh[ed] a word on some political pronouncement with the maddening deliberation of a chess-player'.[10] He also understood the importance of vision in politics: that, as John A. Murphy has argued, 'when a small nation has been placed by the facts of geography and history in uncomfortable proximity to a great power, the people of that small nation, scarred by such a history, crave not only material progress, not only political sovereignty, but a psychological independence as well',[11] and he translated his personal vision of sovereignty into a political reality. He also demonstrated extraordinary diplomatic skills for, while the British resented and resisted his constitutional changes, the clarity with which he had telegraphed his intentions ensured that resentment and resistance never turned into retaliation. De Valera was the architect of the independent Irish state, and his blueprint was a constitution that also 'brought much needed stability after the hectic constitutional changes of 1922–37; a constitution which, on the whole, has operated as a salutary check on the other branches of government and which has promoted the protection of individual rights'.[12]

Éamon de Valera's vision was powerful but blinkered. Powerful because his conception of an Irish republic satisfied the nationalist appetite for independence. Blinkered because he saw independence as an end in itself rather than as a means to an end. Once independence had been achieved, his preoccupations with ending partition and creating some sort of Irish-speaking pastoral idyll were naive and unattainable, remote from the lives even of a majority of those who had identified with his quest for sovereignty. There is a savagely appropriate irony in the fact that it was during his second term as taoiseach that his eyesight disintegrated to the point where he had only peripheral vision. Although he regained power in 1951, with emigrants fleeing from de Valera's Ireland in their tens of thousands, he was ever afterwards on the periphery.

Yet de Valera's Ireland is a phrase too often used only in a pejorative sense: as an umbrella term for everything that was socially, economically and culturally backward about Ireland in the 1950s. Many historians and political scientists, preoccupied with social and economic history rather than with political history, focus less on his achievements than on what he did not try to achieve. In this version of history de Valera stands condemned, not for what he did as for what he never tried to do, a cast of mind well captured by the title of Tom Garvin's book, *Preventing the Future: Why Was Ireland So Poor for So Long?* A more apposite question is *Creating the Future: Why Was Ireland Independent So Soon?* Nor are suggestions that prosperity would have come if de Valera had bowed out earlier well founded – if, say, he, rather than Seán T. O'Kelly, had become president in 1945 and if Seán Lemass had then become taoiseach. It is far from certain that Lemass, who was never popular in certain quarters of Fianna Fáil, would have secured the party leadership in 1945 when O'Kelly was tánaiste. The post-war period would also have been a much more difficult and testing time for any other Fianna Fáil taoiseach than it was for de Valera. Ireland's wartime neutrality had left an enduring residue of resentment – especially among the British and the Americans – and the prevailing economic climate was much harsher than during the international buoyancy of the Lemass years. The defining characteristics of the 1950s – Britain's chronic sterling crisis and its implications for Ireland, high unemployment, the haemorrhage of emigration – these were but some of the circumstances outside the control of any taoiseach, as John A. Costello's two terms of office well testify. Indeed, there is a case to be made that at such an economically depressed and volatile time de Valera's continuance as taoiseach provided an important element of stability. Nor would a Lemass or an O'Kelly have commanded a comparable authority and obedience to negotiate the challenge to the stability of Fianna Fáil and, ultimately, to the stability of the state, posed by the IRA campaign of 1956–62.

Ireland's entry into the EEC in 1973 signalled that sovereignty was no longer an issue because by then independence had long been taken for granted. Yet without Éamon de Valera Ireland would never have achieved independence so quickly, and certainly would not have achieved it before the Second World War, the only international crisis that has so far threatened to overwhelm the independence of the state. For de Valera's Ireland also means a truly independent Ireland, an Ireland spared further decades of corrosive and sterile debate on the pros and cons of the British connection, an Ireland whose people were consequently self-confident enough about their own sovereignty by 1972 to dilute that sovereignty by voting overwhelmingly in favour of joining Europe. There is a fine symmetry, which might have appealed to de Valera as mathematician, about the timing of the joint admission of Ireland and Britain to Europe in 1973 – the same year that British–Irish interdependence in regard to Northern Ireland found first expression in the Sunningdale agreement: for the last year of his presidency was the moment when the doctrine of interdependence he had first dimly delineated in 1920 became the core of national policy.

References

KEY TO ACRONYMS AND ABBREVIATIONS

BMH WS	Bureau of Military History – witness statement
Dáil debs	Parliamentary debates, Dáil Éireann
DIB	*Dictionary of Irish Biography*
DIFP	Fanning, Ronan et al. (eds), *Documents on Irish Foreign Policy vols I–IX 1919–1948* (Dublin, 1998–2014)
IT	*Irish Times*
NAI	National Archives of Ireland
PRONI	Public Record Office of Northern Ireland
TNA	The National Archives of the United Kingdom
UCDA P 150	Éamon de Valera Papers, University College Dublin Archives

INTRODUCTION

1 John A. Murphy, 1–2.

1 FROM BRUREE TO BLACKROCK

1 Farragher, 9.
2 UCDA P 150/1.
3 UCDA P 150/87.
4 UCDA P 150/1.
5 Owen Dudley Edwards, 25.
6 UCDA P 150/87.
7 Coogan, 18.
8 Longford and O'Neill, 5.
9 Coogan, 19.
10 Longford and O'Neill, 6.
11 Farragher, 11.
12 Ibid., 13.
13 Coogan, 18.

14 UCDA P 150/22.
15 Farragher, 17.
16 Ibid., 22.
17 Ibid., 21.
18 Ibid., 33.
19 Ibid., 28.
20 Ibid., 29.
21 Ibid., 19.
22 Ibid., 34.
23 Ibid., 83–4.
24 Coogan, 38.
25 Ibid., 23.
26 Farragher, 58.
27 Ibid., 61–3.
28 Ibid., 35.
29 Ibid., 49.
30 Ibid., 71.
31 UCDA P 150/49.
32 Farragher, 71–3.
33 Coogan, 30.
34 UCDA P 150/41.
35 Farragher, 73–7.
36 Coogan, 32.
37 McCartney (1983), 18–19.
38 Farragher, 83.
39 Longford and O'Neill, 12.
40 Farragher, 89.
41 Coogan, 27.
42 Farragher, 91.
43 BMH WS 687, pdf 21 – Monsignor M. Curran.

2 THE GREENING OF EDWARD DE VALERA

1 Longford and O'Neill, 15.
2 UCDA P 150/42.
3 Longford and O'Neill, 14–15.
4 Gearoid Ó Tuathaigh, 'The Position of the Irish Language', in Tom Dunne (ed.), *The National University of Ireland 1908–2008 Centenary Essays* (Dublin, 2008), 37.
5 Donal McCartney, 'University College Dublin', in Dunne, op. cit., 90.
6 Ó Tuathaigh, op. cit., 40.
7 Coogan, 39.

8 *DIB*.
9 Terry de Valera, 107.
10 Coogan, 11.
11 Foster, 72.
12 Longford and O'Neill, 16.
13 Coogan, 41.
14 UCDA P 150/445.
15 BMH WS Simon Donnelly (IRB Dublin), cited in McGarry (2011), 27.
16 Coogan, 49–50.
17 BMH WS 99, pdf 3.
18 Coogan, 41–2.
19 Moynihan, xxix.
20 *IT*, 9 December 2013, 3.
21 UCDA P 150/445.
22 UCDA P 122/113, Maurice Moynihan papers, 22 February 1950.
23 Longford and O'Neill, 21.
24 UCDA P 150/450.
25 Longford and O'Neill, 22.
26 BMH WS 242, pdf 3–4.
27 Bromage, 21.
28 BMH WS 242, pdf 6.
29 Longford and O'Neill, 23.
30 UCDA P 122/112.
31 Townshend (2005), 69.
32 Longford and O'Neill, 25–6.
33 UCDA P 150/449.
34 Longford and O'Neill, 24–5.

3 ÉAMON DE VALERA AND THE 1916 RISING

1 Townshend (2005), 93.
2 McGarry (2011), 198.
3 Longford and O'Neill, 25.
4 BMH WS 1766, pdf 19.
5 Bromage, 24.
6 BMH WS 157, pdf 20–22, 40.
7 Bromage, 25–6.
8 Terry de Valera, 121.
9 McGarry (2011), 155.
10 BMH WS 157, pdf 36.
11 Townshend (2005), 255.

12 Ibid., 196–8.
13 Coogan, 69.
14 McGarry (2010), 174.
15 Townshend (2005), 199.
16 Coogan, 71.
17 Townshend (2005), 201.
18 Ibid., 246–8.
19 BMH WS 1140, pdf 10 – Patrick Ward.
20 McGarry (2011), 293–4.
21 Longford and O'Neill, 46–7.
22 Ibid., 47.
23 Enright, 4, 68.
24 Barton.
25 Email to the author from a spokesperson for the National Archives, 13 June 2014.
26 Enright, 68.
27 Longford and O'Neill, 48.
28 McGarry (2011), 339.
29 Enright, 69.
30 Longford and O'Neill, 48–9; Coogan, 77–8.
31 Schmuhl, 36.
32 Coogan, 78.
33 Longford and O'Neill, 52.

4 THE ASSUMPTION OF POWER, 1916–19

1 BMH WS 779, pdf 184.
2 Townshend (2013), 43.
3 BMH WS 336, pdf 7 – Garry Holohan.
4 McGarry (2011), 320.
5 David Fitzpatrick, '"Decidedly a Personality": de Valera's performance as a convict, 1916–1917', *History Ireland*, vol. 10 no. 2 (summer 2002), 40–46.
6 BMH WS 799, pdf 197.
7 BMH WS 1043, pdf 432–3 – Joseph V. Lawless.
8 BMH WS 170, pdf 17–18 – Peter Paul Galligan.
9 Brennan, 103.
10 Fitzpatrick, op. cit.
11 BMH WS 510, pdf 43 – Frank Thornton.
12 BMH WS 1734, pdf 4.
13 BMH WS 687, pdf 225.
14 BMH WS 1770, pdf 49–50.

15 Longford and O'Neill, 56–7.
16 Laffan (1999), 96–7.
17 BMH WS 487, pdf 5.
18 BMH WS 687, pdf 226 – extract from Monsignor Curran's diary.
19 Laffan (1999), 110–11.
20 BMH WS 1077, pdf 3 – Thomas McNamara.
21 BMH WS 1103, pdf 11 – Denis F. Madden.
22 Laffan (1999), 110.
23 David Miller, *Church, State and Nation in Ireland, 1898–1921* (Dublin, 1973), 393–4.
24 Fitzpatrick (1983), 110.
25 Kevin J. Browne, *Éamon de Valera and the Banner County* (Dublin, 1982), 55–6. I am grateful to Judge Adrian Hardiman for having drawn these verses to my attention.
26 BMH WS 687, pdf 229–30.
27 BMH WS 400, pdf 45–6 – Richard Walsh, Irish Volunteer organiser in Mayo.
28 BMH WS 4, pdf 12.
29 BMH WS 104, pdf 8 – George Lyons, member of the IRB 1900–1920.
30 Coogan, 99.
31 Townshend (2005), 331.
32 BMH WS 191, pdf 12 – Joseph Reynolds, senior officer, Fianna Éireann.
33 Laffan (1999), 76, 87, 91, 103, 105–6 116–17.
34 Longford and O'Neill, 67–8.
35 BMH WS 722, pdf 18 – Dan McCarthy.
36 BMH WS 945, pdf 5.
37 BMH WS 391, pdf 51 – Helena Molony of Cumann na mBan.
38 Foster, 57.
39 BMH WS 779, pdf 11 – Robert Brennan.
40 *IT*, 26 October 1917.
41 Moynihan, 7–8.
42 See above, p. 26.
43 NAI CSSO Sinn Féin Funds Case 2B 32-118-36, A1.
44 Fitzpatrick (1983), 103.
45 BMH WS 400, pdf 32–3 – Richard Walsh.
46 Townshend (2013), 38.
47 Longford and O'Neill, 70.
48 *Dáil debs*, 272, 6 January 1922.
49 BMH WS 687, pdf 270–79 – Monsignor Curran's diary.
50 Longford and O'Neill, 72.
51 Ibid., 72–3.

52 Ryan, 28.
53 Miller, op. cit., 404, 413.
54 Morrissey, 148.
55 BMH WS 687, pdf 280, 292.
56 Cf. Ronan Fanning (2013), 180–85.
57 *Christian Science Monitor*, 15 May 1918.
58 BMH WS 1280, pdf 74–7 – Éamon Broy.
59 Bromage, 38.
60 Fitzpatrick (1983), 103.
61 Laffan (1999), 145–6.
62 Longford and O'Neill, 80.

5 MISSION TO AMERICA, 1919–20

1 Ward, 167–8.
2 Brennan (2002), 114–15.
3 Bromage, 39.
4 Laffan (1999), 155.
5 Fitzpatrick (2003), 122.
6 BMH WS 779 (Section 3), pdf 18 – Robert Brennan.
7 Bromage, 37.
8 Fitzpatrick (2003), 114.
9 Longford and O'Neill, 84–7.
10 Coogan, 129.
11 See above, p. 50.
12 *Dáil debs*, 22 January 1919, 26.
13 BMH WS 939, pdf 131.
14 *DIB* – Brugha entry.
15 Longford and O'Neill, 87–8.
16 Fitzpatrick (2003), 117.
17 *DIFP I*, 6–9.
18 BMH WS 687, pdf 339–41 – Monsignor Curran.
19 Bromage, 41.
20 Coogan, 131.
21 UCDA P 150/617.
22 Townshend (2013), 83.
23 Bromage, 42.
24 *DIFP I*, 10–11.
25 *Dáil debs*, 1 April 1919, 30–34.
26 *Dáil debs*, 2 April 1919, 36.
27 *Dáil debs*, 10 April 1919, 46–7.
28 *Dáil debs*, 10 April 1919, 67–9.

29 Carroll (1985), 10–15.
30 *DIFP I*, 17.
31 Coogan, 134–5.
32 BMH WS 356, pdf 9 – Milo McGarry.
33 *Dáil debs*, 17 June 1919, 113, 131.
34 BMH WS 826, pdf 17 – Maeve McGarry (as recounted by de Valera).
35 Longford and O'Neill, 96.
36 Coogan, 139.
37 Fitzpatrick (2003), 124.
38 Coogan, 145.
39 Ibid., 150.
40 Carroll (1978), 150.
41 Fitzpatrick (2003), 133.
42 Coogan, 148.
43 Cronin, 83.
44 Fitzpatrick (2003), 129, 125.
45 Longford and O'Neill, 103–5.
46 *DIFP I*, 54–5 – 17 February 1920.
47 BMII WS 767, pdf 64.
48 Coogan, 165–7.
49 Moynihan, 34.
50 Ibid., 41.
51 Longford and O'Neill, 113.
52 Jordan, 68.
53 Fitzpatrick (2003), 192.
54 NAI DE/1/3/13.
55 Longford and O'Neill, 112–13.
56 Ronan Fanning (2013), 243–4.
57 NAI DE/1/3/55.

6 1921: WAR AND PEACE

1 BMH WS 779 (section 3), pdf 111 – Robert Brennan.
2 Ronan Fanning (2013), 246.
3 TNA W.O. 35/90/2.
4 Longford and O'Neill, 115–17; Coogan, 197–8.
5 Coogan, 198.
6 BMH WS 779 (section 3), pdf 110–11.
7 BMH WS 939, pdf 128 – Ernest Blythe.
8 Coogan, 204–5.
9 Garvin (1996), 57.
10 Coogan, 205–6.

11 Longford and O'Neill, 116.
12 Coogan, 200–201.
13 NAI DE/1/3/80.
14 O'Connor, 132–3.
15 BMH WS 767, pdf 82–4.
16 Longford and O'Neill, 119.
17 O'Connor, 134.
18 *Dáil debs*, 241–8.
19 *Dáil debs*, 264, 279.
20 BMH WS 1410, pdf 2–3 – Michael O'Kelly (a lieutenant in the 2nd Battalion of IRA's Dublin Brigade).
21 Coogan, 216.
22 *Dáil debs*, 292.
23 BMH WS 779 (section 3), pdf 132–3.
24 Ronan Fanning (2013), 256.
25 Longford and O'Neill, 124–5.
26 BMH WS 826, pdf 26–7 – Maeve MacGarry.
27 Longford and O'Neill, 129.
28 BMH WS 826 pdf 27.
29 Ronan Fanning (2013), 261–2.
30 Ibid., 262–3.
31 BMH WS 544, pdf 14 – Joseph O'Connor.
32 Coogan, 231–2.
33 *DIFP I*, 235.
34 Ronan Fanning (2013), 264.
35 Longford and O'Neill, 136.
36 Ronan Fanning (2013), 265.
37 NAI DE/1/3/117B.
38 Longford and O'Neill, 136.
39 Ibid., 139.
40 NAI DE/1/3/117B.
41 Longford and O'Neill, 140.
42 Ronan Fanning (2013), 267–70.
43 *DIFP I*, 259–60.
44 NAI DE/1/3/118A.
45 Maye, 188.
46 *Dáil debs*, 94–5.
47 Ronan Fanning (2013), 273.
48 *Dáil debs*, 96.
49 BMH WS 939, pdf 136 – Ernest Blythe.
50 BMH WS 838, pdf 279 – Seán Moylan.
51 Maye, 189.

52 *Dáil debs*, 90–91.

7 CATASTROPHE

1 Regan (2013), 224.
2 *DIFP I*, 272.
3 *DIFP I*, 270–72.
4 Foster, 279.
5 Coogan, 256.
6 Mansergh, 178.
7 *DIFP I*, 274–5.
8 See Bowman (1982), appendix 1, 341.
9 Pakenham, 134.
10 Coogan, 257.
11 *DIFP I*, 282–3.
12 Pakenham, 138–9.
13 Maye, 196.
14 *DIFP I*, 288.
15 *DIFP I*, 293.
16 BMH WS 939, pdf 136 – Ernest Blythe.
17 Colum, 343.
18 Murray (2001), 51–2.
19 BMH WS 687, pdf 576 – Curran.
20 Taylor, 129.
21 *DIFP I*, 290–91.
22 *DIFP I*, 293.
23 *DIFP I*, 299.
24 *DIFP I*, 307.
25 *DIFP I*, 308–9.
26 *DIFP I*, 309–11.
27 Jones, 138–9.
28 *DIFP I*, 317.
29 Jones, 176–7.
30 *DIFP I*, 319–20.
31 Jones, 177.
32 *DIFP I*, 321.
33 Cronin, 107.
34 *DIFP I*, 344–6.
35 BMH WS 979, pdf 37.
36 Regan (1999), 15.
37 Jones, 180.
38 *DIFP I*, 348–9.

39 See Ronan Fanning (2013) for a fuller account of the events of 5–6 December.
40 *DIFP I*, 351–6.
41 Valiulis, 109.
42 Longford and O'Neill, 166.
43 Ibid., 167.
44 Coogan, 283.
45 Ibid., 284.
46 Laffan (2014), 103.
47 Longford and O'Neill, 168.
48 NAI DE/1/3/183.
49 Coogan, 285.
50 NAI DE/1/3/184.
51 Coogan, 285.
52 *IT*, 9 December 1921, p. 5.
53 Longford and O'Neill, 169.
54 *Dáil debs*, 7.
55 *Dáil debs* (private sessions), 101.
56 Regan (1999), 41–2.
57 *Dáil debs*, 43–4.
58 *Dáil debs*, 274–5.
59 *Dáil debs*, 353, 357, 396, 410.

8 A GLASS WALL

1 UCDA P 150/1800.
2 Longford and O'Neill, 182–3.
3 Laffan (1999), 363, 367–73.
4 Regan (1999), 55.
5 Curran, 145.
6 Hopkinson (1988), 58.
7 Valiulis, 127–32.
8 Curran, 173–4.
9 Longford and O'Neill, 185.
10 Curran, 175.
11 Laffan (1999), 364, 374–5.
12 Longford and O'Neill, 187.
13 Coogan, 312–13.
14 Longford and O'Neill, 187.
15 Laffan (1999), 375.
16 Hopkinson (1988), 70.
17 Laffan (1999), 376, 381.

18 Ronan Fanning (1983), 13.
19 Hopkinson (1988), 100.
20 Ibid., 123–4.
21 BMH WS 779, pdf 192, 197.
22 Hopkinson (1988), 134–5.
23 Valiulis, 175.
24 UCDA P150/657; reproduced in Ferriter, 91–2.
25 Hopkinson (1988), 188.
26 Longford and O'Neill, 205–6.
27 Hopkinson (1988), 233.
28 Moynihan, 111–12.
29 Hopkinson (1988), 256.
30 Moynihan, 113.
31 Hopkinson (1988), 257.
32 Moynihan, 114.
33 Hopkinson (1988), 260.
34 Longford and O'Neill, 196.

9 THE PATH BACK TO POWER

1 UCDA P 150/1807.
2 Laffan (1999), 438.
3 Ibid., 436.
4 Coogan, 356.
5 Longford and O'Neill, 226–7.
6 Coogan, 359.
7 Laffan (1999), 437.
8 Bromage, 107.
9 Coogan, 362, 365.
10 Owen Dudley Edwards, 94.
11 Longford and O'Neill, 422.
12 UCDA P 150/1584.
13 Moynihan, 116.
14 Longford and O'Neill, 238–9.
15 Murray (2000), 186, n. 211.
16 Seán Farragher's note of an interview with de Valera, c. 1973.
   I am grateful to Caroline Mullan, the archivist at Blackrock College,
   for this reference.
17 UCDA P 150/1826 – facsimile in Ferriter, 94–5.
18 Keogh (1986), 131, 129.
19 Brian P. Murphy, 148.
20 MacBride, 90.

21 Mannix, 109.
22 Keogh (1986), 131–2.
23 Ibid., 132.
24 O'Neill, 164.
25 Ryle Dwyer, 8–9.
26 O'Neill, 169.
27 Laffan (1999), 442.
28 Cronin, 141.
29 Moynihan, 129.
30 Ibid., 143–4.
31 *Dáil debs*, 22, 1615.
32 Horgan, 45.
33 Garvin (1981), 156–7.
34 Moynihan, 149.
35 Ibid., 150.
36 Ibid., 154–5.
37 O'Brien, 2, 4.
38 Coogan, 388.
39 O'Brien, 20, 26, 1, 37, 35.
40 MacDonagh, 109.

10 THE ATTAINMENT OF INDEPENDENCE, 1932–8

1 Ronan Fanning (1978), 216.
2 Longford and O'Neill, 276.
3 Letter from F. A. Coffey to *IT*, 4 November 1996.
4 NAI CAB 1/4/7.
5 McMahon, 42.
6 *DIFP IV*, 46, 50–51, 74–7, 82–3.
7 *DIFP IV*, 125–6.
8 *DIFP IV*, 210.
9 NAI T/D S. 4469.
10 *DIFP IV*, 4–6.
11 *DIFP IV*, 20–21.
12 Deirdre McMahon, 'Anglo-Irish Relations, 1932–38' (PhD thesis, Cambridge University, 1979), 259.
13 *Dáil debs*, 55, 2270–76.
14 Longford and O'Neill, 278.
15 Canning, 138–9.
16 *DIFP IV*, 88–91.
17 *DIFP IV*, 169.
18 Moynihan, 227.

19 Ronan Fanning (1983), 114–15.
20 Moynihan, 265.
21 Hogan, 152.
22 NAI CAB 1/6/315.
23 NAI CAB 1/37/35–6.
24 Hogan, 263.
25 I am grateful to Sir David Goodall for this information.
26 Canning, 169.
27 Hogan, 274.
28 Terry de Valera, 57; UCDA P 150/101.
29 Terry de Valera, 24.
30 *DIFP V*, 11–17.
31 See Ronan Fanning (1978), 266–9, and Hogan, 386–405.
32 Terry de Valera, 51.
33 Longford and O'Neill, 295–7.
34 *DIFP V*, 31.
35 Moynihan, 331.
36 Fisk, 63.
37 Moynihan, 239.
38 Cronin, 157–8.
39 Moynihan, 265–6.
40 *Dáil debs*, 59, 1535–6.

11 INDEPENDENCE AFFIRMED: NEUTRALITY IN WORLD WAR II

1 *Times Literary Supplement*, 25 January 1980, 77.
2 Lyons, 554.
3 Moynihan, 219–23.
4 Longford and O'Neill, 336–7.
5 Moynihan, 276–7.
6 NAI G2/12/316, 18 August 1936.
7 NAI D/T S 9177.
8 Eoin O'Duffy, *Crusade in Spain* (Dublin, n.d.), 38–9.
9 Moynihan, 319.
10 T. D. Williams, 137.
11 NAI CAB 1/8/76–8.
12 Canning, 185.
13 Ibid., 196–7.
14 Moynihan, 346.
15 O'Halpin (2003), 22–3; Kennedy (2008), 20.
16 Moynihan, 417–20.
17 *Dáil debs*, 71,437.

18 *DIFP VI*, 37–8, 42, 47.
19 Desmond Williams (1969), 25–6.
20 Kennedy, 283–6.
21 Ronan Fanning (1983) 124–5.
22 Desmond Williams (1969), 26.
23 Gerald Stourzh, 'Some Reflections on Permanent Neutrality', in August Schoue and Arne Olav Brundtland (eds), *Small States in International Relations* (Stockholm, 1971), 45–8.
24 Winston Churchill, *The Second World War* (London, Reprint Society edn, 1948), vol. vi, Appendix C, 565, and vol. i, 486.
25 Fisk, 103, 107.
26 *DIFP VII*, 537.
27 *DIFP VII*, 552–3.
28 Lyons, 551.
29 John A. Murphy, 14.
30 Ronan Fanning (1983), 127.

12 DE VALERA'S IRELAND

1 Moynihan, 233.
2 Ibid., 466.
3 Lee, 331.
4 Moynihan, 476.
5 J. A. Costello, *Ireland in International Affairs* (Dublin, 1949), 28–9.
6 NAI CAB 1/4/47-8 and 1/5/183.
7 Murray (2000), 254.
8 Dublin Diocesan Archives – DDA/AB7/Irish bishops/9 June 1932 (uncatalogued). I am grateful to Tim Fanning for this reference.
9 Murray (2000), 262.
10 Ronan Fanning (1983), 130.
11 Cruise O'Brien, 119.
12 NAI T/D S 3066A, 19 June 1934.
13 McCartney (1969), 81.
14 *50 Year Report*, Dublin Institute for Advanced Studies.
15 *DIB*.
16 Moynihan, 436–49.
17 *Dáil debs*, 79, 10, 1091 and 1109.
18 Sir Andrew Gilchrist's report on his conversation with de Valera and Aiken, 27 February 1967; facsimile in Ferriter, 210–13.
19 UCDA P 150/3110; facsimile in Ferriter, 321–3.
20 Moynihan, 235, 468.
21 *Dáil debs* (private sessions), 153.

22 Kelly, 24–5.
23 Bowman (1982), 81, 102.
24 *Dáil debs* (private sessions), 29.
25 *Cork Examiner*, 28 October 1931.
26 Kelly, 39.
27 Ibid., 69–71.
28 Longford and O'Neill, 317.
29 Kelly, 79.
30 Moynihan, 372–3.
31 NAI T/D S 9361.
32 Bew, x.
33 Ibid., xviii.
34 Bowman (1982), 237.
35 *DIFP VI*, 249–50, 237, 239.
36 Fisk, 77–8.
37 Canning, 284.
38 *DIFP VI*, 278–81.
39 *DIFP VII*, 155–9.
40 *Dáil debs*, 78, 135–6.
41 *DIFP VI*, 141.
42 Moynihan, 433.
43 Ibid., 421.
44 PRONI D.715/11/73–4.
45 NAI CAB 277/201.
46 *DIFP VII*, 508.
47 Ronan Fanning (1986), 36–41.
48 Moynihan, 486.
49 Ronan Fanning (1986), 56–9.
50 Kelly, 108–10.

13 MARKING TIME, 1848–59

1 Terry de Valera, 269.
2 *DIFP IX*, xv.
3 *DIFP IX*, 13–14, 82.
4 Kelly, 125–7.
5 McCabe, 21.
6 *DIFP VIII*, 503–4.
7 Moynihan, 506.
8 Keogh (1994), 190–91.
9 Terry de Valera, 266.
10 *IT*, 22 March 1949.

11 Moynihan, 543.

12 Coogan, 257.

13 The following account is based on Ronan Fanning, 'Fianna Fáil and the Bishops', *IT*, 13 and 14 February 1985.

14 Horgan, 150–51.

15 He revealed this in a 1968 interview with Brian Farrell, to whom I am indebted for this information.

16 McKee, 193–4.

17 Coogan, 697.

18 Terry de Valera, 21.

19 McCarthy, 165, 177, 183.

20 Tim Fanning, 134–46.

21 Ibid., 176–8, 191–2.

22 Cornelius O'Leary, *Irish Elections 1918–1977* (Dublin, 1979), 42.

23 T. D. Williams, 'The Politics of Irish Economics', *The Statist*, 24 October 1953.

24 *Dáil debs*, 159, 1614.

25 Moynihan, 327.

26 Chambers, 71, 121.

27 John A Murphy, 9–10.

28 Garvin (2004), 37.

29 Denis Donoghue, *Warrenpoint* (New York, 1990), 156–7.

30 Keogh (1994), 229–30.

31 Kelly, 200–202.

32 Moynihan, 580–84.

33 Ibid., 589–94.

34 *DIB* – Patrick Maume's entry on Jim Ryan.

35 Chambers, 122.

36 Farrell, 96.

37 Longford and O'Neill, 447.

38 Byrne, 59–62.

39 O'Brien, 106–13; Coogan, 674–7.

40 Farrell, 96–7.

41 Coogan, 677–8.

14 LAST LAPS, 1959–75

1 McCartney (1983), 30.

2 Walsh, 136.

3 McCartney (1983), 25, 47.

4 Ibid., 32–3.

5 Walsh, 137.

6 UCDA P 150/98.
7 Walsh, 152–3.
8 Facsimile in Ferriter, 180.
9 Terry de Valera, 271, 278.
10 Longford and O'Neill, xxii.
11 Murray (2001), 39.
12 Bowman (1983), 191.
13 Murray (2001), 41, 65.
14 Terry de Valera, 279.
15 Longford and O'Neill, 464.
16 Ronan Fanning (1983), 203.
17 Terry de Valera, 272–3.
18 Coogan, 681.
19 Moynihan, 599–602.
20 Longford and O'Neill, 461.
21 Horgan, 285.
22 Coogan, 687.
23 O'Malley, 56, 66, 51, 74–5.
24 Chambers, 268–9.
25 Coogan, 678.
26 Terry de Valera, 228.
27 Ferriter, 364–5.

CONCLUSION

1 Robert Dudley Edwards, 7.
2 George Bernard Shaw, *The Devil's Disciple*, Act 3.
3 Ibid.
4 Robert Dudley Edwards, 8.
5 Mark C. Nolan, *Keynes in Dublin* (Cork, 2014), 35.
6 Walker and Fitzgerald, 90, 87.
7 McCartney (1979), 314–15.
8 Longford and O'Neill, 471–2.
9 Isaiah Berlin, *Personal Impressions* (London, 1982), 9, 27.
10 Ryan, 14.
11 John A. Murphy, 14.
12 Hogan, 320.

Select Bibliography

Barton, Brian, *From Behind a Closed Door: Secret Court Martial Records of the 1916 Easter Rising* (Belfast, 2002)

Bew, Paul (ed.), *The Memoir of David Gray: A Yankee in de Valera's Ireland* (Dublin, 2012)

Bowman, John, *De Valera and the Ulster Question 1917–1973* (Oxford, 1982)

—, 'Éamon de Valera: Seven Lives', in John P. O'Carroll and John A. Murphy (eds), *De Valera and his Times* (Cork, 1983)

Brennan, Robert, *Ireland Standing Firm* and *Éamon de Valera: A Memoir* (Dublin, 2002)

Bromage, Mary, *De Valera and the March of a Nation* (London, 1967 edn)

Byrne, Elaine A., *Political Corruption in Ireland 1922–2010: A Crooked Harp* (Manchester, 2012)

Canning, Paul, *British Policy Towards Ireland 1921–1941* (Oxford, 1985)

Carroll, F. M., *American Opinion and the Irish Question 1910–23* (Dublin, 1978)

—, (ed.), *The American Commission on Irish Independence: The Diary, Correspondence and Report* (Dublin, 1985)

Chambers, Anne, *T. K. Whitaker: Portrait of a Patriot* (Dublin, 2014)

Colum, Padraic, *Arthur Griffith* (Dublin, 1959)

Coogan, Tim Pat, *De Valera: Long Fellow, Long Shadow* (London, 1993)

Cronin, Seán, *The McGarrity Papers* (Tralee, 1972)

Cruise O'Brien, Conor, *States of Ireland* (London, 1972)

Curran, Joseph M., *The Birth of the Irish Free State 1921–1923* (Alabama, 1980)

de Valera, Terry, *A Memoir* (Dublin, 2004)

Dudley Edwards, Owen, *Éamon de Valera* (Cardiff, 1987)

Dudley Edwards, Robert, 'Mr de Valera Considered Historically', in the *Leader*, 12 January 1957

Enright, Seán, *Easter Rising 1916: The Trials* (Dublin, 2014)

Fanning, Ronan, *The Irish Department of Finance 1922–1958* (Dublin, 1978)

—, *Independent Ireland* (Dublin, 1983)

—, 'The Anglo-American Alliance and the Irish Application for Membership of the United Nations', *Irish Studies in International Affairs*, vol. 2 no. 2 (1986), 35–61.

—, *Fatal Path: British Government and Irish Revolution 1910–22* (London, 2013)

—, et al. (eds), *Documents on Irish Foreign Policy*, vols I–IX: *1919–1948* (Dublin, 1998–2014)

Fanning, Tim, *The Fethard-on-Sea Boycott* (Cork, 2010)

Farragher, Seán P., *Dev and His Alma Mater: Éamon de Valera's Lifelong Association with Blackrock College 1898–1975* (Dublin and London, 1984)

Farrell, Brian, *Seán Lemass* (Dublin, 1983)

Ferriter, Diarmaid, *Judging Dev: A Reassessment of the Life and Legacy of Éamon de Valera* (Dublin, 2007)

Fisk, Robert, *In Time of War: Ireland, Ulster and the Price of Neutrality* (London, 1983)

Fitzpatrick, David, 'De Valera in 1917: The Undoing of the Easter Rising', in John P. O'Carroll and John A. Murphy (eds), *De Valera and His Times* (Cork, 1983), 101–12

—, *Harry Boland's Irish Revolution* (Cork, 2003)

Foster, Roy, *Vivid Faces: The Revolutionary Generation 1890–1923* (London, 2014)

Garvin, Tom, *The Evolution of Irish Nationalist Politics* (Dublin, 1981)

—, *1922: The Birth of Irish Democracy* (Dublin, 1996)

—, *Preventing the Future: Why Was Ireland Poor for So Long?* (Dublin, 2004)

Hogan, Gerard, *The Origins of the Irish Constitution, 1928–1941* (Dublin, 2012)

Hopkinson, Michael, *Green Against Green: The Irish Civil War* (Dublin, 1988)

Horgan, John, *Seán Lemass: The Enigmatic Patriot* (Dublin, 1997)

Jones, Thomas, *Whitehall Diary: Volume III: Ireland 1918–1925*, edited by Keith Middlemas (London, 1971)

Jordan, Anthony J., *Éamon de Valera 1882–1975: Irish : Catholic : Visionary* (Dublin, 2010)

Kelly, Stephen, *Fianna Fáil, Partition and Northern Ireland, 1926–1971* (Dublin, 2013)

Kennedy, Michael, *Guarding Neutral Ireland: The Coast Watching*

    Service and Military Intelligence 1939–1945 (Dublin, 2008)

Keogh, Dermot, *The Vatican, the Bishops and Irish Politics 1919–39*
    (Cambridge, 1986)

—, *Twentieth Century Ireland: Nation and State* (Dublin, 1994)

Laffan, Michael, *The Resurrection of Ireland: The Sinn Féin Party,*
    1916–1923 (Cambridge, 1999)

—, *Judging W. T. Cosgrave* (Dublin, 2014)

Lee, J. J., *Ireland 1912–1985: Politics and Society* (Cambridge, 1989)

Longford, The Earl of, and Thomas P. O'Neill, *Éamon de Valera*
    (London, 1970)

Lyons, F. S. L., *Ireland Since the Famine* (London, 1971)

MacBride, Sean, *That Day's Struggle: A Memoir 1904–1951*, edited by
    Caitriona Lawlor (Dublin, 2005)

McCabe, Ian, *A Diplomatic History of Ireland 1948–49: The Republic,*
    the Commonwealth and NATO (Dublin, 1991)

McCarthy, Kevin, 'Éamon de Valera's Relationship with Robert
    Briscoe: A Reappraisal', *Irish Studies in International Affairs,*
    vol. 25 (2014), 165–86

McCartney, Donal, 'Education and Language, 1938–1951' in Kevin B.
    Nowlan and T. Desmond Williams (eds), *Ireland in the War Years*
    and After 1939–51 (Dublin, 1969)

—, 'De Valera's Mission to the United States, 1919–20' in Art
    Cosgrove and Donal McCartney (eds), *Studies in Irish History*
    Presented to R. Dudley Edwards (Dublin, 1979)

—, *The National University of Ireland and Éamon de Valera* (Dublin,
    1983)

MacDonagh, Oliver, *Ireland: The Union and Its Aftermath* (London,
    1977)

McGarry, Ferghal, *The Rising: Ireland: 1916* (Oxford, 2010)

—, *Rebels: Voices from the 1916 Rising* (Dublin, 2011)

McKee, Eamonn, 'Church–State Relations and the Development
    of Irish Health Policy: The Mother-and-Child Scheme, 1944–53',
    Irish Historical Studies, vol. xxv no. 98 (November 1986),
    159–94

McMahon, Deirdre, *Republicans and Imperialists: Anglo-Irish Relations*
    in the 1930s (New Haven and London, 1984)

Mannix, Patrick, *The Belligerent Prelate: An Alliance between*
    Archbishop Mannix and Éamon de Valera (Newcastle-upon-Tyne,
    2012)

Mansergh, Nicholas, *The Unresolved Question: The Anglo-Irish*
    Settlement and its Undoing (New Haven and London, 1991)

Maye, Brian, *Arthur Griffith* (Dublin, 1997)

Morrissey, Thomas, *William O'Brien 1881–1968* (Dublin, 2007)

Moynihan, Maurice (ed.), *Speeches and Statements by Éamon de Valera, 1917–73* (Dublin, 1980)

Murphy, Brian P., *Patrick Pearse and the Lost Republican Ideal* (Dublin, 1991)

Murphy, John A., 'The Achievement of Éamon de Valera' in John P. O'Carroll and John A. Murphy (eds), *De Valera and His Times* (Cork, 1983)

Murray, Patrick, *Oracles of God: The Roman Catholic Church and Irish Politics, 1922–37* (Dublin, 2000)

—, 'Obsessive Historian: Éamon de Valera and the Policing of his Reputation', *Proceedings of the Royal Irish Academy*, vol. 101c, 337–65 (2001)

O'Brien, Mark, *De Valera, Fianna Fáil and the Irish Press* (Dublin, 2001)

O'Connor, Frank, *The Big Fellow* (London, Corgi edn, 1969)

O'Halpin, Eunan (ed.), *MI5 and Ireland, 1939–45: The Official History* (Dublin, 2003)

O'Malley, Desmond, *Conduct Unbecoming: A Memoir* (Dublin, 2014)

O'Neill, Thomas P., 'In Search of a Political Path: Irish Republicanism, 1922–27' in G. A. Hayes-McCoy (ed.), *Historical Studies X* (Connemara, 1976), 1

Pakenham, Frank, *Peace by Ordeal* (London, rev. edn, 1962)

Regan, John M., *The Irish Counter-Revolution 1921–1936* (Dublin, 1999)

—, *Myth and the Irish State* (Dublin, 2013)

Ryan, Desmond, *Unique Dictator: A Study of Éamon de Valera* (London, 1936)

Ryle Dwyer, T., *Éamon de Valera* (Dublin, 1980)

Schmuhl, Robert, 'Ambiguous Reprieve: Dev and America', *History Ireland*, vol. 21 no. 3 (May–June 2013), 36–9.

Taylor, Rex, *Michael Collins* (London, 1961)

Townshend, Charles, *Easter 1916: The Irish Rebellion* (London, 2005)

—, *The Republic: The Fight for Irish Independence 1918–1923* (London, 2013)

Valiulis, Maryann Gialanella, *Portrait of a Revolutionary: General Richard Mulcahy and the Founding of the Irish Free State* (Dublin, 1992)

Walker, Antoinette, and Michael Fitzgerald, *Unstoppable Brilliance: Irish Geniuses and Asperger's Syndrome* (Dublin, 2006)

Walsh, John, 'Éamon de Valera, 1921–75', in Tom Dunne (ed.), *The National University of Ireland 1908–2008 Centenary Essays* (Dublin, 2008)

Ward, Alan J., *Ireland and Anglo-American Relations 1899–1921*
(London, 1969)

Williams, Desmond, 'Ireland and the War', in Kevin B. Nowlan and
T. Desmond Williams (eds), *Ireland in the War Years and After,
1939–51* (Dublin, 1969)

Williams, T. D., 'Irish Foreign Policy, 1949–69' in J. J. Lee (ed.), *Ireland
1945–70* (Dublin, 1979)

Acknowledgements

Much the most important primary source for this book is the voluminous collection of the papers of Éamon de Valera that are in the custody of the Archives Department of University College Dublin. I am indebted to all their staff but, in particular, to Seamus Helferty, Principal Archivist, for his unstinting help in dealing so expeditiously with my many inquiries.

I must also thank the National Archives of Ireland, the National Archives of the United Kingdom (where Neil Cobbett was most co-operative), and the Public Record Office of Northern Ireland for permission to quote from documents in their care.

Neil Belton first emboldened me to embark upon de Valera's biography and persistently encouraged me thereafter as did my agent, Jonathan Williams. The enthusiastic response of Julian Loose, publishing director at Faber and Faber, when he read the manuscript meant much to me; I am also grateful to his colleagues, Anne Owen and Kate McQuaid, and to Richard Curry for designing the map. But, yet again, the greatest debt I incurred as the book took shape is to Jill Burrows not only for her superb copyediting and typesetting but also for preparing so meticulous and comprehensive an index.

I want also to thank those who read the book in typescript for all their comments and suggestions: my son, Tim; my brother, Adrian; and my friend, Michael Lillis.

I owe a very special debt to Nora Pat Stewart without whose constant yet unobtrusive encouragement at a difficult time I would never have delivered the manuscript on time. I am particularly grateful to her and to her husband, Trevor, for their frequent hospitality and many kindnesses that included allowing me to commandeer their dining room at Broadwell to put the last touches to the text during a prolonged visit at Christmas 2014.

I am grateful, too, to Adrian Hardiman and Yvonne Murphy for their hospitality at Portnoo and for their enthusiastic engagement in many conversations about de Valera.

Tim Dixon's assistance and advice on some of the more arcane aspects of word processing was invaluable, as was the thoughtful generosity of my niece, Dr Sarah Hennessy, and her husband, John, who gave me a present of computer software that enabled me more readily to overcome the handicap of having to finish the manuscript after I had broken a wrist.

Finally, I am more thankful than I can ever say for the personal support of all my children – Judith, Gareth and Tim – and of Virginia's children – Mark and Caroline.

Index